PRAISE FOR *ACCOUNT-BASED GROWTH*

'In business life, I cannot think of anything more satisfying than creating value for customers and, in the process, creating value for all stakeholders including the Planet. A few years ago, when account-based marketing first emerged, I said that it was a paradigm shift for the marketing domain. I have not changed my view. Please read this book to find out why. Incidentally, both authors are brilliant.'
Professor Malcolm McDonald, Emeritus Professor, Cranfield University School of Management

'Delivering sustainable, profitable growth from your most important customers should be a key part of your strategy. The authors bring their decades of pragmatic experience to bear, laying out why it is so critical to focus on this topic and how to go about it. Read this book; it might well make you rethink your whole approach to profitable growth.'
Kevin Loosemore, Chairman, De La Rue

'Customer success evolved from the idea that a strong relationship with your client matters. Now it's great to finally see a book focused on building those relationships with your most strategic clients holistically. This book takes the virtues of the customer success revolution and builds on it with the other key elements – account management, account-based marketing, and executive engagement – while offering a comprehensive guide with insights from top market leaders.'
Nick Mehta, CEO, Gainsight

'In the subscription economy, retaining and growing with your top customers is essential. Bev Burgess and Tim Shercliff have researched this topic, laid out a framework for account-based growth and explain the challenges that need to be overcome, with the benefit of viewpoints and case studies from across the technology industry. Whether you're a high growth software company or a more mature technology serv
in this book for you.'
Sue Barsamian, board member

GU00505952

'I'm a passionate believer that your company's future prosperity depends on how well you treat a relatively small proportion of your customer base. Get this right, lining the whole company up behind the go-to-market team, and you will prosper. It sounds easy. It isn't. This book explains how to drive profitable growth, co-creating solutions with your best customers and turning them into advocates that help you win your next top customers. A must for CROs.'
Jon Hunter, CRO

'Bev Burgess has established herself as the leading light on client relationship marketing in all its dimensions within the business-to-business sector. The growing complexity of working relationships, between both institutions and individuals, requires new thinking that goes beyond the original idea that account-based marketing is all that is needed to bridge the gap between marketing and sales. Bev and Tim's new book explains why treating client relationship development as a total business concept, requiring the attention, effort and focus of all parts of the organization is necessary to ensure mutual, sustainable value.'
Dr Charles Doyle, Global Chief Marketing Officer, Arup

'Focusing on your most important customers is vital for your future growth. This book explains how to go about it, in clear and practical terms. A must for all CMOs.'
Fran Wilson, Chief Marketing Officer, Boomi

'Bev Burgess and Tim Shercliff have produced the must-have guide on account-based growth. This valuable business bible provides a no-nonsense approach to maximizing the potential of your top accounts and growing your business. It stands out from the crowd because it provides clear guidance on how to align and optimize internally to get the best results in this volatile market, it also helps leaders navigate the very real and unique cultural and societal issues businesses are facing today.'
Stella Low, Chief Corporate Affairs and Communications Officer, HP

'If you believe that selling to existing customers is easier than attracting new ones, this book will help you understand who your most important existing customers are, and how to sell more to them.'
Mike Phillips, Senior Independent Director and Audit Committee Chair, Bytes Technology Group

'This book wonderfully summarizes the importance of strategic accounts to your business and to your top clients. You know the 80/20 rule...well now it's about the 50/3.5 rule! Bev and Tim build the business case and provide the practical examples from both the supplier and the client's perspective. This serves as a guide to help change your mindset and develop a plan to grow your account as a "market of one". This is a must-read for those of us dedicated to focusing on our top clients for the long haul. Bravo!'
Denise Freier, President and CEO, Strategic Account Management Association

'When Bev Burgess codified and defined account-based marketing in 2003, she was way ahead of her time. It's taken many of us in B2B marketing and sales the best part of two decades to catch up with her. Her latest book (co-written with long-time collaborator Tim Shercliff) is similarly visionary, simultaneously elevating and reinvigorating the conversation around key accounts, their criticality to so many B2B organisations, and how to manage them. In essence, it's nothing short of a manifesto for why we need to shake up B2B sales and marketing once more to align with the unavoidable new business realities of 2022, and the challenges of operating in the post-Covid world. This is no work of theory or conjecture – it's packed full of real-life testimonies and case studies, and evidence-based strategies for how to turn these ideas into reality. Read it now and be ready for the future of B2B.'
Joel Harrison, co-founder and Editor-in-chief, *B2B Marketing*

Account-Based Growth

*Unlocking sustainable value through
extraordinary customer focus*

Bev Burgess and Tim Shercliff

For Krett,

with best wishes,

from Bev.

KoganPage

First published in Great Britain and the United States in 2022 by Kogan Page Limited

2nd Floor, 45 Gee Street	8 W 38th Street, Suite 902	4737/23 Ansari Road
London	New York, NY 10018	Daryaganj
EC1V 3RS	USA	New Delhi 110002
United Kingdom		India
www.koganpage.com		

Kogan Page books are printed on paper from sustainable forests.

ISBNs

Hardback	978 1 3986 0746 0
Paperback	978 1 3986 0744 6
Ebook	978 1 3986 0745 3

British Library Cataloguing-in-Publication Data

A CIP record for this book is available from the British Library.

Library of Congress Cataloging-in-Publication Data

Names: Burgess, Bev, author. | Shercliff, Tim, author.
Title: Account-based growth: unlocking sustainable value through extraordinary customer focus / Bev Burgess and Tim Shercliff.
Description: London, United Kingdom; New York, NY: Kogan Page, 2022. | Includes bibliographical references and index.
Identifiers: LCCN 2022030341 (print) | LCCN 2022030342 (ebook) | ISBN 9781398607446 (paperback) | ISBN 9781398607460 (hardback) | ISBN 9781398607453 (ebook)
Subjects: LCSH: Marketing. | Small business–Growth. | Customer relations.
Classification: LCC HF5415 .B77244 2022 (print) | LCC HF5415 (ebook) | DDC 658.8–dc23/eng/20220707
LC record available at https://lccn.loc.gov/2022030341
LC ebook record available at https://lccn.loc.gov/2022030342

Typeset by Integra Software Services, Pondicherry
Print production managed by Jellyfish
Printed and bound by CPI Group (UK) Ltd, Croydon CR0 4YY

To all the business leaders who have inspired us over the years
Bev and Tim

CONTENTS

FOREWORD

We are facing a perfect storm of a post-pandemic world with customer, strategic, operational and organizational challenges in our business lives. We find ourselves dealing with some critical pinch points, including a skills and talent crisis, leadership challenges, economic and political uncertainty and anxiety from a war in Ukraine. But rather than feel overwhelmed by this litany of potential issues, we should grasp this time as an opportunity to make a transformational shift in our business models, redefine our organizations for the next generation of customers and really take the learnings from the pandemic to create a new norm of 'wowing' customers.

What we are seeing coming out of the pandemic is a new currency of trust. As this excellent book argues, current business models that don't put the customer at the centre of their business are increasingly dysfunctional. We have to become obsessed about building strong customer relationships based firmly on trust and built around a single view of our most valuable assets, those customers who will help us grow.

Individual relationships, too, have changed. We have been given insights into all facets of our customers' lives through our recent virtual experiences. We see what books they read, their families, even their pets! As a chairman, director and mentor for many companies, I hear more and more from senior executives about the online meetings they have been having with the CEOs of their biggest customers – CEOs who pre-pandemic would have been 'protected' by armies of assistants and diary managers. They liken them to friendly chats – the 'we're all in this together' feeling – that would never have happened before the pandemic. And they're telling us that they need our help, not just in transforming their own enterprises, but in tackling challenges like recruiting the best talent, embedding equality and diversity and with broader social issues like climate change.

It's interesting how things change. Years ago, no one got fired in B2B if they bought from prestigious brands like IBM or GE. Now I think companies are struggling with what this new world looks like. The prestigious brands have been disrupted and customers buy on different values. Meanwhile, business leaders are asking: Who are our most important customers? How should we serve our biggest customers, who deliver a disproportionate amount of our profits? How should we serve the others?

What should the engagement model be for different customer tiers? How do we engage our employees? How do we simplify and add agility, spontaneity and speed? How do we ensure our offer and our own business has a strong purpose, embracing broader issues around sustainability? How do we become a most trusted brand? Future success emphatically won't be about individually 'fixing' sales, or marketing, or customer success. It will be about mobilizing our entire company to ensure that the customers who give us the license to exist derive maximum value from our products and services, and we invest our resources in them appropriately, with a careful balance between human resources and increasingly sophisticated technology.

Each of these customer relationships should be managed through unique moments of truth. After all, you are building a volunteer army of powerful advocates in customers when you get it right. Those businesses that become trusted to meet and exceed customers' expectations consistently will be tomorrow's global market leaders.

You have to start with small steps. Ask some basic questions. Do you know your revenue per customer? Revenue growth? Customer profitability? And critically, future growth potential? As the research for this book shows, too few have an integrated view of their customers. So, build an approach based on a clear-eyed view of each customer's importance and make sure every single employee is well aware that you only exist if your customers are successful. Integrate and align all functions but especially marketing, sales and customer success. Introduce disciplines such as behavioural psychology and data science and manage the huge complexity.

Within this all-embracing, customer-centric strategy, it will be essential to have a new leadership model, which balances the long-term vision and mission with actually delivering results. Changing gears on this scale will be challenging, so you need shorter-term project deliverables to prove early success and get the momentum going. That could be increasing revenue per customer or driving greater profitability overall.

Invite customers to stand on the stage with the chief executive, telling their story about what you have done for them and what more you could be doing. When people in the organization see the actual benefits from being focused on the customer's outcomes and experience, you will get this amazing, overwhelming drumbeat of customer-centricity permeating every part of the organization's DNA.

Intellectually this all makes perfect sense, of course. But if it were that easy, more companies would be doing it. In order to move to a new model, you will have to change. Undoubtedly, all companies will need help as you are likely to need to change your organization, plans, leadership, KPIs and even incentives to win the trust of customers. So, read the best-in-class case studies and the viewpoints contained in this book to see how others have done it, and the hurdles they have had to overcome.

Learn how they have got ahead of the game by segmenting their customers according to a careful analysis of current and potential growth, and then used this intelligence to take a radical view of resource allocation across these different tiers of customers, leveraging best practice in account management, marketing and customer success and making the most of their executives to accelerate customer value. Create a program of quick wins, celebration of successes, clear results – this will build the internal drumbeat of customer obsession.

I have personally worked with the authors on complex company transformations delivering exponential growth results. This timely book is an essential guide to navigating what will be a daunting yet exciting period of business transformation and growth. The book is written by experienced practitioners with the scars and learnings punctuated with powerful case studies. Take advantage of its wisdom and the pragmatic approaches it offers to have a chance of joining the band of world-class organizations set to thrive in this new world.

Stephen Kelly

Stephen Kelly is a company builder and serial entrepreneur. He is chair at Tech Nation, the UK's leading growth platform for tech companies and entrepreneurs. He is an investor in high-growth companies, a senior advisor to Blackrock LTPC, chair of the Science & Technology Honours committee, the former CEO of Sage, Micro Focus and Nasdaq-listed Chordiant and has been chief operating officer for the UK Government.

ABOUT THIS BOOK

Half of the profitable revenue for many B2B companies comes from just three per cent of their customers. This book explores this phenomenon in more detail and how companies are choosing to respond, particularly with their top customers, but also how they manage the 97 per cent of customers that make up the other half of the revenues. Some companies, as you will read later, have arrived at this imbalance by design and others almost by accident. But whichever it is, although 'the customer is king', to quote an old adage, clearly not all customers are equal.

Over the last 20 years the idea that a company should focus on its most important customers, treat them as a market in their own right and allocate marketing resources to build highly personalized marketing plans has taken hold. Account-based marketing emerged in the 2010s and is now recognized as a key element of B2B marketing. This is particularly true where complex, customized, high-consideration purchases are the norm, sometimes with individual deals worth hundreds of millions of dollars or annual recurring revenues running to tens of millions.

This is not just about marketing, however. It never was. It's about how a company becomes customer-centric across multiple processes and teams. And it's about growth and, more specifically, how to grow profitably with this huge imbalance between customers large and small.

These complex transactions are between companies which establish long-term, company-to-company relationships, as well as executive-to-executive relationships, which often last decades. The technologies and the ecosystems may change at an ever-increasing pace, but the relationships endure.

For example, some companies, recognizing the value of their largest customers, have taken account management to new levels, investing in much more senior executives managing their most important customer relationships.

Sales, too, is going through its own revolution. Customer executives and increasingly sophisticated procurement functions expect their strategic suppliers to understand their business issues and be proactive in bringing them valuable insights and solutions that tackle these issues and challenges and achieve their business outcomes.

Different consumption models have emerged over the last couple of decades, with subscription models and software-as-a-service largely eclipsing on-premise license and maintenance in the software industry and more sophisticated commercial models in services companies, with payments, risks and rewards linked to supplier performance and customer business outcomes.

Whatever the commercial model, retention and growth depend on whether an organization is actually delivering the value and the desired outcomes customers care about in ways that help them achieve their own key metrics.

To confront this, more companies have built customer success teams to attempt to ensure that customers achieve these desired outcomes. Too often, however, these customer success teams are organized around lines of business or divisions responsible for a major product or service, or a portfolio of similar products and services. That makes it difficult to take an integrated view of customer success and the lifetime value being delivered at an overall customer level.

So the central idea in this book is to postulate that companies should take a more aligned view of how they manage, sell to, market to, provide customer success and deliver services to and leverage their executive relationships for their customers, particularly the three per cent or so that are driving half their profitable revenue. They need a holistic view as to how to allocate resources and organize themselves more effectively to deliver profitable, sustainable growth and outstanding value for the most important customers. The impact on long-term profitable growth is significant, as many of the case studies in this book demonstrate.

The book is in four parts.

- Part One makes the case for account-based growth as a key element of a company's growth strategy, and examines account-based growth in practice today, first with a customer's perspective from Vodafone then drawing on the experience of Accenture and Infosys. It introduces the account-based growth framework, combining the elements that need to be better aligned internally and the elements that should be aligned for external engagement.

- Part Two discusses four essential elements that need to be aligned at a company level to implement an effective account-based growth strategy, looking at account prioritization and resource allocation; integrated account business plans; data, technology and operations; and leadership, culture and change. Further insights come from Atos, Cirrus (now owned by Accenture), Fujitsu, Inverta, Kyndryl, Microsoft, SAP and Telstra.

- Part Three examines each of the key customer-facing teams: account management and sales; account-based marketing and customer success. In addition, we look at how a company's executives can sponsor and engage top customers more effectively, with further perspectives from Cranfield University, Deloitte, Micro Focus, Virgin Media O2, Red Hat, Salesforce and ServiceNow.

- Part Four contains an assessment tool to enable companies to assess their own position against the key elements of account-based growth, clarifying the areas for improvement as they pursue an account-based growth strategy.

A note on terminology

Different industries use different terminology, so we have decided to use some terms throughout the book as follows:

- 'customer' to mean either client or customer;
- 'customer success' to signify both customer success and service or value delivery in predominantly service companies.

Also, while this book focuses mainly on technology services, software and professional services, these businesses share many characteristics with other sectors as the lines between industries become more blurred and as the digital revolution permeates almost every industry and every aspect of our lives.

ABOUT THE AUTHORS

Bev Burgess

Bev Burgess is passionate about the critical role marketing can play in accelerating business growth. Her specialism is the marketing and selling of business services, built through a combination of postgraduate study and the privilege of advising over 40 of the world's most influential firms, primarily in the technology and professional services sectors.

Bev's background includes senior marketing roles at British Gas, Epson and Fujitsu and Senior Vice President at ITSMA, where she led the ABM Practice for many years. Bev first codified ABM as a marketing strategy while Managing Director of ITSMA Europe in 2003. She has run her own strategic marketing consultancy and today Bev is a founder and Managing Principal at Inflexion Group, delivering thought leadership, consulting and training to companies around the world that are designing, developing and implementing account-based growth programmes.

Bev holds an MBA in strategic marketing and a BSc in business and ergonomics. She is a Fellow of the Chartered Institute of Marketing and has served as an international trustee.

Her first book, *Marketing Technology as a Service*, co-authored with Laurie Young, was published by Wiley in 2010, exploring proven techniques to create value through services based on an infrastructure of technology. Her most recent, *A Practitioner's Guide to ABM* (with Dave Munn, Kogan Page 2021, 2017), explains how to use ABM to accelerate growth in strategic accounts. *Executive Engagement Strategies*, published by Kogan Page in 2020, explains how to have conversations to deepen executive relationships and build sustainable growth with key clients.

Tim Shercliff

Tim Shercliff is an experienced and energetic business executive and board-level advisor with a strong track record in delivering outstanding results in the technology sector, through an unusual combination of experience in P&L

management of large business units; strategy development and execution in global businesses and complex program management.

Tim has spent more than 40 years in the technology and professional services sectors, the first 22 of which were at IBM Corporation, where he held senior sales, marketing, strategy and general management roles, becoming an IBM Corporate Executive in 2000.

Since leaving IBM in 2005, Tim has worked with over 20 technology and professional services companies, often as a member of or advisor to the executive leadership team in companies such as Micro Focus, Morse, CSC, Nationwide Building Society and Unisys. As a consultant, he has worked with Accenture, Microsoft and Fujitsu, amongst many others.

Since 2005, Tim has owned and managed consultancy businesses, initially Focus2xl Ltd, which he ran for 10 years, and more recently co-founding Inflexion Group, where he is Managing Director.

ACKNOWLEDGEMENTS

We have many people to thank for their help in writing this book.

Our deepest thanks go to the many executives who have collaborated with us to build the case studies and viewpoints that bring the concepts we put forward in the book to life. Alphabetically, by company and first name, they are: Accenture – Arjun Bedi and Stephanie Winters McConnell; Atos – Neil Berry; Deloitte – Paul Legere; Fujitsu – Ian Hunter; Infosys – Navin Rammohan; Inverta – Kathy Macchi; Kyndryl – Andrew Fitzgerald; Micro Focus – Nick Wilson; Microsoft – Rudy Dillenseger; Red Hat – Eileen Egan, Kari Price and Kristin Nordstrom-Waitkus; Salesforce – Aaron Tunesi; SAP – Bill Doyle and Eric Martin; ServiceNow – Gemma Davies; Telstra Purple – Chris Smith; Virgin Media O2 – Mark Larwood; Vodafone – Ninian Wilson. And a big thanks to Stephen Kelly for writing the all-important foreword to this book.

We'd like to recognize some of the leaders in other fields that we have featured in this book, who have been kind enough to give us their time, their viewpoints and their permission to reproduce some of their own thinking: Simon Haywood, CEO of Cirrus and published author on leadership topics, whom we feature in chapter 6; Emeritus Professor Malcolm McDonald, Associate Professor; Dr Javier Marcos Cueva, Dr Sue Holt and Visiting Fellow Mark Davies at Cranfield University School of Management, who run the Key Account Management Forum there, now in its 25th year, and who have written extensively on the topic, as we reference in Chapter 7; Nick Mehta, CEO at Gainsight, who has done significant work in the field of customer success; and Graham Clark, Visiting Fellow at Cranfield and author of several books on both service strategy and leadership, both of whom we feature in Chapter 9.

The people whom we work with every day to support our clients with their own account-based growth programmes also deserve a mention, since we create ideas as we work, and we have the pleasure of bringing them to life with such great people. We'd like to thank Amy, Katherine, Laura and Victoria in particular for their support in conducting and analyzing the account-based growth research study we feature throughout the book. Special thanks also go to our co-directors at Inflexion Group, Andy

McFarlane and Louise Jefferson, for peer reviewing our draft chapters in their spare time!

There are people without whom this book simply would not have been published and to whom we are especially grateful – Laura Mazur, whose help with interviewing, drafting and editing was invaluable as the book took shape, and the team at Kogan Page, especially Chris Cudmore, Heather Wood and Stephen Dunnell for their support along the way.

Finally, we'd like to thank our friends and family for giving us the encouragement and space to write, especially at weekends and on holidays! Katherine, Lauren, Ruth, Max – it was worth it!

PART ONE

Introducing account-based growth

The first part of this book describes what account-based growth (ABG) is and why it is emerging as one of the most powerful strategies organizations can follow to achieve profitable growth. It explains its foundations in the principle introduced by a 19th-century Italian economist who proved that a small proportion of inputs can translate into a disproportionately large amount of outputs. Applied to the business world, it means that for many companies 80 per cent of profitable revenue can come from just 20 per cent of customers – which can be an astonishing revelation for many once they grasp its implications, and, more importantly, act upon them.

Chapter 1 discusses the history of the 80/20 rule, its application to business over the years and how in this complex, uncertain and turbulent world, companies frequently seem to underestimate how dependent they are on a relatively small number of customers for sustainable, profitable revenue growth. And, because the 80/20 rule is fractal – meaning, it repeats itself – the rule can become more like 50/3, with half a company's profitable revenues coming from just three per cent of customers.

The chapter argues for a more aligned and selective approach towards these important accounts, which should be seen as a vital source of growth, particularly when the cost of customer acquisition can be so high. It describes the drawbacks faced by many companies that still operate with functional silos, despite revolutions within individual functions such as marketing, sales and customer success over the last few years.

Chapter 2 moves on to explore how account-based growth works in practice, based on original research carried out for the book among 65 B2B organizations. It shows that the 80/20 rules does indeed apply across the board. Many companies recognize aspects of this and have developed top-account programmes, appreciating that some customers are more important than others to their growth. But too many have yet to align themselves internally around their top customers to maximum effect. This chapter explains the key findings from the research and will help you analyze your main gaps, introducing a simple but powerful framework to achieve account-based growth.

01

The case for account-based growth

When a business starts, it is based on a simple model. It solves a problem for a customer by providing a solution and is obsessed with delivering value to that customer. It's likely that everyone in the team is very well attuned to every customer's needs. There may only be a few customers on the roster, but the business knows them well because its very existence depends on winning them and keeping them happy.

Over time, companies typically grow in two dimensions: find more customers who like what they do, and/or develop new solutions for existing customers. However, even in those early days with only a few dozen customers, a fundamental principle is starting to emerge: some customers will be far more important than others. In fact, a pattern soon develops that will probably reveal that around 80 per cent of profitable revenue comes from just 20 per cent of customers.

Once the pattern starts to emerge, it doesn't seem to change much over time. In fact, it may become even more pronounced.

Fast-forward a few years and guess what: the ratio applies equally in large companies! Take any complex, global technology company. They boast billions in revenues, have thousands of customers, tens of thousands of employees and a complex partner and supplier ecosystem. But the self-same 80/20 rule applies to these companies too. In fact, it is often even more skewed: sometimes 90 per cent of profitable revenues comes from just 10 per cent of the customers.

At Broadcom, a $27bn technology company, this statement from the 2021 annual report illustrates the point further. It shows how concentrated its business is, with a business strategy designed to focus on adding high value to a relatively small set of the world's leading business and government customers. 'A relatively small number of customers account for a significant portion of our net revenue… We believe aggregate sales to our top five end customers, through all channels, accounted for more than 35 per cent and 30 per cent of our net revenue for each of our fiscal years

2021 and 2020, respectively... We expect to continue to experience significant customer concentration in future periods' (Broadcom, 2021).

Broadcom may be an extreme example of the 80/20 rule, but once we started looking further into this topic, we found similar stories of high levels of dependency on relatively few customers everywhere.

The fact that this is happening in multiple companies is not some freak accident. Examine almost any dataset of any size you like and you find that there is an 80/20 split between causes and effects or inputs and outputs. Invariably, companies that do the analysis will find that 20 per cent of their customers provide 80 per cent of their profitable revenue, as illustrated in Figure 1.1.

FIGURE 1.1   20 per cent of accounts drive 80 per cent of revenues

THE 80/20 RULE IS FRACTAL
The 80/20 rule is fractal, meaning it repeats itself, carrying on in descending order. Within the first 20 per cent, another 20 per cent will account for 80 per cent within that dataset, and so on, like a *matryoshka*, or Russian nesting doll.

FIGURE 1.2   The 80/20 rule is fractal

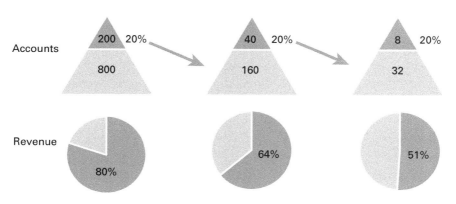

The implications of the fractal nature of the 80/20 rule are profound for business, as we will demonstrate later in this chapter. Before that, though, let's understand the underlying concept further.

The 80/20 rule and its application to business

The 80/20 principle is elegant in its simplicity. Its roots lie in the work done by an Italian economist, Vilfredo Pareto, whose research in the late 1890s showed that roughly 80 per cent of the land in 19th-century England was owned by 20 per cent of the population and that this distribution also applied with mathematical precision across countries and timeframes (Koch, 2017).

For many years, Pareto's work was of interest mainly in the more rarefied circles of academia. In 1951, however, it burst onto the industrial scene through the work of Joseph Juran, a Romanian-born US engineer and management consultant whose name has become synonymous with the emergence of total quality management (Koch, 2017).

Juran had begun to apply the Pareto principle to problems of quality control in the 1940s, demonstrating that 80 per cent of problems stem from 20 per cent of causes, something he called the 'vital few'. In 1951, he published the *Quality-Control Handbook* (Juran, 1951). With little interest shown by American companies, he was invited to Japan, where application of his ideas transformed Japanese industry into a quality powerhouse.

This eventually led to the rise of the total quality management (TQM) movement of the late 1970s/early 1980s in the West, which has since morphed into other quality management approaches such as 'lean' and 'six sigma'. The key components include customer focus, employee involvement, an emphasis on fact-based process, integration and continuous improvement (DeFeo, 2019).

It was not until 1997 that the rule itself and how to exploit it in business came to the fore with the publication of the first edition of *The 80/20 Principle: The secret to achieving more with less* by Richard Koch. A successful entrepreneur, Koch explains how to achieve more with less across all facets of business and life by identifying and focusing efforts on the 20 per cent that really matters:

> For example, the 80/20 principle asserts that 20 percent of products, or customers or employees, are really responsible for about 80 per cent of profits.

If this is true – and detailed investigations usually confirm that some such very unbalanced pattern exists – the state of affairs implied is very far from being efficient or optimal… In this kind of situation one might well ask: why continue to make the 80 per cent of products that only generate 20 per cent of profits? Companies rarely ask these questions, perhaps because to answer them would mean very radical action: to stop doing four-fifths of what you are doing is not a trivial change. (Koch, 2017: 14)

Relevance to account-based growth

Companies frequently seem to underestimate just how dependent they are on a relatively small number of customers for sustainable, profitable revenue growth. Some companies seem to have arrived at this point by design; others by accident.

Because of the fractal nature of the 80/20 rule, they may also underestimate how much more important the customers at the top end of the top 20 per cent – the tier-one accounts – are compared with those at the bottom (Figure 1.3). We reviewed a dataset at an enterprise software company recently to find the top 10 customers out of their top 150 customers contributed on average eight times more revenue than the bottom 10 customers in that same top 150. Despite this, they had a 'top 150' programme covering all 150 accounts, with little differentiation between how those right at the top were treated compared with those at the bottom.

The result of this 'wonky' fractal relationship is startling, as Figure 1.2 demonstrates. In a company that has 1,000 customers, only eight customers will account for just over half the company's revenues if the 80/20 rule applies. In Chapter 2, we will discuss the results of our research in this area, which shows that the average for the companies we surveyed is very close to 80/20. In most cases it is between a 75/25 and an 80/20 split, but in some cases it is more extreme than 80/20.

The result of the fractal nature of the 80/20 rule for each tier of accounts is shown in Figure 1.3. This shows just how concentrated a company's revenues are in a relatively small number of accounts and how important it is to treat the most important customers that make up the top 20 per cent differently, not just from the remaining 80 per cent, but from the rest of the top 20 per cent.

If the customer dataset is based on an exact fractal 80/20 split, it follows that the average revenue from the customers in tier one is 16 times bigger

FIGURE 1.3 The contribution of different account tiers to revenues

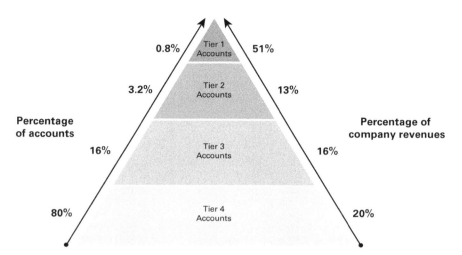

than those in tier two, 64 times bigger than those in tier three and 256 times bigger than tier 4. This is easy to demonstrate. Let's assume that a company has 1,000 accounts and revenues of $1,000 million. In this case, 51 per cent of the revenue comes from just 8 accounts, which is an average revenue of c. $64 million for each (tier one); 13 per cent of the revenue comes from the next 32 accounts, at an average of c. $4 million (tier two); the final 16 per cent of revenues in the top 20 per cent comes from 160 accounts, at an average of $1 million (tier three). Finally, revenues from the bottom 80% have an average of $0.25 million (tier four).

THE FIGURES SPEAK FOR THEMSELVES

Revenues from accounts in tier one are 256 times greater, on average, than those in tier four, ie the 80 per cent of accounts that make up only 20 per cent of the company's revenues (tier four). Consider this: if you lose an account in tier one, you would need to win 256 average-sized accounts in tier four to make up for the lost revenue. Figure 1.4 illustrates this visually.

FIGURE 1.4 Losing one tier-one customer means finding 256 tier-four customers

Table 1.1 illustrates the mathematics that underpins this, showing a company with $1,000 million in revenues and 1,000 customers.

If you are sceptical about whether 80/20, with its fractal nature, applies to you, as many companies have been when we have first engaged with them on this topic, have a look at your own data. We think you might be surprised. You may not be exactly at 80/20 and it may not be exactly fractal, but our experience suggests you won't be far off these ratios. The implications for this level of concentration in a relatively small number of accounts are far-reaching, particularly in relation to your company's growth and profitability and how resources are allocated.

Impact on profits

So far we have been discussing the 80/20 rule in relation to revenues, not profit. In our experience, the picture is even more skewed in companies that measure profit at the account level. Sometimes all of a company's profit is derived from a relatively small number of customers, with the 'long tail' of accounts in the bottom 80 per cent generating relatively little revenue and often no profit at all.

In a recent discussion we had with executives in a large enterprise software company, they shared some analysis that in a total customer base of 7,000 customers, 5,000 of them were 'a rounding' when it came to revenue, and lost them money at the bottom line when direct costs were taken into account. Perversely, the marketing team were generating leads at a ratio of 10,000 leads in this group of 5,000 less important customers to just one lead

TABLE 1.1 The key ratios if the fractal 80/20 rule applies in your company

Company ABC Account Tiers – if 80/20 rule is fractal in your company

	Number of accounts	% of total number of accounts	% of revenue	Average revenue per account ($m)	Ratio from top tier
Tier 1	8	0.8%	51%	$64	1
Tier 2	32	3.2%	13%	$4	16
Tier 3	160	16.0%	16%	$1	64
Tier 4	800	80.0%	20%	$0.25	256

Number of customers (over agreed minimum size)   1,000
Total revenue ($m)   1,000

in their top 10 per cent of accounts. This is obviously crazy – but a real example of the amount of disconnect there sometimes is between, in this case, marketing and sales.

Stability of top accounts

One of the other interesting phenomena is how long these top account relationships endure. Or put another way, if a company analyzes its top accounts this year and compares it with the top accounts of five or 10 years ago, it will tend to find that the same companies keep cropping up. Of course, over this timescale, new companies have emerged as major players and new accounts will appear on the top account list while some drop out, but the churn rate between the tier-one accounts and the next tiers is often remarkably small.

This leads to an important conclusion, which is that companies need to find growth in these all-important accounts, and not rely, certainly not exclusively, on new customer acquisition as the primary source of growth.

You should grow in your biggest accounts, not just defend

Too often companies have not done the analysis to show which customers contribute most revenue and profit. When they do the analysis, they are often surprised about their dependency on a relatively small number of accounts. They also often underestimate the potential of these accounts, taking a wholly risk-averse attitude to pursuing more growth with them.

Of course, there is a need to build risk mitigation into plans for the top customers, because losing one altogether can be very damaging for revenues and profits and will be very difficult to make up for, particularly in the short term, as we demonstrated earlier. However, it is our assertion that risk mitigation does not necessarily mean accepting little or no growth from these top accounts, particularly when the company's portfolio is large and expanding. There is strong evidence from the market leaders that this is something they excel in, with viewpoints and case studies throughout the book, illustrating best practice.

After all, you already have an established relationship and reputation for value delivery with these customers. Even if you have 10 per cent of a customer's spend in the addressable market space you can target, aiming for growth of 50 per cent still accounts for only 15 per cent of their business. Moreover, if you don't grow your share of their wallet, someone else may, potentially having a detrimental effect on your ability to defend your position.

Sustained customer loyalty has a significant impact on a company's fortunes. This concept was first brought to prominence by Bain & Company's Frederich Reichheld and still holds true today. Depending on the industry, research suggests that acquiring a new customer is five to 25 times more expensive than retaining an existing one.

Returning to the 'maths' of the 80/20 rule, 50 per cent growth in one of your most important customers may well equate to acquiring hundreds of smaller customers. At least some of these smaller customers are quite possibly top customers of your competitors, so the chances of success are much reduced, given that they will be defending their base.

It clearly makes sense, in addition to focusing on your current top accounts, to be deliberate in the targeting of new accounts, and do this over a long enough time horizon to be able to establish trust, something Stephanie Winters McConnell, from Accenture, discusses in her viewpoint in Chapter 2.

Trust is not established overnight, of course, but through value delivered and relationships built up over years. So it may be that patience is required to acquire a new top account.

THOUGHTFUL TARGETING OF PROSPECTS

It is likely to be more cost effective to put effort and energy into customers that could become future top accounts than treat the 80 per cent of customers that only account for 20 per cent of your revenues in the same way.

The perils of the long tail

The long tail of large numbers of accounts generating very little revenue can be a challenge for business leaders, particularly if their company strategy and market capitalization is predicated on future growth. One mature enterprise software company recently calculated that the bottom 15 per cent of accounts cost a full 40 per cent of their renewals expenses and that the gross profit generated from the smaller transactions in these customers therefore lost the company money at the net profit level. This realization has caused a re-evaluation about how to move these smaller customers to self-service channels and the rebalancing of resources towards the larger, more profitable customers, upon whom future profitable growth depends.

FIGURE 1.5 The perils of the long tail

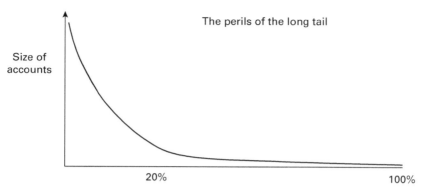

Figure 1.5 illustrates what a company's account profile might look like, with a relatively small number of customers generating 80 per cent of the revenue and a long tail of increasingly smaller and smaller accounts.

Deciding how to grow

Growth no matter what is not a sensible strategy, particularly when the cost of customer acquisition, and, to a lesser extent, subsequent expansion, is so high. Often, the cost of bidding for high-consideration, complex deals can run into millions of dollars, with some of the company's best resources tied up on deals for many months, sometimes years.

The central hypothesis for this book is that, with company-wide analysis and strategic decision-making around the 80/20 rule, the right accounts can be targeted and company resources focused more effectively, leading to stronger growth, lower costs and higher profitability.

While the majority of a company's growth should come from its most important accounts, it is important to focus on finding new customers that could become, over time, part of the top 20 per cent. This deliberate targeting of future top accounts rather than pursuing sales with any and all prospects is a key strategy, discussed in Chapter 3 on account prioritization and resource allocation and throughout later chapters. It demands thoughtful targeting, a willingness to place bets and a disciplined approach.

There have, of course, been significant improvements in how companies strengthen customer relationships, with revolutions in the way that customer-facing functions such as marketing, sales and customer success operate and how executives engage, detailed in the next section. But even where this has happened, it has occurred mainly in their respective silos. And it has often happened without a real company-wide focus on the accounts that matter most now and will matter most in the future. This presents a massive opportunity for companies to build much stronger internal alignment and engage far more effectively with their most important customers to accelerate growth.

Building blocks for success

The last 20 years has seen the emergence of groundbreaking strategies such as account-based marketing (ABM), key account management (KAM), challenger sales (Dixon and Adamson, 2011), customer success and executive engagement strategies, driven by the need to build relationships with companies that can boast revenues rivaling that of many small or medium-sized countries. Recognition of the 80/20 rule, implicitly if not explicitly, has been the driving force behind some of these advances.

Marketing

B2B marketing has been transformed by account-based marketing (ABM), one of the biggest shifts in B2B marketing thinking for decades.

The idea of treating individual accounts as markets in their own right began to take hold as customers grew in size and scale. This has been particularly true where complex, customized, high-consideration transactions have increasingly become the norm, sometimes with individual deals worth hundreds of millions or even billions of dollars over multiple years. These complex transactions are between companies who establish long-term, company-to-company relationships, as well as individual executive-to-executive relationships, often over many decades.

As defined in *A Practitioners Guide to Account-based Marketing* (Burgess, B with Munn, D, Kogan Page, 2021), 'ABM gives marketers a structured process for developing and implementing highly customized marketing programmes based on deep insights into strategic accounts, partners or prospects.' The key is account prioritization and following through with appropriate investment in ABM, focusing on your most important accounts.

Account management

In parallel to the shift to account-based marketing, some companies, such as Accenture and Salesforce, recognizing the value of their largest customers, have enhanced their account management approach to invest in much more senior executives managing the most important customer relationships. This has seen the rise of the customer managing director, general manager or client partner, where a senior executive, often having previously run a major part of the business, has responsibility for a single, hugely significant customer, managing customer lifetime value and, in some cases, profit and loss, at a customer level.

Much of these companies' growth can be attributed to their relentless focus on their most important customers and the trust they have built with them over many years. Both companies, as will be discussed later in the book, have been pioneers in the field.

At Salesforce, the legendary Jim Steele was appointed as the first ever Chief Customer Officer in 2009 and returned once again to Salesforce in 2020 to spearhead the focus on global strategic customers.

At Accenture, the focus on top customers is through the establishment of the Diamond Client Leadership Council, Accenture's global strategic portfolio of clients, described further later in this chapter.

Sales

Selling has been through its own revolution. Gone are the days of sales asking 'open questions' to elicit a customer's requirements and then building solutions to fit these requirements. Customer executives and increasingly sophisticated procurement functions expect their strategic suppliers to know their business issues and be proactive in bringing them valuable insights and solutions, creating competitive advantage for them in the process.

The rise of insight-based sales methodologies, such as 'challenger sales' in the last ten years, mirrors the way that account-based marketing has become the norm for B2B marketing, and was described in the groundbreaking book *The Challenger Sale* by Matthew Dixon and Brent Adamson (2011). *The Challenger Sale* is based on interviews with 6,000 sales reps across a range of industries and territories so that the authors could get a clearer picture of why some sales reps were more successful than others.

The authors found that they could categorize the sales teams into five profiles: relationship builders, hard workers, lone wolves, reactive problem solvers and challengers. While all of these types of reps can deliver average sales performance, only one out of the five, the challenger, delivers consistently high performance. This accords with numerous studies mentioned by

Koch, that show that the top 20 per cent of salespeople generate between 70 and 80 per cent of sales (Koch, 2017).

Notwithstanding these advances in marketing, sales and key account management, the question remains whether companies are focused on the right customers and whether the sales coverage model is being appropriately tuned to the realities and potential of the customer base and prospects. Moreover, many B2B firms operate a complex partner ecosystem, which means that some partners are as important or in some cases more important than the end customers. This too needs to be reflected in the overall approach a company takes to account-based growth with the same focus and allocation of resources in managing these significant relationships. We will consider this in more detail in further chapters.

Customer success

It is one thing to win business in the first place, but quite a different task to retain and grow over subsequent years. Different consumption models have emerged in the last couple of decades, with subscription models and software-as-a-service largely eclipsing on-premise licence and maintenance in the enterprise software industry, and more sophisticated commercial models appearing in services companies, with payments, risks and rewards linked to supplier performance and customer business outcomes.

In response, many of the leading companies, particularly in enterprise software, have built customer success teams to attempt to ensure that their customers are receiving the value they expected and consequently remain a customer and increase their adoption over the long term. These customer success teams are, in our experience, sometimes operating in a silo, not necessarily focused sufficiently on the top accounts and not fully aligned with marketing and sales. Here too, there is opportunity to better align the company's efforts on the most important customers.

Executive sponsorship and engagement

Finally, the way company executives engage with their customer executive counterparts has also been going through something of a revolution, with some companies investing in executive engagement programmes sponsored at the highest level. That said, the opportunity to have a well-focused, well-orchestrated executive sponsorship and engagement programme proves elusive for many companies, with executives being parachuted in to help close deals and fight fires, rather than being focused on long-term growth and mutual value creation with their biggest accounts, or helping nurture executive relationships in carefully targeted prospects.

The business context

There are some powerful forces forcing businesses of all sizes and shapes to carry out a radical rethink about the long-term value of customer relationships and how they interact with their customers. Understanding them is integral to account-based growth success.

These forces include:

1. The changing nature of B2B buyers

As technology increasingly enables a one-to-one relationship with customers, B2B organizations have to do more than just sell effectively. They have to create real insight into what their customers value and make it easy for customers to acquire knowledge about them through multiple channels as they make their way through the buying journey.

High consideration, complex transactions are commonly determined by increasingly large groups of buyers looking to reach consensus before making a decision. In 2015, this was reported as an average of 5.4 people in wide-ranging research by CEB and reported in the book *The Challenger Customer* (Adamson *et al*, 2015). Other research and anecdotal evidence suggest that the number of decision-makers in the buyer group can be as many as 20 to 30 people in very complex sales. In the same book, it was also reported that the buying journey was, on average, 57 per cent of the way through before the customer reached out to potential suppliers, with some commentators now reporting this as 60–70 per cent. Finally, it noted that the number of people involved in the buying process was increasing every year.

There is an inexorable rise in the use of different channels in the B2B buyer-seller journey, consistent with the way that consumers have become accustomed to using multiple channels, particularly online, self-service, to research and make quite substantial purchases. McKinsey, in a report from December 2021 (Harrison *et al*, 2021), charted the rise of 'omnichannel' in B2B purchases, with five channels in active use in B2B buying decisions in

2016 and 10 channels being used by 2021, with all of the additional channels being online alternatives to meeting face-to-face with a salesperson. The report also blows apart the myth that B2B purchases online are only for small, simple transactions, with 20 per cent of B2B decision-makers now willing to make purchases of between $500,000 and $5 million through a single online transaction, up from 16 per cent in less than a year.

Although the really high value transactions of over $10 million are still very rarely made online (4 per cent), the direction of travel is obvious, with the danger that traditional approaches to face-to-face selling are being bypassed, particularly if 60–70 per cent of the buyer's journey has been completed before customers reach out to potential suppliers. This important trend in how B2B business is actually done leads to two conclusions:

1 The integration across marketing and sales, in how they present a consistent set of channels and relevant, personalized content to their customers is increasingly important.

2 For the largest customers, the nature of the relationship between the company and customer needs to be sufficiently strong and deep to be able to influence the decision process much earlier in the sales cycle than will naturally happen because more and more information is available through other channels.

This demands investment in experienced, senior dedicated teams in the largest customers, who spend the time it takes to get to know their customers intimately. By definition, this has to be done selectively. As one seasoned executive commented: 'If we have one managing partner on an account and our competition can afford four managing partners on the same account, on the whole, we're going to lose out. We'll be losing business we didn't even know about before it was too late.'

2. The rise of platform businesses and the impact on B2B

Platform businesses create marketplaces that bring together consumers and producers of value units through interactions that occur on the platform, for example, large aspects of the businesses of Amazon, Google and Apple. McKinsey estimates that 30 per cent of global economic activity – $60 trillion – could be mediated by digital platforms by 2025 (Chung *et al*, 2020). Platform businesses like Amazon, Google and eBay grew rapidly by enabling symbiotic relationships between buyers and sellers in that the more buyers there were, the more suppliers there were. This creates a strong multiplier effect.

It has led to the most successful platform business becoming near-monop-olies, which means that in many of these market segments there are no profits to be made unless you are in one of the top three or even two spots. Everyone else loses money. For example, in the search engine market, one company, Google, holds an 86 per cent market share (Statista, 2022).

The network effects of these platform businesses enable rapid and hith-erto unseen growth rates and almost instant global reach, with the power and speed to change competitive dynamics within whole industries. Despite initially being mainly a B2C phenomenon, the most rapid growth is now in B2B platform businesses.

3. The impact of the pandemic

When the world shut down in early 2020, it was a generational trauma. Although scientists had worried about such a cataclysmic event, no one really saw it coming. For businesses, the impact was devastating. Doors shut abruptly and suddenly building and maintaining relationships and trading online was just about all there was for most B2B businesses.

For B2B companies, it was urgent to climb a steep learning curve in order to stay close to, and support, their best customers – assuming they knew who they were.

The three biggest providers of online infrastructure services or cloud services, Microsoft, Google and Amazon Web Services, saw enormous growth in just a few quarters: taken together, from $27 billion in the fourth quarter of 2020 to $37 billion by the second quarter of 2021. Microsoft Executive Chairman and CEO Satya Nadella stated, 'We saw two years of digital transformation in two months' (Microsoft, 2022).

McKinsey calls this digital explosion the new normal. Its research shows that more than three quarters of buyers and sellers say they now prefer digi-tal self-service and remote human engagement over face-to-face interactions.

Companies that had already invested heavily in close, executive-level rela-tionships with their most important customers reaped the rewards. In the rapid acceleration of digital transformation, there was much work to be done and no time to form new relationships, so companies turned to their pre-existing trusted relationships, driving rapid growth in wallet share in some cases.

4. The need to focus on broader environmental and societal issues

Three companies featured later, Accenture, Atos and Infosys, illustrate how important a compelling, authentic, values-based approach to broader sustainability and social issues has become to developing long-term, mutually supportive relationships with their customers. This is echoed in the customer viewpoint included in this chapter, from Ninian Wilson, CEO of Vodafone procurement.

Accenture has possibly the broadest and most mature response to this, its '360° Value' approach, delivering the financial business case and unique value a client may be seeking, along with striving to partner with its clients to achieve greater progress across these dimensions: client, talent, inclusion and diversity, experience, sustainability and financial. The company applies these same categories of value to how it operates its business to ensure strong, consistent alignment internally and externally (Accenture, 2021). This is illustrated further in the Accenture case study later in this chapter.

Atos describes itself as the global leader in secure and decarbonized digital, with a range of market-leading digital solutions along with consultancy services, digital security and decarbonization offerings; it has an end-to-end partnership approach. It adds that it is a net-zero pioneer in decarbonization services and products, with a commitment to the future extending to carbon neutrality for its organization as well as its customers and partners.

Infosys, too, stresses that, in many cases, it is the alignment around shared values with its customers that enables it to win and retain customers, as much as the compelling nature of its solutions. Its partnerships with *Financial Times* and *The Economist* create opportunities to align with and develop deeper relationships with its top customers around topics of mutual interest and significance.

We know of many companies that, when making major decisions, are using the alignment of values, culture and the approach to sustainability in their potential suppliers as a key factor in their decision process. While the business case and ROI will remain hugely important financial measures, there is no doubt that, over the next few years, a set of measures associated with how a business creates value sustainably and responsibly has become increasingly important, as Ninian Wilson goes on to explain shortly.

The customer and supplier view

Most of the viewpoints and case studies contained in this book are written from the perspective of the supplier, illustrating their views and best practice in different aspects of account-based growth. However, before we learn more about account-based growth from a supplier's perspective, we have a viewpoint from Ninian Wilson, representing the customer's view, based on his many years in procurement and supply chain management from Cable and Wireless, and, more latterly, Vodafone.

VIEWPOINT

Ninian Wilson, Group Procurement Director and CEO, Vodafone Procurement Company

In your experience, how do companies differentiate between strategic suppliers who can really make a difference to their competitive advantage and other suppliers?

The classic approach is to use a variation of the Boston matrix, mapping out your spend with a supplier and how critical they are to your business (Figure 1.6). Your strategic suppliers are those where you are spending a lot and the services they provide are critical to your business. Typically, procurement will sit down with the business executives and review all suppliers, looking at what impact they can have for our business going forward.

FIGURE 1.6 Illustrative supplier matrix

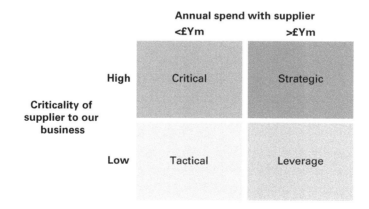

It's useful to also map each supplier's view of us behind this matrix – do they see us as a strategic account? There needs to be a match for it to work. If the supplier sees you as strategic, but you do not, this needs to be worked through.

And when it works, you have relationships that span decades benefitting both businesses and their wider stakeholder communities. Strategic suppliers get more access and engagement across the business – up to the executive committee – collaborating much more closely.

What should companies expect from their strategic suppliers?

There are six key things.

The first is a dedicated account team – the supplier should invest sufficiently to make the strategic relationship work; and customers should reciprocate by ensuring access to the right executives.

Next, an unfair share of their research and development budget – if a customer is really strategic, it should be translated into competitive advantage through access to innovation and assets.

Strategic customers need to be first to receive new products and services, and also be 'first among equals' commercially, as they prepare to build something once (for us) and then sell it many times (to others) later.

Strategic suppliers should be highly connected at all different levels across the business, starting with CEO to CEO, and right through the executive teams and functional leaders in both organizations.

Governance is really important, too. For example, I'd expect the CEOs to meet twice a year and the account director to meet the client quarterly in review meetings as part of the relationship governance. And, by the way, these governance reviews should start with current performance, and then move on to future innovation and opportunities. If the current performance isn't good, you may never get on to future opportunities, of course. If it's all good, you have more time to explore what's next.

It takes a seasoned, experienced executive to run this kind of strategic relationship, and I see that role as the most important one in the supplier. That person represents our voice into the supplier company. They need to be senior enough to know everyone and be able to make things happen on our behalf.

What is best practice from strategic suppliers today?

In addition to the things we've already discussed, I would add executive sponsorship – someone from the supplier's headquarters allocated to you as an account. That sponsor will come to the quarterly reviews, and have full transparency as to how things are going in the relationship. If the account executive is not the right calibre, for example, both sides will see that. There's nowhere to hide. And at Vodafone, we insist that the executive sponsor for our strategic suppliers is either the CEO or one of their direct reports.

The best strategic suppliers are those that stay the course, over the long term, even if the nature of the business changes and the level of the business fluctuates. It's important to see these as long-term plays, sometimes lasting decades, such as the relationship between Ericsson and Vodafone, who sent and received the first ever text message in 1992, and are still technology partners, some 30 years later.

And, typically, what are some of the main faults of suppliers?

A lack of connection internally across the supplier's account team is one that comes to mind. A lack of professionalism can be an issue, for example, not sending meeting materials in advance of the meeting so that the customer has time to prepare. Since we see all our strategic suppliers through a common governance process, it is very easy to see which are less professional and less well prepared.

Leaving issues unresolved is a real problem that can really damage the relationships. The supplier's account executive has to be able to escalate problems and get them sorted quickly: cut a deal, sort it out and move on. Otherwise, everyone takes their eye off the ball and it can prevent future innovation, for example.

A lack of commerciality, and empathy as to what our objectives are, is another issue. For example, as a customer, we'll have objectives to reduce costs over time, so we want our strategic suppliers to acknowledge this and bring us ideas on how this can be achieved rather than try to hold on to the current revenue from the contract. The best supplier's account executives are open. They deliver an excellent service with great product quality at the right price. I don't need to know exactly what profit they're making, but I certainly don't want to hear that they're 'not making enough money' from the account.

Surprises are a no-no. I expect strategic suppliers to give us a heads-up around important changes and announcements in their business. We shouldn't find out about news that could impact our relationship from the media!

And finally, I would say that trying to cut procurement out of discussions is the wrong way to go. Strategic suppliers need to understand the role and positioning of procurement leaders in the wider business.

How important are shared values and a focus on broader social issues when selecting strategic suppliers today?

These are becoming more important for two reasons. The first is that there is a huge interest from customers in how we're running our business today. The second is that access to capital is being regulated by a company's position on environment, sustainability and governance (ESG) issues.

This ESG focus is not going away. Customers are so much more aware of business practices, and it takes around 16 minutes for bad news to go viral, so there's no time to respond after the event – you can't change your agenda in 16 minutes.

For us at Vodafone, we have three main areas of focus: helping to digitize society, driving diversity and inclusion and supporting the planet. I am the executive sponsor for the inclusion agenda, as we want to drive it through our whole supply chain.

And when supplier selection is based on weighted scores in a tender, with most decisions swung by just 3–4 per cent, weightings around ESG can make the difference. For example, we might weight health and safety criteria at around 10 per cent; diversity, equality and inclusion at 5 per cent and care for the planet at another 5 per cent across the whole tender. For suppliers who don't take one of these seriously, it can mean losing the opportunity, even if they have a good track record – they need to put the effort in.

How can companies encourage smaller suppliers, who may have innovative solutions but no prior track record or relationships?

This is the holy grail of procurement – getting access to innovative ideas and capabilities for the future, particularly from up-and-coming companies. It's a key part of the procurement leader's role.

We set up an incubator five years ago as a joint venture with the Luxembourg Government, to help scale-up companies connect better across the business at Vodafone. We've set up a website (tomorrowstreet.co) as a resource to help them.

We also run an annual two-day event called Arch Summit, as a *Dragons' Den*–style event. We have some of the actual dragons from the show come along, together with Vodafone executives, and there's the chance to win a substantial investment or contract with Vodafone for the winners.

It can be difficult for these smaller suppliers to do business with large customers, so you have to recognize this and try to make it easier. For example, we've moved to a two-page contract and 30-day payment terms for small suppliers.

Professional service firms talk a lot about leveraging a broader ecosystem of partners on behalf of their customers. Is this something you think valuable and welcome?

These relationships can be so complex, where you buy from your strategic supplier, they buy from you, and you also go to market together in joint ventures. In these relationships, either party can suggest new partners, leveraging their ecosystem, and then our role as procurement leaders is to orchestrate the ecosystem. That involves everything from finding new suppliers through to getting the right commercial constructs in place.

Finally, what last piece of advice would you give suppliers trying to build long-term sustainable value with their customers?

Keep an eye on how the wider business environment is changing. For example, the whole area of supply chain risk is becoming more of a focus. We may even see companies verticalizing some of their supply chains, in a move back to the business models of 70–80 years ago, as we face increasing global uncertainty. How will that impact our relationships and ecosystems going forward?

Be humble. Even from a global, strategic supplier, I don't want to see arrogance. If you've made a mistake, hold your hands up and learn from it, don't pretend it didn't happen. Do your homework and find out what the key drivers are for the relationship as it evolves.

Ninian has laid out the landscape for strategic suppliers beautifully, from the customer's perspective, offering useful insights and practical advice for both up-and-coming, smaller companies offering new and innovative solutions to large, complex, global organizations.

One large, complex, global company that has a well-defined programme for its top clients is Accenture, whose Diamond client programme has been developed over many years. Like many other companies, they follow the 80/20 rule, with 244 Diamond clients out of 7,000 (3.5 per cent) delivering over half their revenue (Accenture 2022, CFO slides).

The case study below explains further.

CASE STUDY
Accenture: Creating 360° Value

Accenture is a global professional services company with a history tracing back to the installation of the first computer system for commercial use in the United States. Since it went public in 2001, Accenture has enjoyed significant growth, from revenues of $11bn and 75,000 employees, to 2021, when its revenues reached over $50bn with more than 600,000 employees.

The company has leading capabilities in digital, cloud and security, combining unmatched experience and specialized skills across more than 40 industries. It offers strategy and consulting, interactive, technology and operations services – all powered by the world's largest network of advanced technology and intelligent operations centres. Today, its nearly 700,000 employees and ecosystem of 185 partners deliver on the promise of technology and human ingenuity every day, serving more than 7,000 clients in over 120 countries. Its focus is on embracing the power of change to create value and shared success for its clients, people, shareholders, partners and wider communities. As of 2022, it has been recognized among *Fortune*'s World's Most Admired Companies for 20 consecutive years.

Enduring client relationships

Accenture's clients include more than three-quarters of the *Fortune* Global 500. Ninety-eight of its top 100 clients have been clients for over 10 years. Its largest client relationships have only grown in the years of the pandemic. In April 2022 it reported that 70 per cent of its new bookings were sole sourced; and in the two years since the pandemic was declared, it achieved a 50 per cent increase over the prior two years in the number of clients with quarterly bookings over $100 million. Accenture's largest client relationships, which it refers to as 'Diamond clients', comprise more than 50 per cent of its total revenues. These numbers reflect the scale of Accenture's work with its top clients and their level of trust, which sets the company apart. Accenture clients have increasingly taken on bold transformation programmes, often spanning multiple parts of the enterprise and in accelerated timeframes – an approach the company refers to as 'compressed transformation'.

Recognizing the importance of its Diamond client relationships, Accenture has appointed a senior managing director, Arjun Bedi, to lead this strategic portfolio of clients as a member of the company's Global Management Committee (GMC). In his role, Arjun leads an Executive Leadership Team comprised of client account leaders representing the company's three geographic regions – North America, Europe and growth markets – who together bring the voice of the customer to the very top of the company.

Arjun Bedi, Chairman, Diamond Client Leadership Council, commented: 'Trust is at the heart of developing deep strategic relationships. We solve for our client's interest first, and also ensure it aligns with value for Accenture. This requires understanding the industry context and the strategic objectives of the customer in order to provide a view of value across multiple dimensions to ensure a 360° view of value – it means going beyond financial measures to include all dimensions of value that matter to the client.'

Clients value the depth and breadth of the knowledge and experience Accenture's integrated global teams bring to their entire enterprise. They also value Accenture's 'continuous innovation mindset', counting on the company to anticipate and invest ahead of their needs so they can continue to lead in their industries.

This faith in Accenture's innovation capabilities is not misplaced. For example, in fiscal year 2021, Accenture invested $4.2 billion in acquisitions, $900 million in learning and professional development and $1.1 billion in R&D in assets, platforms and industry solutions. Its portfolio of patents and pending patent applications has grown to more than 8,200.

Creating value in all directions

To look beyond financial metrics and deliver broader long-term value for clients, Accenture has set a goal of achieving '360° Value', which it defines as delivering the financial business case and unique value a client may be seeking, along with striving to partner with clients for greater progress on inclusion and diversity, reskilling and upskilling their people, achieving their sustainability goals and creating meaningful experiences for their customers and employees.

As Accenture's website explains, '360° Value makes a positive impact for all stakeholders – clients, partners, shareholders, people and communities. From the financial business case clients are looking to achieve, to the unique impact they may be looking to create, we are focused on delivering 360° Value and helping our clients become the next and best versions of themselves.'

It continues, 'We are now using our new 360° Value Meter with 330 Accenture clients worldwide, and we are activating the capability to monitor and measure the value we are creating together for them across Client, Talent, Inclusion & Diversity, Experience, Sustainability and Financial dimensions.'

It's clear from the Accenture case study and from other public statements from the company that Accenture is very committed to its Diamond clients, right from the top of the company. During Accenture's analyst and investor conference on 7 April 2022, CEO and Chair Julie Sweet confirmed her commitment to these relationships, saying, 'Our strength begins with the clients with whom we are privileged to work. In the last two quarters alone, I have done over 170 client meetings.' (Accenture 2022, transcript).

Sweet explained the impact of these Diamond client relationships on Accenture's growth: 'In March 2020, we had 202 Diamond clients, our largest relationships. Today, we have 244. Consider two facts: 70% of our new bookings are sole-sourced; and in the past two years since the pandemic was declared, we've had 156 clients with bookings over $100 million in a quarter, a 50% increase from the prior two years before the pandemic. This shows the scale of our work with our top clients and their level of trust. (Accenture 2022, transcript).

Adopting an account-based growth strategy is a decision that deserves company-wide engagement. Most companies, over the last several decades, have used segmentation to make choices about where to compete and how to win. However, this segmentation has most often been focused on products, services, industry sectors and geographies – not specifically in relation to customers. An account-based growth strategy demands a similar approach to segmentation: choosing which accounts will drive sustainable, profitable revenue growth; defining what is the appropriate level of investment and approach for each type of account and then following through with company-wide execution.

Good business strategy is always about making choices, and the opportunity to build strategy around accounts alongside choices around services, products, industries and countries is no exception. Good business strategy is also based on data and evidence of what works, appropriately integrated across the company. We are beginning to see a revolution in the way that companies think about their growth, focusing more on the accounts that will make the difference and placing their bets accordingly, often cutting costs overall, while investing more in the most important accounts they have today and those they aspire to acquire.

Now that we've made the case for account-based growth, Chapter 2 picks up the story and explains account-based growth in practice today, with the results of our research in this field and viewpoints and case studies from leading companies.

SUMMARY CHECKLIST

1   The 80/20 rule, with its fractal nature, highlights how dependent many companies are on relatively few customers.

2   Surprisingly, many companies have failed to understand this, and even fewer have built and executed a company-wide strategy to realize the opportunity it presents.

3   As a consequence, companies are often under-resourcing their top customers and putting too much investment into marketing, sales and customer success teams working on the bottom 80 per cent.

4   The mirror image is true for customers, where 20 per cent of suppliers deliver 80 per cent of the value, with only a few of them seen as strategic.

5   Strategic suppliers are vital to customers' competitive advantage, and these customers have high expectations of them, relying on them for major aspects of their business model and to innovate and bring them ideas that will improve their competitiveness.

6   Great progress has been made in marketing, sales, customer success and with executive engagement, but this has largely happened in silos.

7   B2B businesses are subject to a number of forces, eg the change in buyer behaviour, the rise of platform businesses, the pandemic and the importance of aligned values beyond the financial measures.

8   Leading companies have recognized the opportunity that adopting an account-based growth strategy represents, unlocking sustainable value through extraordinary customer focus.

02

Account-based growth in practice

With the case for account-based growth made in Chapter 1, we're now turning our attention to whether it really works in practice. Do companies see 80 per cent of their profits and revenues coming from just 20 per cent of their customers? Are they setting up top account programmes to focus on these customers and build long-term value with them? Do they set out ambitious plans for these customers and then align everyone in the company to achieve them? And what successes are they seeing as a result?

At the beginning of the year we conducted an online survey among 65 B2B companies to find out the answers to these questions, supplementing our survey with additional desk research on each company and 20 in-depth conversations to provide a more qualitative view of approaches to account-based growth today (Inflexion Group, 2022).

ACCOUNT-BASED SURVEY RESPONDENTS

Of the 65 companies that responded to our survey, half came from the software sector, with roughly a quarter from cloud services and software companies (26 per cent) and another quarter from enterprise software (25 per cent). Technology consulting and services accounted for 22 per cent of respondents, while 15 per cent came from professional services and consulting, and 12 per cent from telecoms and networking companies.

Around a third had revenues over $5 billion (31 per cent), and another third were in the $1–$5 billion category (34 per cent). The remainder were from companies under £1 billion.

Most of the respondents were director level or above (82 per cent), with one-third at vice president (VP) or senior vice president (SVP) level (32 per cent), and 8 per cent at CxO levels in their organizations. Over a third (39 per cent) were answering from a global perspective, with 28 per cent answering for a region or business unit within their company. The remainder answered on behalf of their country's operations.

Our key findings from this survey are set out in this chapter, together with a viewpoint from Accenture and a case study from Infosys. We examine the challenges we see companies wrestling with, and our ideas for how to overcome them. We'll explore the way companies structure and manage their top account programmes, how they plan for growth and execute on those plans and how they track their success, before setting out our recommended framework for improving the way account-based growth is delivered today.

Does the 80/20 rule really apply?

Put simply, yes it does.

Practically every company in our research has a top account programme, reflecting the fact that they recognize some of their customers are more important than others. Nearly three-quarters of these programmes are global, while just under half (45 per cent) also run regional and country unit–level programmes (42 per cent). One in five also had a top account programme at a business unit level. On average, there were 185 accounts in their programmes.

Our research showed that within these programmes, two-thirds of companies prioritize their top accounts into tiers – perhaps reflecting the fractal nature of the 80/20 rule – but very few have more than two tiers. But, as we saw in Chapter 1, the accounts at the top of a customer programme are significantly bigger and probably more complex than those at the bottom. Two tiers are likely to be insufficient to distinguish these variations in most programmes.

For example, one US-headquartered technology company with over $30 billion in revenues gets 35 per cent of its revenues from just 25 customers. That's an average of $500 million each, but the fractal nature of the 80/20 rule indicates that most likely the top five accounts are worth an average of $2–$3 billion each. These are definitely worth a tier of their own in the top account programme.

It's also worth noting that just over half of respondents include new accounts as well as existing customers in their programmes (Figure 2.1) as they look for the top accounts of tomorrow from among the accounts they've yet to win or grow.

When we asked more closely about the revenues these top accounts drive for their business, there was a drop-off in those people able to answer. Over

FIGURE 2.1 Top account programmes are the norm

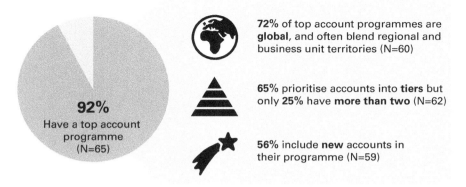

72% of top account programmes are **global**, and often blend regional and business unit territories (N=60)

65% prioritise accounts into **tiers** but only **25%** have **more than two** (N=62)

56% include **new** accounts in their programme (N=59)

92%
Have a top account programme
(N=65)

a third didn't know, and 4 per cent reported that their company didn't track that information. Neither of these situations is very encouraging, as it's hard to know where to apply your resources and investment if you don't know the value of the different customers you could assign them to.

Among the 32 companies that did know both what percentage of customer accounts were in their top account programme and what percentage of annual revenues came from accounts in that programme, the ratio was 3.5 per cent of accounts driving 50 per cent of revenues on average (Figure 2.2). There are several important indications coming from this result.

The first is that the 80/20 rule appears to apply to these companies. In fact, it is somewhere between 80/20 and 75/25. Secondly, it means that a whopping 96.5 per cent of their customers are delivering the other half of their revenue. This has significant implications for how these companies treat their top 3.5 per cent of accounts, compared with how they should treat the other 96.5 per cent.

One large technology company with revenues in excess of $10 billion had recently analyzed its customer revenue data to find that just 2.5 per cent of its customers accounted for 50 per cent of its revenue. This is even more highly skewed than our research results show, with 97.5 per cent of customers driving the other half of revenue. And as we reported in Chapter 1, this is further illustrated by the case of Accenture's 244 Diamond clients – 3.5 per cent of their 7,000 customers – who deliver over 50 per cent of their revenues.

FIGURE 2.2 The universe is wonky and so is B2B business

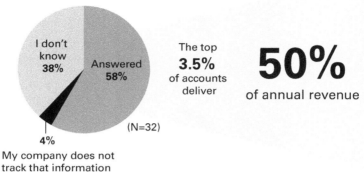

**What % of your annual revenue comes from
your top account programme? (N=55)**

SOURCE © Inflexion Group, 2022. All rights reserved.

It's worth saying at this point that we didn't ask about what proportion of profits are coming from the top account programme, and the reason for this is that most companies don't track that effectively, as we'll see later.

One market-leading company that understands the importance of its top accounts – and has since its inception just over 20 years ago – is Accenture, as we saw in Chapter 1. It demonstrates vividly what can be achieved by a company that recognizes the importance of the 80/20 rule and takes intentional decisions about how it runs its business as a result. Stephanie Winters McConnell, a Managing Director at Accenture, shares her perspectives on the importance of the 80/20 rule for B2B companies and some of the implications for how to manage these all-important relationships with top customers.

VIEWPOINT

Stephanie Winters McConnell, Managing Director, Accenture – Pursuit and Reputation Marketing

Is the 80/20 rule something you have seen operating during your career? Do executives use it to drive decision-making?

Making sure you pay the most attention to clients who are not only going to bring you the most profitable revenue today, but whom you can continue to grow with in the future, is a business construct many understand but few fully implement. Even within the top 20 per cent, there are often big differences between the few clients in the very top tier and those in the bottom of that tier. Decision making about how to partner with these clients and how to identify and allocate the most productive levels of talent, resources and investment needs to be very clear.

I have seen companies that do it incredibly well. They look very closely at their client portfolio not only in terms of where growth will come from, but also what investment they are willing to make to support those clients. These organizations often look to co-invest and co-innovate with their clients because they see the benefit of truly partnering in new ways.

I've seen others that really struggle. They look at short-term successes and don't make the time or investments needed to build a deep partnership.

Ultimately, business partnership and success depend on long-term investment on both sides, mutual understanding and consistency, even when clients temporarily reduce the amount of business they are doing with you. It's often the tough times when deeper relationships and respect are built, and you can demonstrate you are in this for the long haul; it's something clients never forget.

Are companies broadening their focus beyond financial metrics to produce their 80/20 list, looking at other aspects such as sustainability, for example?

There are examples of companies in every industry sector and geography where the focus on sustainability in all its forms has increased to the point where strong alignment with clients is vital. It is a source of differentiation and can determine whom you choose to partner with over the long term.

What benefits can come from applying the 80/20 rule to business growth?

A key driver of business growth is trust; that is fundamental. If you have a trust-based relationship with your most significant clients and you are regarded as a business partner who has the client's vision and objectives in mind, the opportunities for continued growth and expansion can be significant. This has been particularly true over the last couple of years when companies have faced some of the biggest disruptors of this generation.

When the pandemic hit, companies that had put off transforming the way they operated essentially had to figure out overnight how to stay relevant. When you are in that position, whom are you going to turn to? You will turn to a trusted partner you have worked with before, a partner you know will deliver what's needed to help your company survive.

It's about joint accountability and shared vision, with the client knowing that everything you are doing is in their best interest. That deepens the relationship and leads to a willingness to work together in ways that are mutually beneficial.

Have there been improvements in the way companies integrate cross-functionally for their top clients?

Historically, functions such as marketing, sales and delivery worked in silos. Increasingly there is a clear recognition that if all the different teams put the client at the centre, it will result in a more consistent approach with much better outcomes. Looking at the client interactions in a truly integrated way can help shape the client experience. It is happening, for instance, with account-based marketing, where the marketer works closely with other functions to deliver insights, personalized content and tailored thought leadership to these top clients.

There is still a long way to go in many companies to drive client-centric collaboration across all functions. The larger the portfolio a company has, the more important this is and, in my experience, the more difficult it is to achieve. Key to success is using data and insights in a holistic way to drive decisions and smarter outreach, no matter what the functional area is.

How should companies approach the remaining 80 per cent of their clients?

In today's dynamic business environment, it's imperative that clients feel confident their business partners have their best interests in mind, will bring new ideas and help them achieve their goals. Things can happen fast: companies get acquired or divest, senior leaders rotate, geopolitical environments shift and more. Your clients want to know they have a business partner they can rely upon.

While you may invest more in the top 20 per cent of your clients, it's important to strategically nurture and grow the remaining 80 per cent, too. If you're maintaining highly invested, highly personalized relationships with your top clients, selectively target the next 20 per cent, and then work down in tiers. I don't think you can lump that 80 per cent together any more than you can treat the top 20 per cent in the same way. You have to target your efforts intentionally. It may not be nearly as personalized with that next tier down from the top, but you shouldn't treat them in a generic way.

Consistent use of criteria, access to solid internal and external data and, above all, a willingness to act on what the data tell you are all important to make progress in where to target to keep the growth engine running.

What are the most important culture and people levers to drive the right 80/20 behaviour?

Being client-centric requires a common set of objectives, principles and metrics that revolve around the client's goals. In addition, there must be transparency around results, which will build a sense of joint ownership. If I only see my results, but not those of the collective team, it doesn't incent the right behaviours.

And that must start at the top. Leadership needs to reinforce the idea that not only is this approach expected, but it is the way we work. That interaction is important in tone, in style and in process. For example, even with something as practical as setting your client strategy, is there a mechanism that ensures all the different perspectives are included?

While leadership direction is key, it's also important to align processes, metrics and rewards that encourage the sharing of information and a joint accountability towards client outcomes.

How companies manage their top accounts

Selecting accounts for the programme

The first step in terms of managing the accounts in a top account programme is to decide who is in and who is out. Given the long-term nature of many of these relationships, this process should be a robust and rigorous process and not something resembling a merry-go-round with constant changes.

Our research found that the account selection process is dominated by the sales function (Figure 2.3). Marketing and strategy were mentioned by half our respondents, presumably bringing a longer-term and more strategic perspective to the decision making. The poor relations in this process are the customer success and finance teams, while occasionally leadership and operations teams get involved.

So, how do they make this all-important selection decision? What criteria is it based on? What do customers need to do to be considered? Well, there are two leading criteria used: the future growth potential in the account and current revenue from the account – mentioned by 87 and 76 per cent of respondents, respectively (Figure 2.4). Less-used criteria include the company's competitive position in the account, intent data or propensity modelling

FIGURE 2.3   Account selection is dominated by sales

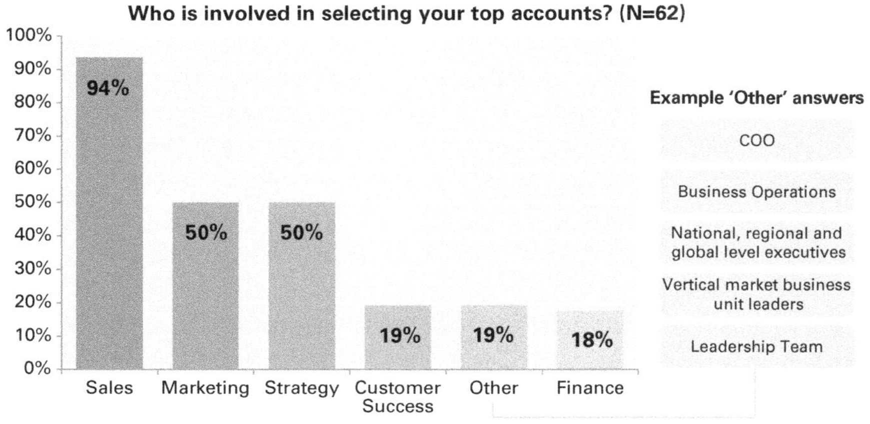

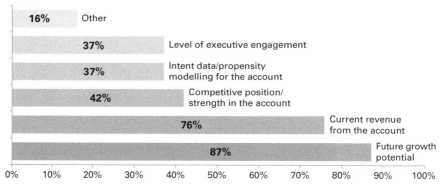

Who is involved in selecting your top accounts? (N=62)

Example 'Other' answers

COO

Business Operations

National, regional and global level executives

Vertical market business unit leaders

Leadership Team

94% Sales
50% Marketing
50% Strategy
19% Customer Success
19% Other
18% Finance

FIGURE 2.4   The range of criteria used to select top accounts

How do you determine which accounts are in your programme? (N=62)

16% Other
37% Level of executive engagement
37% Intent data/propensity modelling for the account
42% Competitive position/strength in the account
76% Current revenue from the account
87% Future growth potential

that might suggest the account is interested in your solutions and the level of executive engagement with the account. These less-used criteria are important because they provide a richer and more nuanced approach to selecting top customers. It's interesting to note that, apart from the current revenue criterion, the same criteria could apply to targeting new prospects, too.

Overall, we were somewhat surprised by the fairly simplistic approach taken to account selection, something discussed further in the next chapter.

Another important point in account selection is that relationships between companies often last for decades when there is a strategic partnership in place, so churn within a top account programme – particularly where accounts are regularly dropped – is something to be avoided. As Stephanie Winters McConnell from Accenture said in her viewpoint, you may decide to retain a top account even during a lean year, where something has happened to leave them unable to work with you to the extent they normally do. This is about long-term partnership and trust.

So, it's a little surprising that when we asked about how many accounts were added to or dropped from the top account programme in the past financial year, the 30 respondents who answered told us that despite maintaining their focus on selection criteria around current revenue and future growth potential, they had seen a churn rate of 25 per cent in accounts during the previous financial year (Figure 2.5). Almost twice as many accounts were added as dropped, suggesting either that more resources were found to cover those additional accounts or that existing resources were stretched to cover more accounts.

Half of our respondents review which accounts are in or out of their programme annually, while another 18 per cent review every six months and 15 per cent quarterly. Of the remaining 18 per cent of companies, most review their account programmes on a more regular or ongoing basis, something one large software company refers to as an 'evergreen' review process.

Over a third of companies said they had no hard and fast criteria for relegating accounts from the programme (or at least didn't know of any), while 59 per cent indicated that it was mostly due to the current or future revenue potential from the account changing – the same criteria dominating the original selection decision.

FIGURE 2.5 Annual churn within the top account programme

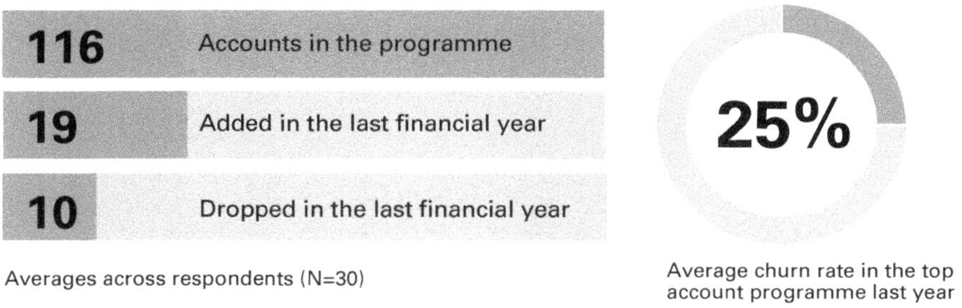

116	Accounts in the programme
19	Added in the last financial year
10	Dropped in the last financial year

25%

Averages across respondents (N=30)

Average churn rate in the top account programme last year

Planning for growth

Everyone who has a top account programme creates plans for these accounts (Figure 2.6), and they report that these plans follow a similar structure to their market or country plans. On the face of it, this seems positive, because top customers need robust business plans.

The vast majority set an ambition to grow their share of wallet in the account beyond the current financial year and articulate how that ambition will be met through a clear action plan. The plans themselves are anchored in a deep understanding of the customers' business imperatives and initiatives – a true customer-centric approach.

Once the plan is created, 87 per cent of companies use a summary of the plan to track progress, mostly running separate governance reviews for these longer-term activities compared to the more short-term deal forecasting and sales reviews in their business (Figure 2.6).

However, there are a number of shortcomings in the current approach to planning. Most do not go so far as involving the customer when they are creating their plan (Figure 2.7), something that would ensure that they've interpreted the account's situation and priorities correctly and prepared an appropriate response. One-third don't articulate how they will leverage the whole company's relationships and resources for the benefit of the customer, nor do they integrate sales, marketing and customer success teams and activities into the plan (Figure 2.7).

In fact, plans are sometimes fairly narrowly conceived, with around a third focusing mainly on revenue objectives rather than broader business outcomes, and not considering how they will compete successfully for the customer's share of wallet they are targeting against named competitors – something you ignore at your peril!

ALIGNING AROUND TOP CUSTOMERS

The good news is that most companies have recognized the value of their top customers and have allocated some of their best talent to look after these accounts (Figure 2.8). This includes the allocation and use of an executive sponsor for top customers from the company's own leadership team, whom the account team brings in to help achieve the growth ambition with that customer.

We have strong views about the kind of people who are needed to lead complex relationships with top customers, and we pick up this point again in Chapter 7.

FIGURE 2.6 Planning for growth – what's working?

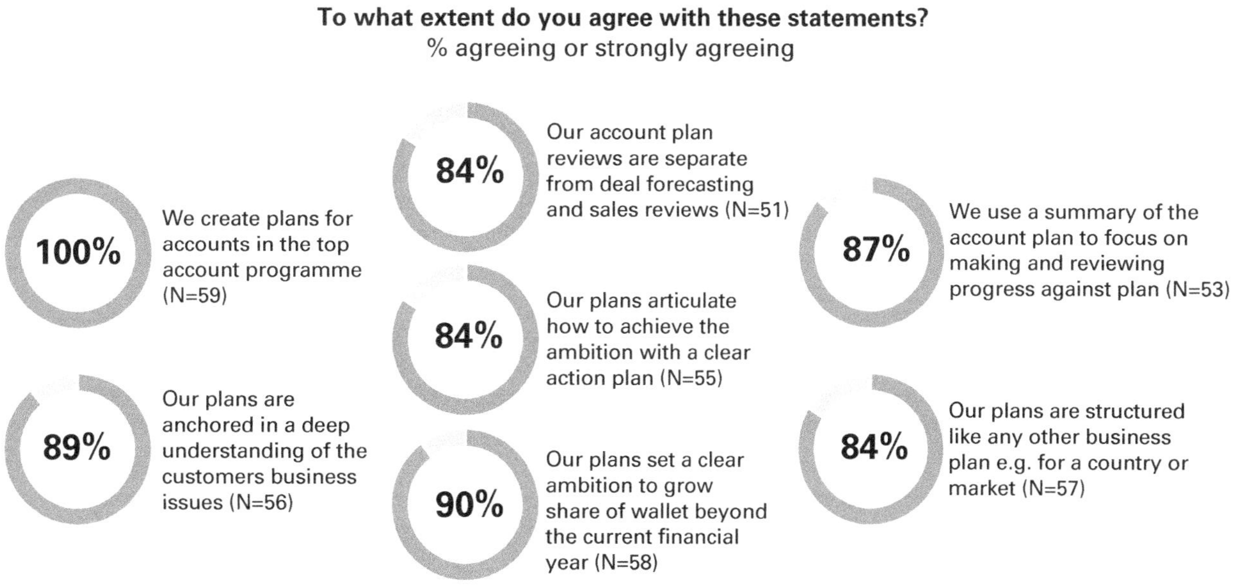

To what extent do you agree with these statements?
% agreeing or strongly agreeing

100% We create plans for accounts in the top account programme (N=59)

89% Our plans are anchored in a deep understanding of the customers business issues (N=56)

84% Our account plan reviews are separate from deal forecasting and sales reviews (N=51)

84% Our plans articulate how to achieve the ambition with a clear action plan (N=55)

90% Our plans set a clear ambition to grow share of wallet beyond the current financial year (N=58)

87% We use a summary of the account plan to focus on making and reviewing progress against plan (N=53)

84% Our plans are structured like any other business plan e.g. for a country or market (N=57)

FIGURE 2.7   Planning for growth – what isn't working so well?

To what extent do you agree with these statements?
% of respondents disagreeing or strongly disagreeing

57%

We involve customers in the development of account plans (N=54)

32%

Our plans articulate how to leverage the whole company's relationships and resources for the benefit of the account (N=58)

29%

Our plans integrate sales, marketing and customer success teams and activities (N=57)

39%

Our plans explain how to compete for share of wallet against named competitors (N=56)

31%

Our plans have success measures that go beyond revenue and profit to track relationships and reputation (N=54)

FIGURE 2.8 Aligning around top customers – what's working?

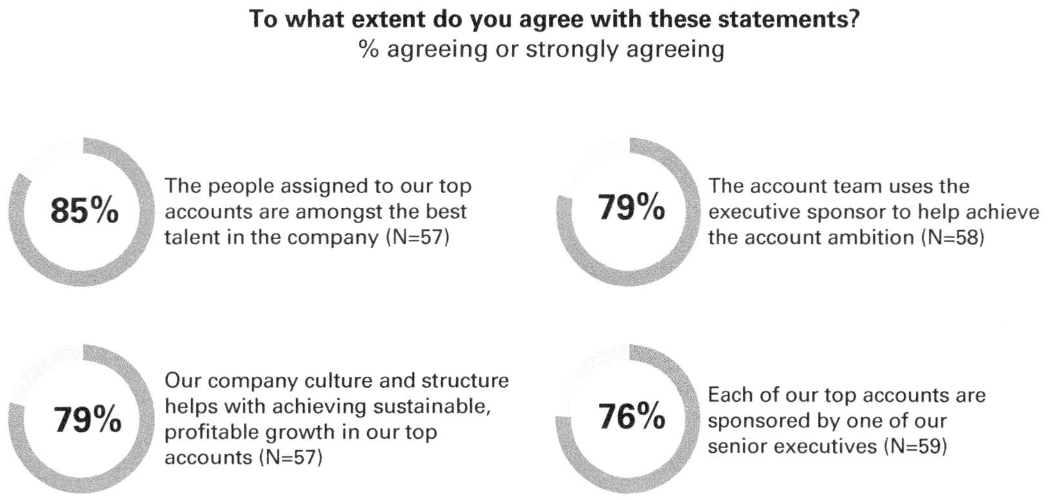

To what extent do you agree with these statements?
% agreeing or strongly agreeing
85%
The people assigned to our top accounts are amongst the best talent in the company (N=57)
79%
The account team uses the executive sponsor to help achieve the account ambition (N=58)
79%
Our company culture and structure helps with achieving sustainable, profitable growth in our top accounts (N=57)
76%
Each of our top accounts are sponsored by one of our senior executives (N=59)

SOURCE © Inflexion Group, 2022.

Going one step further, many companies have set up their company structure and culture to support this focus on achieving sustainable, profitable growth with their top accounts.

Interestingly, three-quarters of companies are stopping short of allocating more than half of their sales, marketing and customer success teams onto top customers (Figure 2.9), despite the fact that the value of each of these customers will dramatically outweigh that of customers outside of their top account programme, who could be served by a more tech-touch and even self-service approach in many instances to improve the company's overall profitability. And the time the executive sponsors for these customers spend calling on executives in the account could be increased, with a third of companies saying that the sponsor calls on less than a quarterly basis.

And, despite the structure and culture of companies broadly supporting this focus on top customers, incentives and reward systems lag behind, with 42 per cent of companies saying that theirs are not aligned with achieving sustainable, profitable growth in top accounts.

But perhaps of most concern here, in this era of big data and artificial intelligence, is the fact that most companies do not have a single view of customer data for their top accounts across marketing, sales and customer success, making it difficult to orchestrate a personalized and seamless experience for their top customers. Approximately one-third say that they do not use data on these accounts to make better decisions for their customers. We have a lot more to say on this in Chapter 5.

Measuring success

As we saw earlier, in Figure 2.7, one-third of companies told us their plans do not track measures of success beyond revenue or financial performance. The result is that the long-term relationships being built, and the reputation created in top customers that can drive loyalty, advocacy and, ultimately, more profitable growth, are not tracked in these businesses at an account level.

Most measure revenue (93 per cent) and growth in revenue (78 per cent) for top accounts, which brings us right back to the most common factors used to select a customer for the top account programme in the first place (Figure 2.10).

It's a different story when we look at profitability. Just under half of companies measure gross profit at a top account level, while only one in five is able to measure the net profit contribution coming from their most

FIGURE 2.9 Aligning around top customers – what isn't working so well?

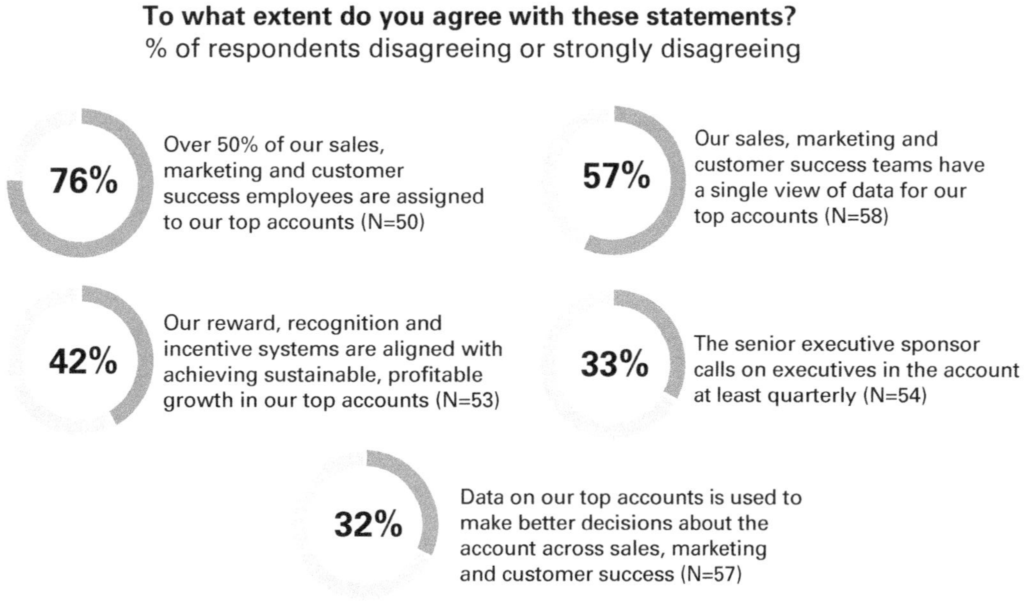
To what extent do you agree with these statements?
% of respondents disagreeing or strongly disagreeing
76%
Over 50% of our sales, marketing and customer success employees are assigned to our top accounts (N=50)
57%
Our sales, marketing and customer success teams have a single view of data for our top accounts (N=58)
42%
Our reward, recognition and incentive systems are aligned with achieving sustainable, profitable growth in our top accounts (N=53)
33%
The senior executive sponsor calls on executives in the account at least quarterly (N=54)
32%
Data on our top accounts is used to make better decisions about the account across sales, marketing and customer success (N=57)

SOURCE

FIGURE 2.10 Tracking financial performance by account

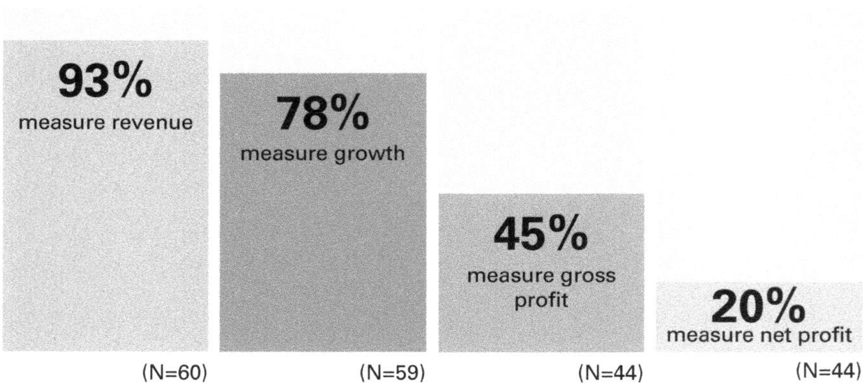

93%
measure revenue

78%
measure growth

45%
measure gross profit

20%
measure net profit

(N=60)   (N=59)   (N=44)   (N=44)

important customers. Clearly there's a lot of work to do here. Without this information, decisions about how much to invest in these top accounts and where to allocate resources are being made in the dark. For example, marketing might be generating leads in the wrong accounts, and the cost to serve smaller customers could be depressing the overall performance of the company.

What market leaders do differently

When we dig into our research and look at the responses of 10 companies recognized as market leaders, they appear to do a few things differently to the rest of the survey respondents, although these are indications rather than statistically significant differences.

For example, when looking at the structure of their top account programmes, they are more likely to focus on existing customers and prioritize them into tiers, and twice as likely to have more than two tiers in their programme, reflecting the variations in scale across top customers.

They select accounts more collaboratively, with sales and marketing appearing to work together to make these selection decisions. They also involve their strategy colleagues more than other companies do. And while they too focus on current revenue and growth potential as key selection criteria, they are twice as likely to take into account their competitive position in the account and more likely to think about current levels of executive engagement with the customer.

When building their plans for growth in these top accounts, they appear to be involving their customers more in the planning process. Their plans also integrate sales, marketing and customer success teams and activities more often, as well as articulating how to leverage the whole company's relationships and resources for the benefit of these top customers.

Almost all of these market leaders have executive sponsors calling on top customers at least quarterly, and they believe that these sponsors help to achieve the ambition for the account. This is an emerging and powerful practice in its own right, as we heard from Ninian Wilson in Chapter 1, and should be a key part of your engagement approach for top customers.

In addition, market leaders appear to be slightly further ahead in building the structure and culture they need in place to serve their top customers, and they are more likely to have focused their incentives and reward systems on driving sustainable, profitable growth in these accounts.

Infosys is one of these market-leading companies. Like Accenture, it has recognized the importance of repeat business from its top customers, and changed the way it selects, manages, aligns around and tracks its top accounts. The case study in this chapter explains some of the main actions the company has taken so far, and points to what's next as it builds long-term partnerships and wider value for society with its top customers around the world.

CASE STUDY

Infosys: Driving account-based growth

Infosys is a global leader in next-generation digital services and consulting. Founded in India in 1981, it serves clients in more than 50 countries as they navigate their digital transformation.

Applying the 80/20 rule

The concept that the top 20 accounts account for 80 per cent of revenue is a principle that Infosys recognizes, according to Navin Rammohan, Vice President, Segment Head Marketing at Infosys. It is why the company embarked a few years back on what has become an ambitious programme to increase both the loyalty and the 'stickiness' of these top strategic clients. The other driver for the programme was to reposition Infosys as a strategic transformation partner rather than be seen only as an IT operations or outsourcing provider.

As Rammohan explains, 'It has always been the case that these 20 per cent of our clients are really important to us, and they continue to give us a lot more revenue than all the others put together'.

Tracking measures

Those top accounts are tracked by measures in three categories. Revenue measures include opportunities identified, deals won, profitability, productivity and growth. Relationship measures include the number and quality of C-level relationships and engagements, plus relationships created with new buying centres in the account. Reputation measures cover things like the customer's perception of Infosys's digital technology capabilities, and its willingness to act as a testimonial and speak on Infosys's behalf.

The company also drills down more deeply into those top-line measures to get a clearer picture on account performance. For example, it calculates the proportion of revenues coming from digital operations such as cloud, data analytics, cybersecurity and modernization projects in a bid to boost that side of its business significantly.

Identifying top accounts

Infosys operates through a vertical industry structure including financial services, industrial manufacturing, retail, public sector and telecoms, among many others. Each vertical business unit leader works with their leadership team to select the top tier of existing customers within their focus industry, and agrees target new logos. The top accounts will display certain characteristics, including how fast they can grow, and the potential for Infosys to have a bigger proportion of digital business within each one.

There are regular conversations within the business operations teams and regional heads to keep an ongoing check on how the top accounts are performing.

Assigning resources to accounts

Infosys categorizes its sales operations into two types: what it terms the hunting and the farming community. The hunters target those new accounts that have the potential to become top players in the portfolio. Since 95 per cent of the company's revenue comes from repeat business, however, the farmers focus on cultivating existing accounts.

The account teams are structured to reflect that objective. Account executives sit at the lowest level, charged with developing insights and exploring opportunities. They are overseen by account managers, with general engagement managers (GEM) above them and the master customer owner (MCO) of the account at the top. The MCOs report to the regional industry leaders, who, in turn, answer to the heads of the vertical businesses.

The marketing team is closely integrated with the business operations management within these sectors and agrees which of the top tier accounts in a particular vertical will fit the criteria for targeted account-based marketing (ABM) treatment.

Service delivery specialists used to be assigned to the individual accounts and managed by the account MCO. That has changed, with a relatively new centralized delivery operation with staff reporting to the central service line head for each business.

Some of the biggest accounts can consist of over 200 people. There is an initiative to allocate human resources (HR) specialists to each of the top accounts to manage the staffing intricacies of what can be very large teams.

Promoting internal alignment

Getting everyone pulling in the same direction for these top accounts can be challenging in a company with such a global reach. There is close collaboration between the marketing and sales sides of the key accounts, enhanced by the well-respected ABM programme. For instance, the ABM team meets regularly with their account MCOs, and with the business and industry heads once a quarter to look at account performance. There is a quarterly report for every account to examine how the dial has shifted in terms of key measures across the revenue, relationship and reputation categories.

Rammohan would like to see closer ties with the service delivery specialists, for good reason: 'After all, they often have much more knowledge about the intricacies of each account than anyone else. So, we go to them for insights or to fill any gaps in understanding because they have such a strong grasp of a customer's internal functions. They can also help generate customer advocacy and testimonials because of the close relationship they have with client executives.'

Building a different mindset

Rammohan believes that this different approach to top accounts requires a change in mindset. For his own team, in marketing, he is emphasizing four priorities. The first is something called a unifier mindset, where the marketer acts like the chief integration officer because they have knowledge about different aspects of what's happening in different parts of the organization and help to align them.

The second is the business partner mindset. Every marketer should understand the account very well, be able to speak to a customer and speak to sales colleagues in the language that they understand. It's important not to become narrow-minded and think of yourself as just a marketing person, but become a businessperson and partner to your own colleagues and the customer.

The third priority is to develop a learning mindset. This is about an appetite for development, getting familiar with new tools and technology, finding new ideas that could be of value to your colleagues or your customer.

The fourth and most important thing for any marketer is having an empathetic mindset. To be a great listener, understand, put yourself in the shoes of the account team or the customer, then come with solutions that can really help move the partnership forward. For example, this is where purpose-led initiatives can be so powerful, working together to drive the environmental or societal goals of both organizations.

Enhancing external engagement

This closer internal alignment and change of mindset is shaping Infosys's approach to customer engagement. Sales and marketing create a joint engagement plan, with marketing activities designed to resonate and help deliver value in line with the account objectives. Rammohan calls this approach 'unmarketing'.

For example, a strategic, multi-year partnership with *The Economist*, announced in October 2021, combines the digital services and capabilities of Infosys with the magazine's global policy research, insights and events expertise, while a partnership with *Financial Times* will investigate immersive journalism. Rammohan is also encouraging joint corporate social responsibility (CSR) projects with these top accounts, leveraging the company's extensive expertise in community-oriented work in partnership with customers for the benefit of wider society.

As Rammohan says, 'Because these are such interesting projects to talk about in a story-led way, they create a different perception within the account about Infosys and open the door for long-term, mutual value for our company, our customers and the communities we all serve'.

Raising your game

The implications of our research

Our research into current account-based growth practices today indicates a number of significant ways that companies could raise their game and drive more long-term, sustainable and profitable value with their top customers.

Here are the top 10 implications we see arising from the results. You may want to review this list in the context of your own business to highlight any gaps you feel need addressing.

1 The universe is wonky, and so are B2B companies. Our results demonstrate that the 80/20 rule is alive and well. This means that the accounts in your top account programme have a disproportionate impact on your current and future success, and so deserve extraordinary focus from all customer-facing teams.

2 Most companies run a top account programme. Two-thirds prioritize these accounts into multiple tiers. Given the fractal nature of the 80/20 rule, accounts at the top of your programme are worth much more to you than those at the bottom. A programme with more tiers will allow you to reflect this variation and invest your resources more wisely.

3 Account selection is currently dominated by sales, using a range of criteria to decide which accounts are in the programme. Wider collaboration across sales, marketing, customer success and other teams, leveraging an agreed range of criteria, would result in more balanced and objective decision making, plus stronger awareness and buy-in across your company on the accounts that matter most.

4 Churn in top account programmes is high at 25 per cent. Stronger governance and discipline in reviewing accounts in the programme with a focus on reducing churn will help you build long-term partnerships and deliver mutual, sustainable value with your best customers.

5 Everyone plans how to grow their top accounts, but plans generally aren't created collaboratively internally, with customers or with taking competitors' share of wallet in mind. By co-creating your account plans, you will build a shared ambition with your customer and enable a tighter alignment as you execute your plan, increasing your chances of success.

6 Executive sponsors are in place and engaged, connecting regularly with customer executives. This executive engagement is powerful in unlocking budgets, accelerating opportunities, and co-creating solutions so make sure this is orchestrated within your overall engagement plan for the account.

7 Companies report they allocate their best talent to top accounts, with a quarter of companies allocating more than half of their total resources. Decide if you have assigned enough of your best resources to your top accounts, and consider using technology and self-service options for your less important accounts.

8   Culture and structure support account growth, but incentives and rewards don't always drive the right behaviour. Review your incentive plans to make sure they encourage internal alignment and a focus on delivering long-term value for your top accounts.

9   Many companies lack a single view of their top accounts and one-third aren't using data for better decision making. Explore how your teams are using data today. Then build a roadmap that leverages your current technology and identifies any additional investment needed to build a single view of your top accounts and create actionable insights for your customer-facing teams.

10 Most companies track revenue and growth, but fewer measure the gross or net profitability of their top accounts. Find out what you are tracking today and identify the gaps in your awareness of how your top accounts are contributing to your profitability. Make a plan to fill the gaps, enabling more effective decision making across your business.

A framework for account-based growth

To help companies think about how to improve their approach to account-based growth with their top customers, and achieve the kind of success that Accenture and Infosys have seen with their programmes, we've created a simple but effective framework, shown in Figure 2.11. It illustrates the key elements that need to be considered to fully realize the opportunities to grow profitably and sustainably in the accounts that matter most.

The foundations of the framework include the four key elements that need to be aligned across the company; the middle of the framework includes the four teams that need to engage externally in a coordinated fashion. Each of these eight elements has its own chapter in the rest of this book, building on best practice today and illustrated with more viewpoints and case studies from senior leaders from across a number of B2B sectors.

This account-based growth framework can set businesses on the right track to growth by exploiting the 80/20 principle and articulating what needs to be done to drive long-term, mutual, sustainable and profitable growth with their top customers.

FIGURE 2.11 A framework for account-based growth

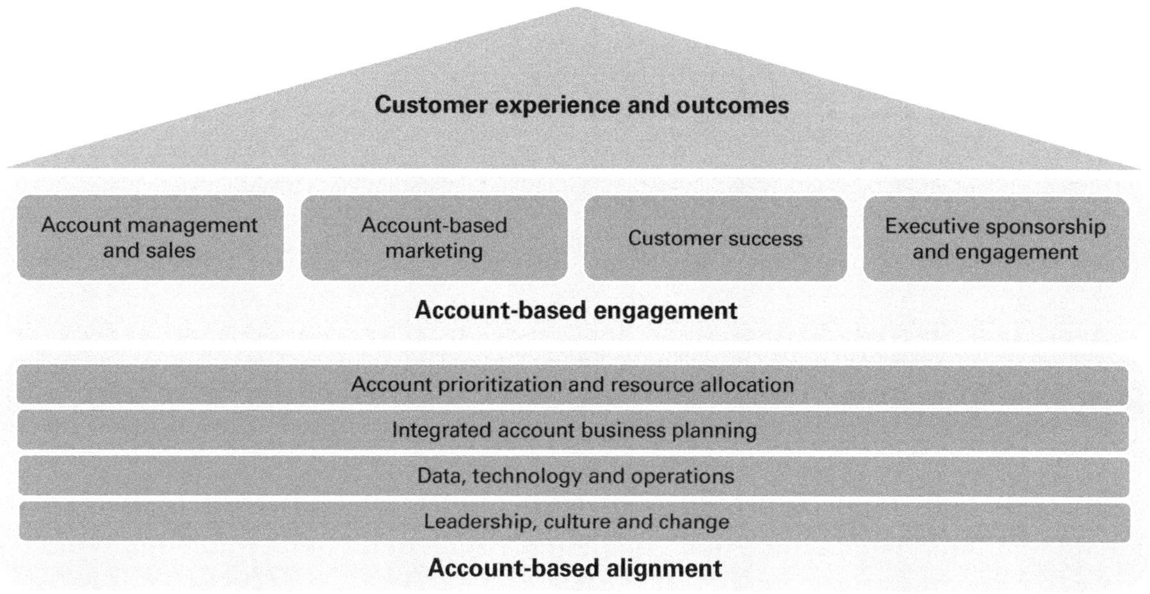

Customer experience and outcomes
Account management and sales
Account-based marketing
Customer success
Executive sponsorship and engagement
Account-based engagement
Account prioritization and resource allocation
Integrated account business planning
Data, technology and operations
Leadership, culture and change
Account-based alignment

SOURCE

SUMMARY CHECKLIST

1 Our research shows that 3.5 per cent of accounts are driving 50 per cent of revenues on average, which means a whopping 96.5 per cent of customer accounts are delivering the other half of a company's revenue.

2 Practically every company has a top account programme, showing that they recognize that some of their customers are more important than others.

3 While most companies are tracking the revenue contribution and growth of their top accounts – reflecting the criteria used to select them in the first place – few are measuring the profitability of the individual accounts.

4 There are a number of opportunities to improve the way companies plan for growth with these top customers today, and how they execute their plans.

5 Some companies are well underway in establishing an extraordinary focus on their top accounts to drive long-term value through a partnership approach.

6 Internal alignment around these accounts, together with orchestrated engagement with customer executives across sales, marketing and customer success teams – plus your own executive leadership – are key to success.

PART TWO

Aligning internally for growth

Now that you have a solid understanding of the powerful impact the 80/20 concept has in the B2B world, you can begin to consider how to put it at the heart of your company's growth strategy, with all the opportunity that creates and the organizational changes it implies. This next section will guide you through what can seem like a daunting change management programme. Taken step by step, however, it will help you redefine your approach to your market and better allocate your resources for sustainable growth.

Chapter 3 starts the process by considering account prioritization and resource allocation. First you need to know what you don't know, by collecting account data to give you a precise view of how the 80/20 rule applies in your organization. It explains what questions to ask, and of whom, to reach this essential starting point.

It offers a systematic and objective way to choose which of your customers – and those potentially lucrative new targets – will be central to your growth ambitions. It outlines a possible data-led account tiering system, based on tried and tested scoring techniques, and discusses how to build an appropriate resourcing model.

Chapter 4 argues for a more integrated, business-like and longer-term approach to account planning. We call this integrated account business planning to reflect the need for integration across the company and to develop a workable business plan. The chapter highlights the weaknesses in many current account planning practices, including the tendency for them to be the preserve of sales rather than integral to all the teams that touch the customer. It explains how to create different types of plans for different customer tiers, drawing on the expertise of all relevant parties and with the backing and active participation of senior executives to ensure there is comprehensive buy-in. It lists the key sections that a good plan should contain, and shows the importance of having a strong narrative with a bias to action.

Chapter 5 is all about the data and how you use them. You can't be truly customer-centric if you don't have a holistic picture of what's going on in each account. That means collecting internal and external data from a range of sources that provide real and actionable insights. This chapter explores how to go about building a single view of the customer in the face of a proliferation of different technologies and different functional approaches. It highlights the importance of having a single operations team that focuses on cutting across all these divides, and makes the case for establishing a customer health index.

Finally, Chapter 6 explores what role leadership, culture and change management play in realigning the whole company towards its customers. It details the rise in agile working practices, which can bring customers into the heart of the organizational management system through ruthless prioritization and simplification, along with flexibility to change course quickly when necessary. It concludes by offering a pragmatic way to structure and implement a change management programme to pursue an account-based growth strategy.

03

Account prioritization and resource allocation

By now it should be clear what the 80/20 rule is all about and how it applies in B2B companies as they derive significant portions of their profitable revenue from a relatively tiny percentage of their customers. Hopefully, we've convinced you that this fact is too important to ignore, and that it makes sense to put it at the heart of your company's growth strategy over the coming years. So, what do you do first?

Well, if you don't know your own company's 80/20 ratio, it makes sense to start there. Just how much of your annual revenue and profit is coming from each of your accounts and how has that changed over time? With this starting point established, you can begin the process of selecting the most important accounts, establishing a top account programme, and potentially tiering them to represent the fractal nature of the contribution they will make to your success.

In this chapter, we recommend an objective and systematic way of prioritizing both the existing customers and new targets. All too often, these decisions are made on an informal or emotional basis, or rely on too few criteria, as we saw in Chapter 2. We offer a data-led approach, proven to be effective and used by many leading companies around the world.

We also discuss how to make decisions around resourcing your top accounts once they are identified, emphasizing the need to assign your best talent to the accounts that matter most across sales, marketing, customer success and your executive team.

Not all accounts are equal

Understanding your own 80/20 context

We've lost count of the times that we've discussed the 80/20 rule with business leaders and been met with a general understanding and acceptance of the principle but a wild denial that such an extreme ratio could exist among their customers. And yet, we know the universe is wonky, and that some version of the Pareto principle will be at play.

So how do you change this mindset and start making the case for an account-based growth strategy in your own company? With data. The first thing to do is to understand your own version of the 80/20 rule.

Our survey suggests something between 80/20 and 75/25 is going on in the 32 companies that tracked these data among the 65 responding to the survey. We've seen some companies with profiles even more extreme than this.

And there's a lesson in itself – not all companies track revenue, growth and profit by account. It sounds unlikely, but even with the extensive technology systems most companies run on today, it can be difficult to get a clear view of exactly who your customers are and what they are contributing to your financial performance and wider impact as a business.

For example, how do you define a customer or account? Is it a company that has spent money with you during the past quarter, year or three years? Is your definition consistent across geographies and business units? Are the various subsidiaries within a conglomerate like Tata or GE all one customer or many?

To get a clear view of your customers, start with your customer relationship management (CRM) system. If it's not a straightforward query to make in the system, you'll likely need to work with your sales operations team and the finance department. Even these two groups may be working from different lists, potentially coming from different systems, so there may be some consolidation needed at this point. We look more deeply at this challenge of getting a single view of customers across functions in Chapter 5.

Within your total customer or account portfolio, you are likely to have some in a top account programme. Again, we've already seen in Chapter 2 that almost all companies have such a programme operating mainly at a global and sometimes regional level, and it is common that accounts will already be prioritized and tiered within it.

The proportion of all customers who fall into your top account programme may give you your first indication of how the 80/20 rule is playing out for you. From our survey (Inflexion Group, 2022), we know that, on average, 3.5 per cent of accounts fall into a top account programme, and therefore 96.5 per cent of customers are outside of it.

Mapping your existing revenue and profitability

As we saw in Chapter 2, it isn't always straightforward to get a clear picture of the proportion of your revenues and profits that are coming from each of your customer accounts.

IGNORANCE IS NOT BLISS

While 93 per cent of companies track revenues captured from each customer in their top account programme, this falls to 78 per cent tracking revenue growth year on year, and 45 per cent measuring gross profit. Just one in five track net profit at the account level. And if this is the view for top accounts, what is being tracked for the other 96.5 per cent of customers?

SOURCE Inflexion group (2022)

Some of the issues may lie in the way that revenue and profit are calculated and allocated in your CRM and finance systems. Companies have historically been very 'inside-out' in their thinking, focusing on product lines or capabilities, and tracking revenue and profit against these. But often it isn't that simple, as global companies have multiple dimensions upon which they run their operations, including geography, industry sector and product or service line. In these cases, there is often a dominant approach to managing and reporting profit and loss (P&L) and a shadow P&L. It's not always clear where the customer sits in all of this.

There may be a view of how the P&L is broken down by customer in that geography. Where customers cross geographical boundaries, as many top accounts will outside of most of the public sector, there needs to be an agreed approach to calculating the proportion of the account's revenues and costs derived from each geography.

To understand what proportions of your revenues and profits are coming from different customer accounts, you'll likely need to continue working with sales operations and finance colleagues. The good news is that you know what questions to ask. It's now about analyzing the data you have available to come up with the answers and demonstrate just how the 80/20 principle – and the fractal ratios within it – are playing out in your company.

Clarifying your ambition for key growth accounts

Once you know your starting point, it's time to set an ambition for how much growth you'd like to see coming from your existing accounts – and which ones will provide the lion's share of that growth.

Thinking back to some of the statistics on the likely size of different tiers of accounts we explored in Chapter 1, those at the very top of your top 20 per cent will be around 16 times larger than those at the bottom of that group. This makes them important for two reasons. First, if you lose one, you'll need the equivalent of 16 more from the bottom of that tier to fill the hole left behind. Second, while you think that the revenues they contribute are high, they can still grow, as either the customers themselves grow (with your help) or you increase your share of their wallet. And we know it is much less costly to focus on these accounts than to try to win new ones.

So, these top accounts can drive a significant proportion of your future revenues, and you should be confident in putting an ambition together for their growth. How much of your revenue will they account for in three years? Will the proportion change? Do you want it to be more or less extreme than it is today?

Inevitably, there will be some churn in these top accounts – although we know that many B2B companies have top account lists that remain relatively unchanged for decades – so you also need to consider where the next accounts will come from to sit in your top tier. There may be some accounts in your lower tiers today – the 96.5 per cent – that are ripe for accelerated growth, perhaps as they themselves disrupt and outperform their industry sector (think Airbnb, Uber, Zoom). These should be carefully nurtured, or incubated, as they grow.

Or you may identify companies like these that are not yet your customers but should be. Or perhaps companies that resemble some of your current top tier accounts today, who can be pursued to bring in new revenues.

Developing a portfolio approach to where your growth will come from is a sensible next step. How much will come from your existing top accounts, versus from selected customers outside your top tier today, or from totally new accounts? The ambition you set for each will help you select the specific accounts that will meet your goals, and it's this account selection and prioritization process that we'll explore next.

Account selection and prioritization

Current practice

All too often, selecting customers for a top account programme is a politically charged, informal and emotional affair. The best companies put significant rigour behind their decisions. The worst have no clear criteria or process, ending up with a fluid list of key customers that is forever changing. This makes it hard for customer-facing teams, such as marketing, sales and customer success, to maintain alignment on where they should invest their time and resources. Inevitably, marketing target campaigns and generate leads from people in the wrong accounts, sales end up chasing deals in the wrong companies and customer success and delivery teams focus too much resource supporting customers who are already unprofitable.

Internal alignment around your top accounts begins with how you select them in the first place. Ideally, this will be a data-led, collaborative effort. From our research, we know that it is not.

Outside of a few market-leading companies, the account selection process is dominated by sales, as we saw in Chapter 2. Marketing and strategy teams get involved around half the time, while customer success is broadly overlooked, mentioned by just 19 per cent of companies in our research. Finance comes even further behind, again mentioned by fewer than one in five companies, despite the dramatic impact we know these decisions can have on long-term revenue and profit.

We're advocating that you pull together a team from across these functions to work through a structured selection process with objective criteria and data-led decision making. We'll explain how shortly, but let's return for a moment to how these decisions are made today.

Far and away, the most common reason for selecting and prioritizing an account for a company's top account programme is the combination of future growth potential in the account and current revenues coming from the account today (tricky, if you aren't tracking revenue by account!). This is, in effect, a version of the long-established Boston Consulting Group (BCG) two-by-two matrix for growth, which looks at market size and market growth rates to help companies decide where to invest. We've illustrated this adaptation in Figure 3.1.

FIGURE 3.1 Account prioritization by current and potential revenue

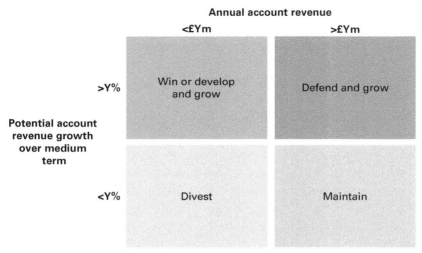

FIGURE 3.2 Directional policy matrix applied to top account selection

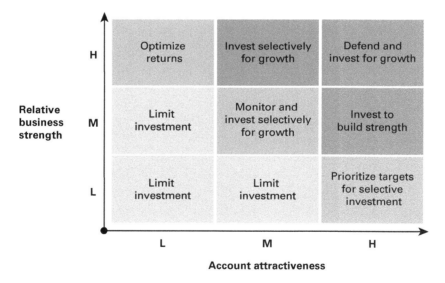

A better way

Our preferred, and a more sophisticated, approach for prioritizing the right customers for your top account programme is to use the directional policy matrix developed by McKinsey for GE (see Figure 3.2).

The advantage of using the directional policy matrix is that it introduces the two key elements that need to be considered, namely whether the account is going to be worth investing in and what we can hope to achieve (the account attractiveness, x-axis) and how likely this is to succeed (the relative business strength, y-axis). The whole point of having a top, strategic account programme is to direct resources to the most fruitful customers, which, since all firms, however large, have finite resources, means some accounts or market segments will receive less resources.

In our experience, the best way to determine which accounts should be in a top account programme is as follows:

1 Agree the ambition and business objectives for the top account programme;

2 Build the long list of accounts that *could* be included in the programme, based on some simple parameters;

3 Define measurable criteria for each axis of the directional policy matrix and create a model;

4 Populate the model to identify the top accounts for your programme;

5 Finalize the accounts and tiers in your top account programme.

Once this is done, you can allocate appropriate resources across account management, sales, marketing, customer success and executive engagement and sponsorship. This is covered in a later section entitled 'radical resource allocation'. But before we get to this, let's work through the approach.

This approach sounds simple, but it isn't, for a whole variety of reasons, many of them structural, cultural and political. It is also quite likely that your company already has some kind of top account programme, which may or may not be delivering the results you need, so your starting point needs to be understood to devise the best approach. In the more detailed explanation below, we have written this from the perspective that you are either starting a programme from scratch or you need a major revamp of an existing programme that isn't working as it should.

1 Ambition and business objectives
   As we've explained already, the maths of 80/20 makes it difficult to grow overall if you are not growing in your most significant accounts, particularly where churn in your customer base is relatively low. Your ambition for your top accounts therefore has to be to grow. How you express this will vary between companies, but it could be that you have multiple ways to express your ambition. For example, you could aim to

have the portfolio of top accounts overall grow at an average of, say, ten percent compound annual growth rate over the next three years, and then have different growth ambitions for each account, or for different tiers of accounts, which support this average. At the account level, we will discuss this more in the next chapter.

Beyond an overall growth ambition, you may have additional business objectives, which could be related to:

- The level of profit, either at gross or net level;
- Win rates, sole source contracts or churn;
- Take-up of new solution and service offerings;
- Brand recognition and reputation measures;
- Net promoter scores, customer success measures;
- Membership of strategic advisory boards.

The basic premise here is that you should be achieving superior results across a whole range of measures in your top customers. After all, if your top customers don't think much of you and don't continue to buy your solutions and services and act as your greatest advocates, you've got bigger problems!

Being explicit, up-front, about what you hope to achieve from the top account programme is important, because it creates a framework within which all other discussions about which criteria to use and which accounts to prioritize can be reviewed, leading to potentially less debate downstream.

2 Build the long list of accounts

There are going to be arguments about which customers are in a top account programme in a company of any reasonable size and complexity with multiple stakeholders representing regions/countries, product or service lines and industries. Everyone will have a view as to why their account should be in or out. Before having this debate, it is worth creating a longer list of accounts based on some very simple parameters which people will not argue much about. This can be as simple as existing annual or monthly revenue over a certain level plus asking every stakeholder to nominate any accounts they wish that don't qualify on the basis of historic revenue, for example where a major deal is being pursued or there is some future event, such as an acquisition, which means they should be included.

The benefit of having a relatively 'benign' approach to the long list is that every key stakeholder has had input so you should not have to keep revisiting it.

3 Define measurable criteria

Armed with clear ambition and business objectives creating clarity on what needs to be achieved and a long list of accounts that could be prioritized, it is now time to create the measurable criteria that will drive a scoring system along each axis of the directional policy matrix. Having completed this exercise many times over the last twenty-five years, we know that the selection of a sensible number of objectively measurable criteria is not straightforward for many companies. Based on this accumulated experience, here is our proposed approach:

- The key stakeholders should empower a small team to create the criteria for each axis. This team needs to use the ambition and business objectives as a reference point to identify criteria for market attractiveness and relative business strength.

- The thing to remember here is that you are trying to find criteria that will genuinely delineate between different accounts by creating a wide variety of scores on each axis. If, having run the criteria, the long list of accounts end up bunched together, you've not achieved much!

- Each criterion needs a weighting and an approach to scoring. So, for example, if one of your market attractiveness criteria is 'total spend on consulting services' (assuming you are in the consulting business), you may give it a weighing of 50% and potential scores of 1, 5 and 10, with appropriate revenue levels for each score. If an account spends less than $20 million each year, it would score 1; if it spends $20–50 million, it scores 5; and if it spends more than $50 million, it scores 10. Your other criteria on the market attractiveness axis would make up the remaining 50% and have scoring systems appropriate to each criterion.

- This is repeated for the relative business strength axis. An example of three criteria for each axis is shown in Tables 3.1 and 3.2, together with the scoring applied to three different accounts.

- It is best to aim for no more than three or four criteria for each axis, but in order to get to this point there is often a much longer list before it is whittled down. This is best done through a series of facilitated workshops, with time between the workshops to test the emerging criteria with data, in order to establish whether the boundaries between different scores are sensible and, crucially, whether there is data that can be used

TABLE 3.1 Accounts scored against attractiveness criteria

Account attractiveness criteria	Weighting	Score 1	Score 5	Score 10	Account A	Account B	Account C
Total spend on consulting services	50%	<$20M	$20–50M	>$50M	10 × 50% = 5.0	5 × 50% = 2.5	10 × 50% = 5.0
High growth market leader in their sector	30%	Below average	Average	Above average	10 × 30% = 3.0	5 × 30% = 1.5	10 × 30% = 3.0
Progress towards carbon zero targets	20%	Carbon neutral	Investing strategically	Early stage	5 × 20% = 1.0	10 × 20% = 2.0	5 × 20% = 1.0
Totals	100%				9.0	6.0	9.0

TABLE 3.2 Accounts scored against business strength criteria

Business strength criteria	Weighting	Score 1	Score 5	Score 10	Account A	Account B	Account C
Access to senior decision makers compared with competitors	40%	Worse	Same	Better	10 × 40% = 4.0	5 × 40% = 2.0	1 × 40% = 0.4
Supplier status in the account	40%	Tactical	Critical	Strategic	5 × 40% = 2.0	10 × 40% = 4.0	1 × 40% = 0.4
Match of ESG policies and values	20%	Unaligned	Some alignment	Completely aligned	10 × 20% = 2.0	5 × 20% = 1.0	5 × 20% = 1.0
Totals	100%				8.0	7.0	1.8

to create a reasonably objective score for each account. The veracity of the data as well as the agreement on the criteria to be used is vital if the resulting analysis is going to meet with stakeholder approval.

- The process to get to no more than three or four criteria is iterative and can be time consuming, but it is time well spent, because it will avoid arguments later. Once the empowered team has agreed the criteria and tested them with data, they should seek approval from the key stakeholders that they agree with the criteria to be used and the source data which will be used to populate the directional policy matrix.

- A model needs to be built, usually in the form of a spreadsheet, to hold the scores for the long list of accounts. This should ideally enable data to be fed from internal and external sources to drive the model, with a way of representing the data visually.

4   Populate the model

Once you have criteria agreed and signed off by your stakeholders and you have a working model and data sources identified, you can now populate the model. This involves running all the accounts from your long list through the model and attributing the scores to each, using the criteria for each axis. This can be an intensive exercise, with the elapsed time largely determined by your ability to access data easily and assimilate it into your model.

With the model populated, you can then represent the data visually, which, if you have been successful in choosing criteria that delineate effectively between different accounts, will result in a distribution of these accounts across the two axes. A simplified version of this is illustrated in Figure 3.3. If they all end up in the middle of the matrix, your criteria or scoring system need revisiting!

5   Finalize the accounts and tiers

The most important accounts will be in the top right corner of the directional policy matrix. You may wish to include these in the very top tier of your top accounts programme. Accounts that are equally attractive but where you are slightly less strong might be good candidates for your second tier. And the accounts that are slightly less attractive, but where you are competitively strong, could be in your third tier. Remember, you can improve your relative strength in an account, but you can't do much to improve its fundamental attractiveness to you.

FIGURE 3.3 Plotting accounts for the top account programme

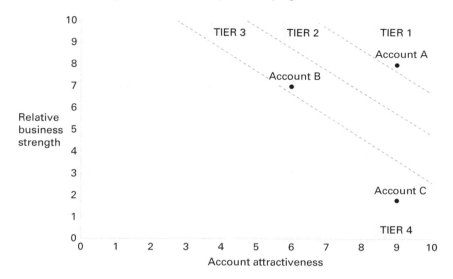

Grouping accounts into tiers within your top account programme is helpful because it will make it easier to decide on the appropriate allocation of resources to each tier and to the approach taken to drive growth. In addition to the three tiers illustrated in Figure 3.3, we have shown a further tier of targeted new accounts as tier four – accounts that are attractive to you, but where you have a lower relative business strength. We have also added in examples of the percentage of total company revenues each of the top three tiers might represent, linking back to the fractal nature of the 80/20 rule explained in Chapter 1. This is illustrated in Figure 3.4.

Of course, you may be analyzing quite a high number of accounts, so different visualization techniques may be required.

The next stage is to agree the shape of your top account programme, which accounts fall into which tier and what that means. How many tiers you have within your top account programme should emerge from analysis of the data, but one thing is almost certain, that the 80/20 principle will be operating here too, so accounts in the top tier of your top account programme may be much more important than those at the bottom. In our experience, large global companies with recognized top account programmes have at least three tiers, which reflects different expectations, different approaches and significantly different allocation of resources, including how executives spend their time.

FIGURE 3.4 Illustrative tiering for a top programme

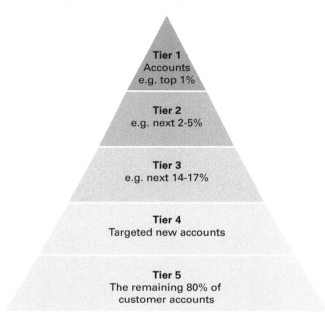

The setting of ambition, business objectives, building a long list and agreeing criteria and data sources to analyze your accounts should stand you in good stead for a rational, evidence-based agreement with executive management and your key stakeholders. These same executives and stakeholders may well have used these techniques before in market segmentation for countries, industries or products, but it may be the first time they have tried to apply the thinking to individual accounts. Ultimately, the point of the exercise is to make good business judgements with good data, making sound business decisions as a result. We would argue this is so important that the whole executive team sign off on it, with input from the key functions and not just be the domain of sales, which seems to be the way many companies operate today.

Of course, someone will always have the final say as to whether an account will be included in the programme, and often this is regional or global business leaders, as in the case with Kyndryl. As a new company, recently spun out of IBM as one of the biggest 'start ups' of all time, it has been working through exactly this process to decide where to place its bets for future growth. Director of Account-Based Marketing, Andrew Fitzgerald, shares his perspectives on account selection.

VIEWPOINT

Andrew Fitzgerald, Director of Account-Based Marketing, Kyndryl

To provide some context, could you tell us a little about Kyndryl?

Kyndryl was spun off from IBM's IT infrastructure services and became an independent publicly traded company in November 2021. We design, build, manage and modernize mission-critical technology systems that our global base of more than 4,000 customers depend on every day. We are a 'start-up at scale', but we also have a long and established history from being part of IBM. We are no longer restricted to being able to offer customers the IBM technology ecosystem, and with our independence comes freedom of choice, so we get to define the market for ourselves and decide where the potential is.

What are the key issues that typically determine which accounts to prioritize to fuel a company's future growth?

In my experience those decisions are typically too simplistic and based on historical revenues, often complemented by knowledge and insights from others involved with the customers such as account teams, sales and executive leadership. It's as though the thinking is 'because we have achieved a certain level of revenue yesterday, we expect it to be consistent now and in the future'. That sometimes turns out to be the case, and sometimes it doesn't.

We are changing the approach to that. What we are now doing is looking to use the whole idea of customer lifetime value, or future potential, in conjunction with the revenue we do today. We have invested time and effort to pull together a data platform that enables us to take this longer-term view, coupled with revenue and profitability. This, in my opinion, is what should drive the choices you make.

How do you take a data-based view of future growth potential?

We are collecting a vast array of customer data. Initially, it involves straightforward information like revenue and profitability but, ultimately, we want to expand to include lots of other data-points such as delivery and infrastructure operations for those organizations. Then we will marry these insights with external data-points about the company's IT landscape, to help us understand their needs, and also to spot future opportunities.

For example, many organizations have already made strategic choices about who their cloud hyperscale partner is going to be. But when you look at what's actually going on, their reality doesn't always match up to their strategic intent. So, the more you can understand that, the more it enables you to use that data to help customers deliver on their strategic choices.

How easy is it to source data and evidence to support the decisions you need to make?

We are a company that serves large corporations and government bodies who all have a very complex set of needs. We have a good understanding of many of them based on relationships developed over many years. Our new freedom to operate as an independent company enables us to concentrate on growing the support we're able to provide to our significant base of existing and new customers.

So, what we are trying to engineer is a data-based view of where we are today and where the future possibilities are in these customers. The more data you can bring from both internal and external sources to these conversations, the better choices you can make. Selecting the right accounts and then making the right choices about how to work with them are inextricably linked. The data informs the accounts you pick in the first place, but then you have to see that same data through to the level that says, for those accounts we picked, how are we going to grow the business? Otherwise, you get a disconnect between selection and potential growth.

Internally, we face the challenge of any large corporation in collecting the right pieces of data in the right format that is consumable and actually delivers actionable insights. There are suppliers that will not only provide you with external data but help build the tools you need to analyze it. Having said that, this is all about enabling better decision making. Individual judgement is still hugely important, but the more data you can provide to help the decision-making process, ultimately the better choices you make.

Who should be involved in making these strategic decisions?

Our business model gives a lot of independence to our country organizations. We collect the data globally, developing matrices that map customer revenue and profitability against growth potential. Then we share that information with the country organizations and account teams, to combine with their first-hand knowledge of the customers.

We are giving them a tool to help them make better decisions, but in the end our go-to-market teams have to prioritize. How should they deploy the sales, account-based marketing and delivery resources to best effect? And then we sit down with the account team, look at the data and discuss what the customer's landscape looks like. What do we think the future potential growth opportunity is, and how do we address it from a sales, marketing and in some instances a delivery perspective?

We are a new company and starting afresh in many ways, so everyone is open to finding new, faster and more efficient ways to operate. Our conversations with country and account teams have been hugely positive and thought-provoking into how we make better choices and ultimately better support our customers.

What are some of the key challenges that can arise in the overall process of prioritizing accounts and allocating resources?

You have to decide where to place your bets. If your strategy is to service a relatively small pool of very big organizations, fine. Equally, if yours is more of a volume strategy, doing smaller deals effectively, that's fine too. It's about the clarity of that choice and how you execute against it. Most of us only have so many resources, and you can't do everything. It's important to focus.

Another challenge a lot of organizations face is how to avoid what can be unproductive, sometimes emotional battles during these discussions. A common, data-based 'single source of truth' helps remove some of that emotion and helps to draw the right conclusions with enough detachment.

That's why we are very deliberately trying not to bring old ways of thinking and behaving into our new situation. Instead, we're building a new culture, which is probably the most interesting and important challenge we face. We are considering quite deliberately what we want that culture to be, because everything will flow from it. Most companies don't have the chance to do that. We are very fortunate to have the opportunity.

What about new accounts?

The process we've described works extremely well for existing customers, but may not work as well if you plan to include new accounts in your top account programme as you seek to win and grow them. For example, in the sample criteria we discussed earlier, you may fall down in the number and strength of the executive relationships you have today relative to your competitors. So, it may be best to run a specific exercise to decide which new accounts to pursue.

One company we work with is doing this by targeting the customers of a specific competitor, where it has recently leapfrogged that competitor in terms of the services and solutions it can offer following an acquisition. Another focuses specifically on disruptive, high- growth new companies that are rapidly building market share in their chosen sector. Each of these companies uses a slightly different set of criteria to evaluate the new logos it would like to build into its future top 20 per cent of accounts.

You won't want to treat these new accounts in the same way as existing customers. For example, the way you invest resources into these accounts will be different – they won't need a customer success manager yet, and you may be allocating a deal-based marketer rather than a dedicated account-based marketing resource. You may allocate a sales leader rather than an account manager at this stage. But you may still want to invest in these new accounts more than you do in the bottom 80 per cent of your existing customers.

This conversation about investment per tier is exactly where we need to go next.

Radical resource allocation

Where are your resources today?

Once you have prioritized the accounts that are most important to you, it's time to follow this through with decisions about how you deploy your resources most effectively. In this context, we mean primarily the resources from sales, marketing and customer success, all collectively responsible for sustainable, profitable growth.

Our research into top account programmes revealed that only 20 per cent of companies are measuring net profit at the top account level. There are two potential reasons for this: either they are not measuring gross profit by account (although 45 per cent said they were), and/or they are not measuring the discretionary expense directly associated with these accounts.

The research findings support our experience that understanding the investment of sales and marketing resource, let alone customer success teams, when it comes to tiers of accounts is not typically something companies do very effectively.

The main reasons behind this apparent lack of insight into where these expenses are being allocated are twofold:

1 The budgets for individual functions, such as marketing and sales, are produced in isolation from each other and largely distributed along functional lines not allocated to tiers of accounts.

2 Accounting systems that measure discretionary expenses accurately are typically rolled up by role, function and country.

There is often a lot of inertia in budget setting and accounting systems, so it is not uncommon to find that the information needed to start to look at the appropriate allocation of resources, once the account prioritization is done, is a somewhat laborious and manual exercise. Once completed, it invariably produces a few surprises.

But, given the skewed nature of where a company's revenue and profits typically come from, shouldn't every company be able to answer this simple question? *'Across the agreed company-wide tiers of customers, what proportion of our resources and expenses are focused on each tier across sales, marketing and customer success, and what impact does that have on our growth and profitability?'*

We also asked companies in our research whether more than 50 per cent of their sales, marketing and customer success resources were allocated to their top accounts, which, as we mentioned earlier, drive 50 per cent of the revenue. Only 24 per cent said this was the case. Of course, whether 50 per cent of these resources *should* be dedicated to your top accounts very much depends on your individual business and where you are in your growth journey. There is no one right answer.

However, many companies often find they have their customer-facing resources over-allocated to the 80 per cent of the customers that only drive 20 per cent of their revenue, and under-allocated to the top 20 per cent. Additionally, even within the top 20 per cent, resources are not skewed enough towards the top few per cent that drive 50 per cent or more of their revenues.

If this is not aligned properly, it creates some odd effects and leads to tension between sales and marketing in particular. Marketing creates 'marketing qualified leads'; sales never pursue most of them. As we saw in Chapter 1, one large enterprise software company was producing marketing-generated leads at a ratio of 10,000:1 in the bottom 80 per cent of customers compared with the top 20 per cent. Most of these leads went nowhere.

The reason this happens is partly because of a misalignment of prioritization of the accounts, and a lack of follow-through on alignment of resources.

But there is something else going on too, which is that sales often 'qualify out' opportunities that they have not previously been involved in, *unless they already know at least some of the customer decision-makers*. This is a problem if the sales coverage model is to cover the bottom 80 per cent of the customer base through an online, channel partner or inside-sales model, where customer interaction is low-touch and low-cost.

One way to think about this is, if the prospect in question is actually a top customer of one of your competitors, they have a significant advantage, so sales may well be right to qualify the opportunity out. And if they are routinely going to qualify them out, marketing needs to stop sending them leads and either find another channel to market or spend their time elsewhere.

Some resources are, of course, not allocated to any particular account tier, particularly in marketing, which builds and maintains the company's brand, digital presence and channels, and produces content and campaigns that apply to multiple tiers. Increasingly, with the move to 'omnichannel' buying, marketing directly 'owns' some of the channels to market, with companies more willing to make higher value transactions online, as we saw in Chapter 1. Even so, an allocation of these broader marketing costs in proportion to the revenue generated from each tier can be instructive and provide a focus on what is being done to support and drive revenue in each tier and whether the proportions of expense and resources are in balance with the size of the opportunity.

A way to capture the output of this resource and cost baselining exercise is shown in Table 3.3.

Place your bets

Every company has finite resources, so, armed with this new insight, the next step is to create a model, using the same table, for where you should allocate resources based on your overall company growth strategy and taking into account many of the trends we discuss in this book. It is an exercise in placing appropriate bets in terms of resources deployed and expenses incurred.

As well as quantity of resources, once this initial modelling is done, there needs to be a company-wide agreement as to the best way to go to market in the accounts that make up the different tiers. We pick this up again in more detail for the top accounts in Part 3, but Table 3.4 illustrates the considerations that need to be thought through and then executed with discipline across sales and account management, marketing, customer

TABLE 3.3 Account resource allocation by tier

Account tier	Number and % of accounts	% of company revenue	% of company gross profits	% of total GTM expenses	Profit/loss % based on GTM expenses	#GTM direct resources	#GTM assigned resources
Tier 1: eg top 1%							
Tier 2: eg next 2–5%							
Tier 3: eg next 14–17%							
Tier 4: target prospects							
Tier 5: Bottom 80%							
Totals	100%	100%	100%	100%	100%	#	#

TABLE 3.4 Illustrative go-to-market (GTM) approach by tier

Account tier	Sales and account management	Marketing	Customer success (or service delivery)	Executive engagement and sponsorship
Tier 1	Executive-level KAM leads account team, with dedicated sales teams provided by each relevant BU and geography	Dedicated strategic account-based marketers (ABM-er), acting as account CMO plus deal based-marketing (DBM)	Dedicated customer success manager	CEO or direct report acts as sponsor
Tier 2	Senior level KAM leads account team, with aligned sales teams provided by each relevant BU and geography	Strategic ABM-er works across 3–5 accounts plus DBM	Shared customer success manager	CEO direct report or C-1 level acts as sponsor
Tier 3	Account Manager (farmer) allocated to 1–3 accounts	ABM-er for 3–5 clusters of 5–15 accounts each plus DBM	Customer success high touch team as needed	C-1 level acts as sponsor
Tier 4: Prospects	Challenger-sales led (hunters)	Cluster ABM or Programmatic ABM plus DBM	Customer success hightouch team as needed	CEO or direct report acts as sponsor
Tier 5:	Omnichannel approach, Challenger-sales if deal is qualified	Programmatic ABM, segment or solutions marketing plus DBM	Customer success mid or tech touch	No assigned executive sponsors

success and executive engagement and sponsorship. It is overly simplistic because companies will be in different states and use different terminology, but it should at least prompt a debate about how aligned go-to-market resources are.

A few words of explanation are needed: KAM stands for key account manager, a term we will expand on in Chapter 7, but which implies a general manager responsible for the top account, covering a range of different job titles that different companies assign, such as account managing director or client partner.

Customer success is a term predominantly used in the enterprise software business, but increasingly creeping into usage elsewhere. In technology services companies, service delivery manager is more commonly used, and in consulting and professional services firms, the role might be client delivery partner. Whatever terms are appropriate to your particular industry segment and business can be substituted, the main point being that it is important to be clear what the approach is in each case and ensure understanding, buy-in and alignment.

Finally, regarding this table, the term 'omnichannel approach' is used to describe the range of channels that companies are investing in to serve a wide customer base. However, top tier accounts also want to buy from you in the way that suits them, so this is not to imply that omnichannel is only relevant for smaller accounts. As we have seen in Chapter 1, there is a trend for B2B purchases being made online to increase in value every year.

The end result of this exercise may or may not be radical, but it will enable the organization to take a company-wide view of how its resources are being spent across the various teams, and whether that makes sense against growth and profit objectives. It should also reduce tension between different teams.

The 'holy grail' outcome here is to identify where you are over-allocating resources, causing you to re-evaluate how to reduce the 'cost to serve' in the bottom 80 per cent of the customer base and to be able to increase the resources dedicated not just to the most important customers today, but also to develop a more forensic and targeted investment in a group of prospects or smaller customers that could become the top customers of tomorrow.

Since we know that acquiring a new customer, assuming they are already an established company, will usually mean winning against incumbent competition that will be defending their position, it is likely that a disproportionately higher level of investment is required here, with different tactics, which are described in the chapters on key account management and sales, ABM and executive sponsorship and engagement.

Companies that get this right start with what needs to be invested in key account management or strategic account-based marketing in their top accounts, within whatever budget is available. This is a long-term play, but the results can be remarkable, with the same top customers generating the long-term profitable revenues a company needs over the long term.

To do the whole account prioritization and resource and expense allocation exercise properly in a large, complex company takes a surprisingly long time, because the data required to drive all the decisions are not necessarily readily available. In addition, the data driven discussions, which, as Andrew Fitzgerald commented in his Viewpoint earlier, need to be used as the basis for thoughtful conversations with people who understand the individual customer situation more intimately before a final decision is made.

Executive management needs to sponsor this resource allocation exercise, and it should be undertaken at a time when the results of the exercise can be factored into the company's next budget or planning cycle as well as into more strategic, mid-term growth plans for the company overall.

If executive management is sceptical about the benefits of the exercise, it might be worth piloting in a single country or business unit. Nine times out of 10, the results contain some surprises that will cause better decisions to be made about where resources are allocated, and the experience will draw interest and attention from across the company.

There may well be some kind of crisis that stimulates the need to make this assessment: a change in leadership, acquisition, private equity buy-out or company turnaround. All of these events tend to force people to take a more fundamental look at their operations, so this can be the perfect time to review the resources allocated and find ways to reduce costs, often an imperative in any of these circumstances.

Even if it is not caused by an existential crisis, it is still a very instructive exercise to build better alignment and understanding across the various teams, and can be sponsored by the chief operating officer, chief revenue officer or chief customer officer, depending on the way your company is organized. The chief finance officer is also likely to be acutely interested in the results too. How to make the change to a more account-based growth strategy is the subject of Chapter 6, examining the challenges from a leadership, culture and change perspective.

Fujitsu, by way of contrast to the $20 billion start-up Kyndryl, has embraced an account-based strategy for many years, with concentration on a relatively small number of very large accounts. Ian Hunter shares his story in the case study in this chapter, this time from his vantage point in a large region in Europe rather than globally.

CASE STUDY
Fujitsu: Optimizing account focus

Fujitsu is a global IT services company headquartered in Japan, operating in over 100 countries with over 124,000 employees. Established in 1935, it is ranked eighth worldwide by revenue, with a leading portfolio of IT services, solutions and products aimed at helping customers on their digital transformation journey. Fujitsu's core purpose is to make the world more sustainable by building trust in society through innovation.

Ian Hunter is Head of Marketing for Northern and Western Europe, encompassing the UK, Scandinavia, Benelux, France, Portugal, Spain and Ireland. Although the company doesn't operate explicitly on the 80/20 principle when prioritizing accounts, he recognizes its validity. 'I do think it's absolutely true that you get 80 per cent of your profit from 20 per cent of your customers. And while it is not something overtly applied to our working practices, it does flow through how the company operates.'

Identifying and categorizing accounts

In terms of selecting priority accounts, the head of each country is ultimately the decision-maker. Their role is defined as 'owning' sales, with P&L responsibility, so they are mandated and challenged to come up with the strategic accounts for their territory. There are a number of broad parameters in choosing these accounts, including existing turnover, potential for growth and potential for selling in new propositions and service lines.

In 2021, the number of strategic accounts for the region as a whole was 40. A small number of these were deemed global strategic accounts, which attract additional scrutiny from Japan HQ and go through governance processes to manage behaviour and performance at a global level. Then, there are about 200 'focus' accounts, which have been identified as offering particular opportunities over the next 12 months and carefully nurtured as the source of future strategic accounts within a given period. Finally, roughly 20,000 accounts make up the remaining bulk of the account universe, and are assigned sales, marketing and delivery strategies according to their status.

There is no one universal process for collecting data to select these key accounts in a federated culture like Fujitsu – it varies by country. For example, in the UK there are a variety of sources, including external databases of contracts coming up for renewal, Fujitsu's own purchase records, account profitability data and input from the account teams. As Hunter explains, 'We have very good internal data about how existing accounts perform, and which ones should be on the list. Plus, we track which of those accounts that we targeted in the year are coming to fruition, and prioritize them for next year accordingly.'

Allocating resources

How resources are allocated depends on the classification and characterization of the account and where the centre of gravity lies. The biggest strategic accounts are operated through individual P&L statements and allocated what Hunter calls the 'golden triangle' of sales and account management, delivery and marketing. These are overseen by an account director, while smaller accounts are run by a service delivery manager. Opportunities in new accounts are classed as sales initiatives and run by sales leaders rather than account managers.

In terms of marketing, while a few of the topmost accounts will have dedicated account-based marketing (ABM), Fujitsu mainly operates a more agile approach. Fujitsu has evolved to ABM-as-a-service (ABMaaS), which enables account teams to consume specialist ABM services on demand and marketers to scale. As Hunter says, 'Since most of the work is deal-based, we focus on applying ABMaaS to specific opportunities that we want to put additional support behind. Our mindset is that ABM is just part of the way we do things and we have a fixed budget for it. So, except in the case of a small number of the largest accounts, we are putting "parts" of people onto ABM activity. We prioritize where we put people based on where we see the big specific opportunities we can help with, pulling in centralized specialist resource to support local marketers as part of the ABMaaS model.'

He encourages the marketers to create sensible and pragmatic plans that resonate with sales objectives and address customer challenges. The guiding principle is to be firmly customer focused, argues Hunter: 'If you know the names of your customers and what business you want to do with them, plus what you want them to think and feel, then you can write your marketing plan. And you do that either as a sector, or an industry, or for one account, and move your resources to reflect whatever is going to generate the best returns. If you are really smart, it will be different every year because you are flexing resources to align with what's really happening in the business.'

Pulling in the best people for each account applies across the board. In service delivery, for example, there are a range of metrics including net promoter scores to monitor performance. It's all linked into what Hunter says is a very customer-focused culture, which is the basis for every activity, and where quality of service delivery is the key to growing the business: 'If you are very clear about your priorities for the business, everything else happens in terms of allocating the best resources in the most focused way.'

Executive engagement

Executive sponsorship has a prominent role to play in customer relationships. The executives who run each country in the region have ultimate responsibility for the customer, so they ensure that the right executives are matched to the right account, although how they engage varies according to the country's customers and culture.

Strengthening executive engagement is done in a number of ways, notes Hunter. One important route is running executive engagement programmes targeting various C-suite members in customer accounts (such as CEOs, CIOs and HR leaders). For example, Fujitsu runs advisory boards with CIOs in a number of countries in the region. At the next level down, there are executive discussion evenings around topics customer executives care about, and, increasingly, tightly focused seminars for small groups of senior people.

Critically, the Head of the Region, Paul Patterson, has set the tone for the strong focus on customers. Hunter concludes: 'He is really clear that the country heads should concentrate on growing the business, and is equally clear that service delivery is key to that growth. We put a strong focus on customer experience and taking proactive ideas to our customers. And we make sure that we talk about the portfolio we are going to deliver in the context of the customer and the outcomes they are trying to achieve.'

Fujitsu is a great example of a global business making account prioritization and resource allocation decisions at multiple levels – by country, region and, in some cases, globally. The beauty of the 80/20 rule is that it applies everywhere, so no matter what your own sphere of influence is in your business, you can apply the thinking we've outlined in this chapter to your operations to drive long-term growth with your most important customers.

SUMMARY CHECKLIST

1 To adopt an account-based growth strategy, you really need to start by understanding your version of the fractal 80/20 rule. To do this, gain agreement as to what you need to measure, and work with your colleagues to understand where your revenue and profits come from at an account level.

2 Based on a more detailed understanding of the 80/20 rule at your company, you can start the process of prioritizing the accounts that you are going to bet on being the most significant for you in the years ahead.

3 Agree the overall ambition for your top accounts, together with business objectives you wish to achieve.

4 Develop an objective, data-led account prioritization approach and model that assess the attractiveness of an account and your business strength relative to competition.

5 Decide on your selection criteria carefully and gain agreement across the business for their relative importance and the scoring model you will adopt for each, together with the source of the data you will use to make the exercise as objective as possible.

6 Use the results of the exercise to foster discussion with the relevant executives across marketing, sales and customer success or service delivery to make choices about which tier to put your customers into.

7 Depending on the size of your company and the scope of your exercise, you may want as many as five tiers, including a tier for targeted prospecting, where you could use the same methodology and tool but with different criteria.

8 Once you have your accounts split into the appropriate number of tiers, it's time to look at how you allocate your customer-facing resources today and how this stacks up with the opportunity you see within each tier for sustainable, profitable growth.

9 As well as looking at quantity of resources and expenses, you need to assess the appropriate resourcing model for different tiers of accounts, recognizing that the expectations of your customers and your ambitions will differ significantly between tiers.

10 Place your bets and make sure you monitor the results of your investments, both at the individual account level and for each account tier.

04

Integrated account business planning

The previous chapter explained how to choose the right accounts. Once prioritized, we need a plan for each of the top customers to maximize the opportunity in each. This chapter discusses the vital role that account planning should play – but too often doesn't – in ensuring that an organization does a much better job of exploiting the potential of its most valuable customers.

Based on our experience and building on the research findings in Chapter 2, it is our contention that, on the whole, account planning has not adapted to the huge significance of these top customers. We believe companies should be taking a more integrated, business-like and longer-term approach to their top tier customers – the three per cent of customers who may well account for more than half of their company's sustainable, profitable revenue.

That's not what we see in current account planning practice, so we're proposing a different approach, which we've called *integrated account business planning*.

- *Integrated* in the sense of integration across the company, particularly sales, marketing and customer success, but also in how executives engage effectively. We know of some companies where the sales-owned account plan is entirely separate from the customer success plan and others where there are multiple customer success plans. This cannot make sense.

- *Business* in the sense of highlighting that the plan should be a real business plan, much as you would construct for a business unit, country or an industry sector.

It seems that account planning across the board is still largely the domain of sales and its benefits remain largely elusive. One executive, who had spent nearly 20 years in sales operations and enablement roles in enterprise software, told us that account planning had never really delivered the benefits expected despite huge efforts and millions of dollars in investment across the business. It's a view we share and hear all too often.

This chapter discusses the way that account planning is done today, drawing on our research and observations.

We then propose the key elements of integrated account business planning, with a viewpoint from Rudy Dillenseger, from Microsoft, bringing to life some of the challenges in account planning, particularly how you move it from being a sales-led activity to a more rounded business initiative.

One size doesn't fit all in account planning, of course, so we explore what is appropriate for each tier of customers before focusing on two key elements that need improvement: the process of building and reviewing plans and the plan content and structure.

Finally, the chapter ends with a case study from Atos, which has adopted account business plans for its largest customers and explains the key elements of its approach.

Account planning today

Our research into current practice in account planning across 65 B2B companies is revealing. It focused on account planning in top accounts, not account planning across the entire company, so the results need to be reviewed in that context.

In top accounts, virtually everyone reports they have an account plan, which suggests that it is seen as a key element in driving growth. For those accounts, 25 per cent strongly agree that their account plans are structured like other business plans: for example, for a business unit, industry or country. It would suggest that in these companies business plans for top accounts are being produced that will stand up to scrutiny. We know from our work with some of the largest and most sophisticated companies that this is indeed the case.

Even more companies report that their plans state a clear ambition to grow share of wallet beyond the current financial year. However, 38 per cent of companies say that their plans do not explain how to compete for share of wallet against named competitors, suggesting there is some rigour missing and that there is an internal focus not properly tested.

Just over 80 per cent say their account plans are based on a deep understanding of the customer's business imperatives and initiatives. This is testament, we think, to the massive impact that account-based marketing has had, and is something that the Atos case study really focuses on.

LACK OF CUSTOMER INVOLVEMENT

One of the really interesting findings, however, is that, despite claiming deep insight, only 7 per cent strongly agree that they involve customers in the development of their account plans, with the majority stating that they do not involve customers in the process. This opportunity for better collaboration with customers is significant.

A plan is only as good as its execution, and 80 per cent of companies report that they do have clear action plans to help them realize their ambition in the top accounts. However, these plans are usually owned within the sales function. When it comes to integrating sales, marketing and customer success, around 40 per cent do not agree that their account plans provide this integration, and 30 per cent do not believe their account plans leverage the whole company's relationships and resources for the benefit of the customer. So there is a significant opportunity for greater collaboration and integration, which is discussed later.

We have found that today account plans themselves fall largely into three camps.

Camp 1. Account plans built from standardized templates. These templates may or may not be linked to data pulled from underlying CRM systems, but they do tell a story, at least from the sales perspective, for what should happen in the account. There are countless templates to choose from, from multiple vendors.

On the whole, templates start with the customer's business situation, vision and challenges, then position the company's portfolio in the context of the customer – an outside-in view that has been heavily influenced by the rise of account-based marketing, as we've already said. However, our experience, in common with other researchers, suggests that companies often overestimate their understanding of the customer's world.

There is always a risk that many account plan templates try to capture too much information and at levels of detail that make them time-consuming to complete in the first place and even more difficult to maintain, leading to unwieldy documents that, despite the volumes of data, don't ever seem to quite get to the point! For top accounts, 'the point' should be: 'How are we going to realize our ambition of sustainable, profitable growth, taking wallet share from competitors and building mutually beneficial, long-term partnerships, based on shared values?'

Camp 2. Account plans built on a bespoke basis to suit the specific customer and often based more around the ambition that could be realized with the account. They are more holistic in that they have greater vision, are over a longer time horizon, and involve a broader perspective than just sales.

In large account teams, sometimes involving hundreds of people across multiple geographies, the need to build a way to articulate the many different aspects of the account plan so that it can be conveyed to a large team means that a PowerPoint document is more likely to be produced, with a concise executive summary, dashboard and execution plan, to keep everyone on track.

Sometimes these account plans draw information from underlying CRM systems, but often they stand alone and are not directly linked to the CRM data.

Camp 3. Account plans that are built in or around CRM systems, such as Salesforce or Microsoft. These pull together data stored in the CRM system in order to create a dynamic view of the account that is accessible to multiple functions. The amount of data and functionality of these plans varies, but can be incredibly rich, with the tracking of literally hundreds or thousands of data-points in the largest plans.

In some companies, an overall account plan, suitable for executive review, is created as a PowerPoint, drawing in underlying data from the CRM system. If implemented well, this can provide the ambitious, holistic, integrated business plan that works well for top accounts.

The danger, however, is that account plans are just 'collections of data' rather than a cohesive story on how to achieve an ambition – something we discuss later.

EXPLOIT THE CRM SYSTEM

Given the significant investment in CRM systems, the ideal situation is surely to use the power that a CRM system has to keep track of a large number of moving parts, combined with the ability to create a clear narrative for the account that is accessible to everyone involved.

Introducing integrated account business planning

Market leaders are building integrated account business plans for their most important customers that:

- are anchored in a deep understanding of the customer's relevant business priorities based on sound research and analysis;

- focus on customer outcomes and metrics important to them, which have been debated and agreed with the customer executives;

- have a clear three-year ambition to grow share of wallet against named competitors, with really stretching ideas;

- articulate how to achieve the ambition, with desired outcomes and clear actions, tied to individuals with challenging but realistic timescales;

- are built and executed collaboratively across sales, marketing and customer success;

- have a one-page executive summary to focus on the 'big rocks' and the progress being made;

- are consistent with company culture, reward, recognition and incentives, balancing the short term and long term;

- are sponsored by an engaged senior executive who helps the team and reviews regularly.

There may well be a need for lots of supporting information, but integrated account business plans should be ambitious, clear and simple in order to get everyone focused on how to get from the current situation to a future state.

Rudy Dillenseger has been involved in account planning in a variety of roles at Microsoft over many years. He gives us the benefit of his experience in his viewpoint.

VIEWPOINT

Rudy Dillenseger, Global Director of Sales Strategy and Enablement, Microsoft Services

In your view, what's wrong with the way most companies do account planning for their top customers today?

One of the problems companies have when they are planning for the year is that salespeople can take almost a reverse-engineering approach to their quota.

What do I mean by that? Let's say they have a $10 million quota for the year. They look at how to retire that quota by creating pipeline in the fiscal year with win rates to achieve their targets and to do that within the constraints of the organization, such as which products they can sell. They look for accelerators and what type of products can be ditched if they don't influence the quota. To me that's what's wrong with so many sales executives' plans. They are not creating proper account plans but more like a quota retirement plan.

Doing account planning once a year and then rarely revisiting the plan so it becomes your one truth is just wrong, in my opinion. What you should do, particularly with your biggest customers, is what I call evergreen planning: keep it fresh because something is happening with customers every day. If you want to create more opportunity, you have to think differently and emphasize business outcomes, not just focus on meeting your annual quota. What I mean by this is that the overall opportunity at the account is usually greater and you can create a pipeline that far exceeds your quota by looking at the total addressable market and focusing on customer current and future challenges.

How do you get salespeople to become more involved in solving business problems for their customers?

It's about providing a different angle so that you can overcome their initial scepticism.

I think the best way to do this is in workshops, where you can have people from the account team in the room, or more often virtually since the pandemic. You should start by asking them what they *could* be doing with their customer but without mentioning any products. They need to think outside the boundaries of their everyday job and make the sky the limit: what sorts of ideas and capabilities *could* they propose to their customer? Depending on the portfolio of your company, obviously you will get different results. But, ideally, by the end of a workshop you might get between 10 and 15 initiatives that would deliver better outcomes for their customers. Often, you can come up with potential projects worth tens of millions of dollars.

How important is having a shared ambition with your customer?

You have to share what you are trying to achieve with the customer if you want to make progress. Customers need to buy into the idea of you having bigger ideas, where you can help them much more broadly. It takes a mind shift with the sales teams and also time to build trust with customers and educate them about what you can do.

I think you have to work in partnership with customers to get to the best solution for them. The problem can be that some customers come with a preset idea of what they want and how it should work. But it's based on what they know, not what they don't know, so you have to have the confidence and the contacts to expand their horizons. You need to try to understand what they are trying to achieve, what objectives and business challenges you can help with so you can identify potential initiatives. If you are not challenging your customers' thinking, then you are just going to be another vendor.

The way I look at it is this: if you are just basically servicing a customer, you get between a 20 and 30 per cent win rate; when you start to teach your customer beyond what they think they want, that rises to 50 per cent; if you go beyond that to really understanding what they want to achieve and their decision criteria, you can see an 80 per cent win rate.

How do you keep everyone on the team aligned around the customer?

The first thing you need is to have something actionable and be clear about who is going to be taking action and when, so it's not like you are shooting a rocket at the moon in one step. You should use executive sponsorship to open up conversations with customer executives and back up the account team, particularly when you want to validate any big ideas with the customer.

I think the more you document information about the account and the more you share, then the more collaboration you get and great things can happen. After all, if a customer is spending a billion dollars on IT every year and you have only a small proportion of that, there is so much room to grow by evaluating your total addressable market into the account as well as opportunities to expand the budget when demonstrating tangible business outcomes.

My philosophy is that it's always easier to sell the next million than the first million! So, you need to be ambitious with your existing big customers and propose to do more with them. This takes courage on the part of the sales team, but with the right support and executive sponsorship, it can really make a big difference.

Microsoft have a well-defined approach to transformative planning with their customers, which they use themselves and encourage their partners to use too. This is called Catalyst, and is described by Microsoft as an envisioning and planning programme to build, plan and execute business transformation strategies with a proven, innovative approach. It has four defined steps, described below.

MICROSOFT CATALYST

Inspire

Start by finding the transformation strategy that's right for you. Define and prioritize your strategy using development activities, then foster ideation and drive decision making with an envisioning workshop.

Design

Next, build a compelling case for change by discussing business and technological impact. During this, you'll quantify the ROI and financial benefits, including revenue growth, cost savings and employee efficiencies.

Empower

Help others across your organization see the value in your business transformation story by creating visual assets and immersive experiences – promoting buy-in and getting alignment on commitments.

Achieve

In this final stage, go from envisioning to execution. Bring in the resources you need to execute your strategy and carry out your business transformation across departments – and then measure its success.

It is interesting to see Microsoft, as well as other software companies, taking a much more business-outcome perspective on how they work with their customers. Salesforce, as we will see in Chapter 9, are also becoming much more consultative in their approach.

Some common failings with account planning

Rudy Dillenseger makes a compelling case for the kind of forward-looking, ambitious account planning we think is vital to drive growth in top accounts. However, before we look further at the best way to approach planning, let's examine some of the common failings.

COMMON FAILINGS

We have found that companies often fail in their approach to account planning because they:

- don't really understand the customer's key challenges and how they can deliver value against them;

- lack ambition and underestimate the opportunity for growth by not fully understanding the addressable market space in their customer;

- are too short-term focused on this quarter and this year, driven by inappropriate incentives and company culture;

- allow the plans to be 'owned' by sales, so they are not leveraging the company's overall strengths;

- create over-complex templates containing too much information and so people merely pay lip service to the plans, partly because they are so unwieldy;

- have too many plans for too many accounts and pursue a one-size-fits all approach;

- do not have executive sponsorship to regularly review the plans, so outcomes are not achieved.

Integrated account business planning in practice

One size doesn't fit all

Different types of plan should exist for different customer tiers. As we have explained in previous chapters, the 80/20 principle is fractal, which means that an account at the top of one tier is much larger than an account at the bottom of the same tier, often by as much as 16 times.

Therefore it makes little sense to have a single level of sophistication for accounts that are so different in their magnitude or growth potential. In a large, established company, we think there should be at least three levels of plan:

- a full-blown, executive-sponsored, integrated account business plan for the largest customers, probably reserved for the top 3 per cent of accounts;

- a comprehensive plan to a standard template for the next tier, which may account for the remaining top 20 per cent of accounts;

- the rest – the 80 per cent of accounts that drive less than 20 per cent of revenues, where the best approach might well be opportunity plans, focused on winning the next deal, rather than trying to do anything much more sophisticated at the overall account level.

The middle tier is interesting for a couple of reasons. First, it may contain future top customers, so some of these accounts may need to be treated more like existing top customers, with appropriate focus and investment; second, these accounts may not be as significant at the global level, but could still be very significant for a country or market-facing unit, which may lead to executive sponsorship from a country-level executive rather than a global-level executive.

In many industries, such as in financial services or pharmaceuticals, where globalization is the norm, many of the largest accounts in a given country will be subsidiaries of a global entity. In this case, some companies have established a 'parent-child' hierarchy for their plans, with a requirement incumbent on the team responsible for the 'child' (or subsidiary) to be properly linked to and part of an overall global 'parent' plan. In these circumstances, there has to be a standardized process and template to enable consolidation.

Our work leads us to propose three areas that will help improve the impact and effectiveness of account planning as you make the shift to integrated account business planning:

- the process of building and reviewing plans;
- plan content and structure;
- leadership, culture and change.

The first two of these are dealt with in this chapter. The third area, 'leadership, culture and change', is the subject of an entire chapter in its own right, Chapter 6, since the ability to have the right leadership, a supportive, agile culture and a willingness to make the changes necessary to pursue an account-based growth strategy affect all elements of account-based growth, not just planning.

The process of building and reviewing plans

The way plans are created and reviewed needs to change, particularly for the top few per cent of customers.

At the very least, the creation and review process should be owned company-wide. This approach and ownership is a recognition of the importance of the top accounts, putting them on a par with products, countries and industry segments, and is a vital step in realizing the opportunity for sustainable growth. It may lead to significant changes to the way the management system at the top of the company operates and how company executives spend their time. It will certainly send a clear message to the sales, marketing and customer success organizations.

Ideally, the customer should be involved in creating the plan or at least validating key parts of it. There are two important points here. First, the nature of top accounts is often that the same accounts remain important over many years, even decades. It follows that there is often a symbiotic relationship between a company and its top customers, where the customer has a vested interest in ensuring that the company really does understand its business priorities and can bring to bear all the company's capabilities in order to achieve its goals, as suggested by Ninian Wilson in Chapter 1. This being the case, it is vital to involve the customer executives in the planning process.

The second point is the need to involve teams from across sales, marketing and customer success or value delivery. Each has a different perspective on the account and brings a variety of knowledge and expertise to the table, all of which needs to be accommodated in the integrated account business plan if the growth potential in these top accounts is to be realized.

As an example, the individual charged with customer success or service delivery may be brilliant at making sure that targets are met, but may be less good at translating that into value statements or ensuring that customer executives understand this value and share their experience with others. Marketing colleagues can help to communicate this value and develop public advocates across the account. Marketing may also be the best source of reliable data regarding the addressable market size at the customer level.

In these complex accounts, there are numerous relationships that need establishing and nurturing. In one case we came across recently, the company tracked over a thousand relationships, with nearly one hundred deemed significant. With all these relationships to manage, sales need all the help they can get!

Ambition for the accounts should be agreed at senior levels, leveraging the whole company's resources for the benefit of the customer. Salespeople typically have a relatively high percentage of their remuneration based on achievement of an annual or even quarterly quota. Every experienced salesperson on an incentive plan has worked out that they will earn more if they can overachieve against their target. So there is a natural tendency for sales-people to temper their view of what might be possible in the account longer term and to focus much more on the current deals that will help them make their quota rather than longer-term, transformational deals.

These deals might help them grow the account significantly over time, but can take more than one year to close and, in some cases might, in fact, slow down or even jeopardize this year's revenue objectives being met. This behaviour isn't the fault of the salesperson but is a common issue that needs to be addressed and overcome. Senior management has to take responsibil-ity for whatever the ambition is for these large, important customers and be able to make and support the appropriate judgements between immediate revenue opportunities and longer-term growth.

The sign-off and review process should focus on progress against planned outcomes to deliver the ambition. The executive sponsor ought to join line management and the account team in these reviews. Note that one company we know of has called the reviews 'Account Transformation Boards'. We like this because it sends the right signals in terms of their importance and purpose.

It is often said that 80 per cent of business success is in the execution and not in the planning. Planning for top accounts is no different. The energy and attention that is applied to how the plan is to be executed, as well as rigorous and regular reviews of progress against the desired outcomes and actions, is vital. Without this, plans are likely to be less convincing in the first place and, even if well thought through and constructed, will lay in the cloud equivalent of the bottom drawer.

The sign-off and review process needs to address this, both for the indi-vidual accounts but also to realize one of the great benefits of having senior company executives focused on their biggest customers: they get to experi-ence first-hand what it is like being a customer of their company. They gain invaluable insights, are told a few home truths and can take company-wide actions that will have benefits broader than just for the individual customer. The best executive sponsors are regarded by the account team as 'in the tent', rolling up their sleeves and supporting the team in their objectives, not just reviewing the plans.

Reviews should be held at least quarterly, with a quarterly cadence around maintaining the plan and ensuring it is up to date. These account reviews will include people who actually interact and have knowledge of the customer with a first-hand, valid opinion. The danger with large companies, with multiple layers of management, is that decisions are taken by people once or even twice removed from the account situation. It is always better to have decisions made by people properly connected to the customer.

Reviews should be separate from sales forecasting and deal reviews. Over the years, many companies have tried to combine strategic reviews of an account with reviews that are focused primarily on closing today's deals and building tomorrow's pipeline.

Most mature sales organizations have an established cadence around sales forecasting and deals, which rolls up from seller through the first-line sales manager through to business units and onto the sales president or chief revenue officer. There is constant pressure in the system to make this month, this quarter and this year's numbers. Typically only salespeople are in the reviews. Even if others are present, salespeople are in the hot seat. Try as we might, it seems that it is fruitless to attempt to combine this sales cadence with a broader review of progress against the desired outcomes and actions undertaken to achieve the longer-term ambition and signed off in the plan for the account.

We are arguing that a different cadence needs to be in place to review account plans because, without it, the executive sponsor will not be connected to the account, will not be sufficiently involved in order to help the account team, and will not be able to remove any blockers that are in the way. This separate review process is also important to bring the whole team together, pooling their knowledge and expertise and adjusting their plans and actions based on the experience and insight gained. The reviews need to be focused on measurable progress and properly sponsored. Without them, the carefully crafted plans are destined to be plans that are never fully executed.

Finally, and perhaps most importantly, reviews of progress need to be held with the customer executives who have helped shape the plan. These 'external quarterly business reviews' focus on what value and outcomes have been delivered in the last quarter and what value is planned to be delivered in the next quarter, and enable supplier and customer executives to carry out a review in the context of a longer-term partnership, looking further ahead. Ninian Wilson described the governance in place at Vodafone in Chapter 1 and how vital it is to the health of the strategic supplier relationships.

Plan content and structure

Every business has some kind of template for its account planning, many of which we have reviewed in conducting research for this book. What we are proposing is a way to bring the plans more in line with an approach to business planning based on some of the current shortcomings we have discussed. This should give you reason to reflect on whether your account plan templates are adequate for the top accounts or whether they need to be updated to drive the outcomes you require.

CUSTOMER INSIGHT

If there is one thing that shines through as being the foundation for a good plan, it is that the plan is based on deep customer insight, something all market leaders invest in by working with the relevant customer executives, investing in the research to be able to do this credibly. But well before this, the foundation should be laid by the account team in building a comprehensive picture of the customer's world. Strategic marketing tools and techniques are required here to make sense of what otherwise would simply be a collection of facts and figures. Too often we have seen hugely detailed account plans with voluminous data about the customer, yet precious little actionable insight that links the information we have gathered with how we can add value.

Chapter 8 on account-based marketing provides much more detail on the best way to create and leverage customer insight. But a good place to start is with the 'wheel of customer understanding', shown in Figure 4.1, which creates an analytical framework to get to the heart of customer insight and helps think through the linkages between different aspects. Refined over 20 years by Cranfield University Key Account Management practice, it focuses the account team on the right topics and recommends the selection of appropriate analytical tools such as PESTEL and the nine-box SWOT, together with ways to assess and quantify value.

The whole approach to value analysis and planning is explained further in *Implementing Key Account Management* (Marcos *et al*, 2018), which offers a comprehensive framework, tools and checklists to assess plans against best practice.

AMBITION

Great insight means nothing if it is not matched by ambition. Alongside deep customer insight, ambition is the next major component of an integrated account business plan. Creating a clear ambition demands strong leadership and collaboration with the customer, with a shared vision of where the business partnership could go and the areas where you expect to

FIGURE 4.1 The wheel of customer understanding

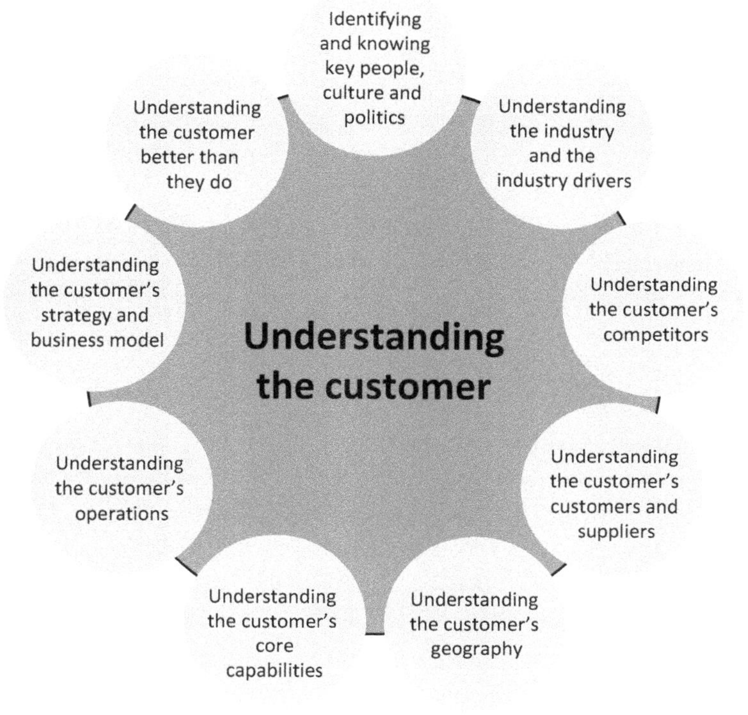

SOURCE Reproduced with kind permission from Marcos *et al* (2018)

be able to add value to the customer and win business, given the right conditions. Internally, the financial ambition should ideally be expressed in relation to increased wallet share against named competitors.

Our experience is that a three-year time horizon is a good one to use both to think expansively about the art of the possible and plot what needs to happen in order to realize your objectives over the next several quarters. In order to be in a position to go for a big prize, you need to earn trust and reputation for value delivery in strategic areas first. And when opportunities are complex and high-consideration deals are costly to bid for, you may need to use the argument that a smaller strategic deal should be given priority and properly resourced in order to open up more significant opportunities. We expand more on this in Chapter 7.

STARTING POINT

Given that this is one of your top accounts, you should be able to articulate your starting point in terms of share of wallet, competitor position and strength of relationships. As we saw in our research, going the extra mile to really understand how you are positioned against key competitors is not always captured. In order to understand share of wallet, you need to assess the size of the addressable market for your business at the customer level and how much of it you control.

What is important is an honest assessment of how this starting point, in all its elements, relates to the insights you have into the customer's world and your ambition, because the whole point of having a plan is that it gives you a way to get from your starting point (A) to your realized ambition (B).

CHOICES

All good strategic planning makes choices, and a good plan for a top account is no exception. As we have seen with some of the best account plans for top accounts in companies we have worked with, the fundamental choices are about 'where to play' and 'how to win'. You will build greater trust with your customer if you are clear about where you can and cannot help them, particularly if that enables you to forge stronger partnerships.

How this translates for your own company will depend on how broad your portfolio is and how you maximize the value you can deliver in relation to what the customer is trying to achieve. Typically, you are more likely to cement your relationship and grow it further if you can aggregate your company's products and services, and those of your partners, into an overarching value proposition that resonates well with the customer's priorities, based on your insight and discussions or workshops with customer executives.

Once you have decided where to play and how to win, in both cases considering collaborating with partners as well as likely responses from competitors, you need to consider which existing, partner-sourced and future capabilities you will need to bring together to make your plan work. In a complex firm with significant capabilities, this is not a trivial task. In fact, in our experience, focusing the relevant capabilities of the firm on the needs of a single customer, even a really important one and over a reasonably long time horizon, is really hard. This too was reflected in our research.

This is for two reasons. First, each of the business units that contains the capabilities you are trying to focus on a single customer has its own priorities, so may not buy into your vision for your customer. Second, the account team leadership may not have the breadth of understanding of all of the company's capabilities, particularly in companies that have grown rapidly and/or by acquisition. Executive sponsorship and a collaborative management system will help, but it is still a big challenge. We pick up this theme again in Chapter 6.

DISRUPTION

We live in unpredictable, volatile times. It is important that, as well as thinking creatively with customers about how to strengthen the partnership, we spend some time analyzing what could derail us.

This really involves three dimensions:

- disruption to the macroeconomic and political situation, which could affect our customer, our own company and our competitors;
- disruption in customers, such as changes in ownership or leadership, mergers and acquisitions or major strategic reviews;
- competitive responses that could impact our plan, particularly when it becomes clear what strategies we are pursuing. This needs to cover current key competitors and the emergence of new competitors who could be a threat, but could equally be open to partnership with a well-entrenched strategic supplier.

The end point of this is to create a thoughtful and prioritized set of possible risks and dependencies and the mitigating actions that can be taken or, alternatively, the early warning signs to monitor.

OUTCOMES AND METRICS

There needs to be a sharp focus on outcomes and metrics in your plan.

Once the plan is seen as a way to get from A to B, the outcomes, describing shorter-term milestones as well as the overall objectives for the account, can be summarized in a dashboard, pulling together the metrics around financial and operational performance, including customer health and expectations.

As we have seen in our research, companies do a better job of measuring and tracking 'hard' but lagging measures like revenue, but are less good at systematically tracking metrics around reputation and relationships, both of which may well be leading indicators and the key to sustainable profitable growth.

MAKING IT HAPPEN

Building an execution plan, with deliverables, actions, milestones and clear accountability, is essential. Without it, the plan will not be executed. The way this is done will reflect the way that a company runs its own management system, with many organizations adopting agile practices. As a practical example, we know of one global account lead who, in order to keep a constant focus on building deeper relationships with key individuals, held a weekly, 30-minute 'stand-up' where the account team members were asked to provide an update on relationship building.

This is far removed from the more traditional concept of a quarterly plan review. While it is indeed important for everyone to take stock every quarter, a weekly or bi-weekly check on progress against key actions is much more likely to keep everyone focused on execution, and not lose sight of the big picture.

Plan narrative

Notwithstanding the fact that plans for top accounts are likely to be quite comprehensive, it is also important to be able to create a short, clear narrative that describes the journey from A to B, with an executive summary forming the basis of executive sponsor reviews.

Probably the best way to do this is to accept that much of the analysis that has gone into the production of the plan is really supporting information and should be contained in appendices rather than being a key part of the narrative. If the plan is too long, there is a temptation for the presenter to spend too much time covering lots of detail before getting to the point. This is sometimes to avoid being grilled too much on the trickier aspects of the plan, such as what we are trying to achieve and what we are actually going to do! It should be possible to explain the plan and review the actions in 45 minutes or less. This won't be possible if it is longer than 15 slides.

Too many account planning templates fall into this trap, producing 50–60-page documents without a clear narrative.

Our proposed structure is more akin to a business plan, has a clear narrative, is relatively short and contains the following sections, as we laid out in this chapter:

1 **Executive Summary** (plan on a page).

2 **Customer Insight:** How do we create value based on our insight?

3 **Ambition:** Where do we want to be in three years?

4 **Starting point:** Where are we now and where are our key competitors?

5 **Choices:** Where do we want to play and how will we win?

6 **Disruption:** What could derail us?

7 **Outcomes and metrics:** What will we track?

8 **Making it happen:** What do we need to do to realize our ambition?

Of course, all companies will have their own view of what is important for them and should create templates that reflect that and are signed off at a senior level in the company. These plans can have significant impact on a company's overall success, as the Atos case study illustrates.

CASE STUDY
Atos: Integrated account business planning in practice

Atos is a global leader in digital transformation, with 109,000 employees and annual revenue of circa €11 billion. It offers a range of market-leading digital solutions along with consultancy, digital, security and decarbonization services. It is the European number one in cyber security, cloud and high-performance computing, providing tailored end-to-end solutions for all industries in 71 countries.

Choosing top accounts

The key strategic accounts have traditionally been those that make up a significant portion of the company's revenues, according to Neil Berry, Head of Global Account and Deal Based Marketing Centre of Excellence. However, over the last few years, other factors such as the propensity to grow an existing share of the account are increasingly becoming important in terms of selection. Decisions are not made on a clear 80/20 percentage split – although the strategic accounts do account for a large percentage of the current revenue and are vital to future growth.

That selection is integral to the company's account-based marketing (ABM) strategy, notes Berry: 'Those accounts are the ones that we will look at from an ABM perspective first, but we do always qualify in a very specific way. It is not necessarily based on just what revenues they bring in, but whether we can generate opportunity from them as well. For instance, is there the potential for global growth or potential to expand the portfolio within the account?'

Approach to account planning

How account plans are developed has evolved extensively over the last few years. While the process for those not considered strategic can be less rigorous and more ad hoc and might employ local support, the big accounts in the strategic portfolio undergo a more exacting, global/regional treatment. They are run through what are called account business plans plus (ABP+), which are built using more extensive account planning tools and will be regularly checked for progress, growth potential and intentions, so that the leadership teams on the executive committee can oversee the results. They emerge from interactive workshops attended by all those with the required skills, with systems and processes in place to execute them.

Account leadership can play a pivotal role in a successful outcome, says Berry. The best account leaders develop a tightly structured approach, constantly checking on progress, running workshops and setting up different streams of activity with different teams: 'You can always tell who is going to turn out to be a fantastic client account director. It's those people who really invest in the business planning upfront, who pull all the relevant people and expertise together and make it work.'

Along with sales, this can include, among others, marketing, procurement, those responsible for partnership management roles and delivery/solutions specialists. The board-level executive sponsors for the big accounts will normally be part of the process as well, to ensure they have a broad grasp of account strategy and direction.

A careful eye is kept on those promising accounts that are heading towards a tipping point in terms of potential, and, with these, account leaders have to up their game, including deploying the company's powerful ABM skills to encourage more reach. As Berry explains, 'The best account leaders are the ones who are able to think differently and embrace the idea of growth rather than just hitting the numbers and then getting on to the next quota. That's what makes the difference.'

Galvanizing the company around the customer

Putting the customer at the centre of the business demands a careful combination of process and, more elusively, leadership. In terms of process, the more successful account leaders set up different work streams running in the background of the plan based on particular activities, regular quarterly reviews and the agility to change course depending on what's working and what isn't. They make sure changing customer needs are reflected in the plan content and execution.

Style of leadership can also make a difference. Berry recalls one account leader whose charisma and organizational skills galvanized everyone involved: 'They would develop the plans and then build a tight execution plan which pinpointed what needed to happen and who should do it at every single point. Whether it was someone on consulting, customer experience, infrastructure, sales, finance or whatever, they would map it out and make those people responsible for the job. Significantly, they would galvanize them through their charismatic leadership so that not only did they buy into the account business plan, but they would pull together as a team to try and achieve it.'

As he adds, 'I think people could see that they wanted to grow the business and have people be part of that journey with them. And it wasn't a one-way street because they would always reciprocate with others.'

Just being known for getting things done can also energize people around the account, Berry points out: 'People rally behind these sort of people because they are successful. They're inspirational leaders and are always interesting to work with.'

Executive sponsorship

Executive sponsorship operates at a higher relationship level, with top executives brought in at pivotal points of account activity where those C-suite conversations can be leveraged to achieve certain objectives. As always, it can depend on the individuals how it actually works, says Berry: 'Some executive sponsors will be more active and involved in the details of what's happening, whereas others will be more hands-off and check in every so often or if they are needed.'

Measuring plan effectiveness

The approach to measuring the effectiveness of each plan for the top accounts can vary. From a business perspective, the net promoter score is regularly used to gauge customer intent, along with measuring growth within the accounts and the outcome of financial targets. Account leaders also have a number of ways to judge success, although the business is looking for ways to increase more consistency of approach here.

Major challenges in integrated account business planning

There are a number of challenges Berry identifies. One is not just having the right people involved in account business planning, but having the right *number* as well. Get too many people involved and you run the risk of dilution, particularly if people's attention gets pulled in too many directions. Too few, and execution is at risk. As Berry says, 'For me, the challenge is not so much about the actual building of the plan but the continued execution. This can be one of the hardest tasks and demands perseverance.'

Time, as always, is another constraint. It can be difficult to get the right people in a room together every few months to review progress and make sure the strategic focus doesn't get blurred. This can be ultimately frustrating for those who want to do a good job but don't feel they have enough time to do what they should be doing properly and just start ticking boxes.

Customer insight

Finally, how to capture valuable and actionable account insights is something that can always be improved, he says. Sometimes the best insights into what's happening with key accounts come from direct face-to-face conversations, which, of course, stopped during the pandemic. He would also like to see more 'sense checks' carried out directly with clients to test that the assumptions underpinning the account business plans are correct from the customer's perspective.

He concludes, 'You should not underestimate the value of having really good insight into an account. For example, if the immediate transaction is a contract renewal with a customer, this doesn't actually give us an insight into what the customer will really value. Sure, it tells you what someone signed up for two years ago. But it doesn't tell you what they could potentially be signing up for next, and it is an ideal opportunity to expand the range of services, as long as these can be packaged in such a way that they add value. Insight is the key to whether we are really well aligned with our top customers, and the account business plan is the best way to make sure the company stays on the same page.'

Collectively, the top customers may account for 50 per cent of a company's revenues. As such, they need the attention of the whole company, given their significance. They are, after all, the ones with the money! Well-researched plans, which are living documents and which lead to better collaboration internally and engagement externally, are vital to mitigate risk as well as to create sustainable, profitable growth.

They should be afforded the same effort and be subject to the same scrutiny as a country plan or a business unit plan, thus ensuring a strong connection between senior executives running the company and the executives in the most important customers – something we will build on in subsequent chapters.

SUMMARY CHECKLIST

1 Plans for top accounts need to be owned on behalf of the company, not be purely the domain of sales.

2 Different types of plans are appropriate for different tiers of customers and should be tailored to that effect.

3 The plans for the top accounts should be subject to the same rigour and commitment as plans for other aspects of the business, and include an executive summary, customer insight, three-year ambition, starting point, choices, possible disruptions, outcomes and metrics and a clear action plan.

4 Plans need to be built with the key teams that touch the customer as equal partners, drawing on their expertise and skills and knowledge to build a more complete picture.

5 Involving the customer in building deep customer insight is vital, particularly as it will deepen relationships and build trust as well as clarify for both parties the choices that have been made about where to play.

6 An integrated account business plan should have a strong ambition, signed off on behalf of the company by a senior executive who should play an active role in helping the team realize the ambition.

7 The plan should create a compelling narrative that is clear and easy to follow, with a bias to action and the emphasis always on doing what it takes to realize the ambition.

8 As important as the structure and content of the plan are, so is the commitment to review it regularly, and with the customer, to make sure progress is being made and to course-correct based on any experience gained.

05

Managing data, technology and operations

It's difficult to have an extraordinary focus on your customers if you have no data on them. Equally, it's possible to have so much data on them that you don't know what to do with them. For many companies, piecing together the important data on accounts and individuals they've gathered from different internal and external sources so that they provide some actionable insight is like putting together a jigsaw puzzle without having the original picture as a guide. How do you know which piece fits where? What picture are you trying to build? What will you do with it once you've built it?

As consumers, we are used to our suppliers knowing us, understanding what we like, and responding accordingly. Whether we're listening to music on Spotify, watching box sets on Netflix, or selecting a book from Amazon, they're one step ahead of us. Almost without thinking, we expect the same from our business partners. They should know all about the public announcement we made to the market yesterday, understand what it means for our strategy and priorities and build on our last interaction with them to offer us something useful – whichever part of the organization and through whatever channel we decide to engage with them.

In this chapter we'll look at how B2B companies are faring at building this sophisticated view of their most important customers, and how different technologies can be leveraged to provide and augment it through ongoing interactions with the account. We'll explore what data companies need to capture to create a rounded picture of their customers, where it can be sourced and stored and how to analyze it effectively to create actionable insights that drive growth. Finally, we'll touch on how to use data and technology to continually improve your engagement with top accounts by managing your performance across sales, marketing and customer success teams, supported by a single, integrated operations team or centre of excellence.

Building a clear view of the customer

As Kathy Macchi, EVP Consulting at growth consultancy Inverta says in her viewpoint in this chapter, building a single view of the customer is the holy grail right now for many B2B companies. Having acquired different systems to support the various teams across the organization – CRM for sales, automation systems for marketing, project management systems for service teams and accounting systems for finance – it can be all but impossible to combine the data coming off them and look at it from the lens of an account rather than by internal function.

Why this is important

As we've said, our expectations for being recognized, understood, valued and served intelligently have been raised by many of the technology-enabled experiences we have as consumers. As Chris Adlard and Daniel Bausor state in their great book, *The Customer Catalyst* (2020: 97): 'well-integrated technology platforms and data provide the essential cornerstone for great customer experiences'. They explain how systems and processes at the back-end of an organization (such as the CRM database used by the account team) should be integrated with front-end systems and processes (such as the company's website) to provide a seamless and intelligent experience for the customer. Their view is that 'without integrated systems and processes, in both B2C and B2B environments, customers quickly cotton on to the fact that doing business with the respective company can be laborious, inconsistent and even painful' (Adlard and Bausor, 2020: 98). And at that point, the customer will go elsewhere.

Adlard and Bausor quote Clive Humby, a British mathematician and entrepreneur in the field of data science and customer-centric business strategies. In 2006 he coined the phrase 'Data is the new oil'. Michael Palmer, of the Association of National Advertisers, expanded on Humby's quote, saying, 'Data is just like crude. It's valuable, but if unrefined it cannot really be used. It has to be changed into gas, plastic, chemicals, etc to create a valuable entity that drives profitable activity; so must data be broken down, analyzed for it to have value.'

We like Adlard and Bausor's conclusion (2020: 108) that 'data should be used to give organizations a far better insight into their customer base, to make smarter decisions about how to serve them better and, therefore, ultimately to drive more sustainable growth. The winners of tomorrow will be those who can get as close to their target customer groups as possible by using their own data, and data they can procure outside of their organization to better understand and serve their customers.' This is even more important for your top customers, as we have already explained.

What you need to know

We've already covered some requirements for data on account selection in Chapter 3 and on integrated account business planning in Chapter 4. Both of these key processes rely on accurate data to be successful. So what data do you need more broadly to build a 360° view of your top accounts?

- **Firmographics.** This is the corporate equivalent of demographic data for individuals, and includes data such as company size, structure, location, ownership, revenues and growth.

- **Technographics.** This is a combination of the words 'technology' and 'demographics' and covers the technology a company is operating, including its installed base of hardware as well as the software systems it uses, such as enterprise resource planning systems from SAP, workflow from ServiceNow or CRM from Salesforce.

- **Psychographics.** These are the more human data around the beliefs, values, motivation, perceptions and behaviour of your customers.

- **Intent data.** Leading analyst firm Gartner (2022b) defines intent data as enabling marketers to 'understand what an individual or company will likely do or buy next, based on behavioural information collected about an individual's or company's online activities.' These data often use a keyword or topic to identify buyer intent signals, such as an online search for 'digital transformation'.

- **Experience data.** As defined by experience management specialists Qualtrics (Temkin, 2020), these include the experience expectations, interaction perceptions, journey perceptions, relationship attitudes, ad-hoc diagnostics and choice preferences of your customers in relation to your company and its solutions.

This comprehensive array of data can be drawn from a range of sources, typically categorized as first-, second- or third-party. First-party data are those coming from your own systems, such as the customer profile, contact and sales data held within your CRM system; the engagement activity on your website or with your marketing campaigns; the billing and payment information in your accounting systems; or the product usage, adoption rates and satisfaction survey scores held in your service or customer success management system.

Second-party data are effectively someone else's first-party data, sold to you privately or given to you, perhaps by a partner (with the permission of the account or individuals where legally required).

Third-party data are other companies' data aggregated together. You typically buy them from outside sources that are not the original collectors of those data. Many large data aggregators exist to pull data from various other platforms and websites where they were generated, paying publishers and other data owners for their first-party data. These data are often bought and sold at scale in real time, or programmatically, and are the basis for many account-based marketing (ABM) campaigns run at scale today, particularly where the data identify prospect organizations that fit an ideal customer profile and are showing signals of intent around keywords of interest to the marketer's company.

In summary then, there is no shortage of data. But as Kathy Macchi says in her viewpoint in this chapter, just because you can collect them doesn't mean that you should.

The internal teams in your company who need to align around your top accounts should all be consulted on the data they need to perform their roles and drive long-term sustainable growth with the customer. In our case study for this chapter, Bill Doyle explains how SAP developed 10 internal personas who would need to access customer data, each one having a specific use case when extracting information from a single view of the account.

We know from our own research (Inflexion Group, 2022) that SAP is ahead of the curve with the Crystal Ball engine they've built to capture, analyze and distribute data on customers across its teams. Over half of the 58 companies we surveyed disagreed with the statement 'Our sales, marketing and customer success teams have a single view of data on our top accounts' (Figure 5.1).

It's easy to assume that this is because they don't have access to the right technology infrastructure to achieve this single view. But in our experience it is more likely to be a lack of enablement in using existing technology across the business – where people just don't feel trained or empowered to use the tools available to them – combined with some missing core skills in the area of data analytics and data science.

FIGURE 5.1   A single source of truth?

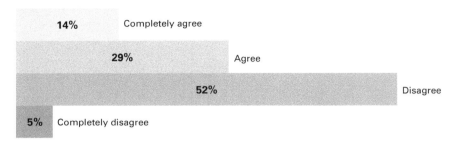

To what extent do you agree with this statement? (N=58)
Our sales, marketing and customer success teams have a single
view of data on our top accounts

14%   Completely agree

29%   Agree

52%   Disagree

5%   Completely disagree

VIEWPOINT

Kathy Macchi, Co-founder and Executive Vice President, Inverta

Why is it so important for companies to have a single view of the customer?

Because of e-commerce leaders like Amazon, your customer expects it. The expectation is present not only to acquire new customers but to retain existing ones. Unified data is needed to ensure a positive customer experience – from employee interaction all the way to the web and digital experience.

However, the proliferation of marketing and sales technologies creates more and more pockets of siloed data. That leads to teams having their own views into what's happening with the customer, and making their own, disparate interpretations.

Only a single view of the customer allows teams to create personalized, unified customer experiences. The challenge for companies is how best to utilize their data to create exceptional customer experiences. This is where the art and science of marketing merge.

As an example, one of the better ABM programs I have worked with started with the ABM leader saying, 'Why do we market to our top customers like we have no idea what they own, when we have sold them a huge amount of their infrastructure? We have a clear opportunity to add strategic value to our relationships with top accounts if we just spent time understanding their needs and applying what we know about them to provide more relevant help.' At its most basic, the challenge is assembling all you know about your customer in one place and being able to activate on that knowledge.

Where are companies today in achieving this view?

They are struggling because of an unwillingness to start simple. Have your marketing and sales executives decide what intelligence they really need. Continue the discussion for 30, 60 or 90 days to be sure you've identified the data that's really important. More data doesn't necessarily mean more insights.

The data you focus on should allow your teams to have something relevant to say (message) or offer (help, services, products, information) that benefits the customer.

Several years ago, when predictive lead scoring was the hottest thing on the market, I suggested trying some of the new technology to a client of mine. What he said next made an impression on me. He said he didn't want to go down that path yet, even though he knew the predictive lead scoring solutions to be effective. He wanted his team to roll up their sleeves, understand the data and build a model on their own in their marketing automation system. In a year, when they understood the underpinnings of the data, he would then consider putting in a predictive technology.

The same can be said about account insights. If you do it manually first, you'll have a better understanding of what data is truly important before building an elaborate, expensive solution.

Deciding what you need to know manually before you start investing is good practice. What other best practices are important?

First, take inventory of your sales and marketing technology. Do the tools serve your go-to-market strategy? Are they well adopted and being leveraged to their full value? Tools get purchased over time and not all are worth their investment.

When I hear, 'I have all this tech, but what do I do with it? Am I getting the most out of it?' I remind my clients that how you deploy your technology-powered capabilities will shape the way you practice marketing. It affects how customers experience your brand. It underpins your processes and frames your marketing strategies. When configured correctly, technology drives innovation, agility and experimentation. But too often, navigating the deluge of tech brings too much of a challenge to be productive.

In summary, make sure you do a thorough technology assessment. Understand how each technology maps to the goals of your marketing and sales organization. Decipher how each technology fits into your strategy, which tools to keep and which to sunset. Map all the data flows and integrations – this is key to building a single view in the future. Build out a maturity model to outline a clear path on where you are and where you want to be. Document how each tool can and should be used. Finally, ensure all staff are trained on how to use the tools and that your processes and tools are aligned. When you follow those steps, you'll be well on your way to getting a single view of the customer and feeling confident in your technology investments.

If your go-to-market is about growing your biggest accounts rather than customer acquisition, what are some best practices for that?

Companies that focus on growing their biggest accounts are companies where a few accounts contribute to a significant portion of their revenue. Their total available market may total 1,000 accounts, and their top accounts may be 100 or fewer.

This effort is going to be less about data-driven technology to identify and target ideal customer profiles and more about building executive relationships and understanding the unique initiatives that drive their account's business. This exercise would include gathering insight into the account's leadership and understanding the different factors that are clear and present for the account. This type of insight is qualitative and manual, and while you could use technology to help you with some of it, you could also hire an external agency to research and build account and executive profiles. It might be more cost-effective and help you build better executive engagement programs.

However, technology can play a significant role when determining whether or not your accounts are 'in market' or 'out of market'. Monitoring accounts and identifying when there is a spike in interest for topics could indicate when to initiate conversations with your stakeholders.

Additionally, technology and data play a role in reporting. When data is in silos across the organization, getting the data in a timely manner to act on it is critical and often a sore spot for most marketers.

Finally, it's critical to understand the difference between whether something requires a report, a dashboard or analytical work. They serve different purposes and are often conflated. It's important to get clarity on the questions you are attempting to answer, and which is the best vehicle to deliver that information.

What are some of the main challenges companies are facing in terms of their technology?

You must always be asking the question, 'Is this tool going to help me reach or connect with my specific buyers?' Organizations can forget why they purchase technology. While tools are typically purchased to extend reach and drive down the cost of acquiring a customer, you need to test the premise of the solution against your marketing strategy.

Another challenge is that the scope of marketing has grown by an order of magnitude. To support marketing's new responsibilities, you must differentiate between activities that are stable and scalable and those that require an agile, experimental approach. About 70 per cent of software in the technology stack should be core, required technology. The remaining 30 per cent is innovative and experimental. In the evolving technology landscape, the challenge is to quickly determine what edge tech drives business results, and transition those to core tools. Integration is the critical component; only with robust integrations will the systems be able to work together and share data.

What's your advice for companies leveraging their existing systems to build a single view?

There are three areas to consider.

First, it's about asking the right questions and knowing what data will show the answer. Then, you can consider how often the data should be updated and plan the measures you will take when the data requires different activities, responses, or offers.

Second, I often hear from marketing and sales leaders about the amount of investment they've placed in creating a single view of their accounts. However, months or years later, their marketing and sales outreach hasn't changed. It's critical to get buy-in early from teams about what they will do differently with a single view of the account. Driving change across an organization takes a concerted and sustained effort, but it appears to have become a forgotten element once the systems are built and in place. Remember, the point of getting a single view of an account is to bring more insight to marketing and sales teams so they can better grow and support their customers. If nothing changes, all that effort was for naught.

Finally, vet the ideas and activities that teams believe will make a difference when they have insight from a single account view. Personalization is a great example of this. Many teams go down the path of hyper-personalization based on the insights gathered and the systems they have in place. However, they find that there isn't content created to support that level of personalization. Organizations need to be realistic about what activities they can support with their budget and resources.

How can cross-functional teams improve top account performance using key metrics and dashboards that represent a single view of their account?

Insights fuel conversations. One of the advantages of technology is that it gives the marketer, salesperson, customer success and technical support teams a shared vision to discuss and to create a mutual plan of action around. With the data finally in one place, it provides a single window into the customer and allows the teams to agree on what they can do to grow and support the customer. It becomes a coordinated effort, and the customer benefits from one cohesive approach.

Impactful metrics and dashboards are the ones that provide an overall customer score based on a handful of key metrics related to the customer journey. This allows the team to understand overall customer health but then drill into areas where there might be concerns.

When considering holistic account views, it's necessary to balance information that's 'nice to know' with information that provides actionable insights. Ideally, a single account view enables you to market and sell differently based on the insights that it's providing. Just because you can track, gather and analyze data doesn't mean you should.

Leveraging your existing technology infrastructure

There is such a proliferation of technology available today claiming to help companies identify, understand and serve their prospects and customers that it's easy to see why people either over-invest in this area and build highly complex technology stacks or are bamboozled to the point of doing nothing. Blissfully's 2020 SaaS trends report (2020) stated that enterprises have, on average, 288 different SaaS applications in use across their businesses.

Adlard and Bausor (2020: 100) assert that 'investing in new technology systems does not, on its own, ensure seamlessly integrated customer experience…a significant investment must be made in integrating existing systems into new applications'. Their recommendation is to simplify, wherever possible.

So, what are the common elements of an existing technology infrastructure that most sales, marketing and customer success teams use to understand and manage top accounts? We list a few here, but each company will have both more and different solutions in its technology stack.

CRM systems

By the end of 2020, the global CRM applications market was worth $45.7 billion in license, maintenance and subscription revenues (Pang, Markovski and Markovska, 2021). According to the report by *Apps Run the World* (Pang, Markovski and Markovska, 2021), CRM systems include applications for sales force automation, marketing automation, customer service and support management such as email automation. Social media management, customer experience management, activity and participant management are among some of the newly available functionality. Salesforce is the most common platform, with around a third of the market, followed by Adobe, Oracle, SAP and Microsoft.

One of the main challenges with many CRM systems is the fact that there are often multiple and differently structured instances of them across a business, combined with inconsistent, missing or duplicated customer data. Adlard and Bausor comment that these systems, 'once heralded as the vanguard of customer-led business strategies and customer-centric technology decisions, have been misused to the point of creating bad customer experience'. They quote Ed Thompson, VP and Distinguished Analyst at Gartner, as saying, 'the vast majority of CRM projects have no benefit to the customer'.

Marketing automation

Marketing automation is software that handles routine marketing tasks without the need for human action. Common marketing automation workflows include email marketing, behavioural targeting, lead prioritization and personalized advertising. Some of the leading platforms include Marketo, Eloqua and Hubspot.

Adlard and Bausor also take a dim view of the claims of marketing automation vendors. They say 'it is interesting to note that the marketing automation platforms that underpin most programmatic marketing campaigns today purport to offer "better customer experiences". In fact, in most cases, they merely provide more sophisticated ways of tracking individuals' (primarily digital) interactions with a vendor.' They go on to say that 'in the worst-case scenario, they simply offer a more sophisticated form of email delivery and web registrations, which is why analyst Gartner, puts them in the "customer relationship lead management" category.'

Traditional marketing automation systems were built to track individual leads rather than account data, with the result that too much energy can be spent matching leads to accounts in many of these systems when trying to build a single view of your most important customers.

ABM platforms

Unlike their marketing automation cousins, the more recent category of ABM platforms have been built with companies, not leads, in mind. Gartner (2022b) defines the ABM platform as 'a technology that enables marketers to run ABM programs at scale, including account selection, planning, engagement and reporting'. Examples include 6sense, Demandbase and Terminus, all of which Gartner classifies as sector leaders.

Forrester (2022) claimed at the end of March 2022 that the ABM platform market had reached maturity, to the point where it is hard to distinguish what's unique about each vendor's offering. It said that 'this has caused vendors in the space to explore adjacent and nascent capabilities ... these include owned proprietary data, deeper machine-learning assistance, and fully embedded email capabilities'.

Forrester (2022) notes that 'consolidation within both the ABM platform category and the broader marketing and revenue technologies categories has created a data arms race'. Traditional data providers are adding applications on top of their data, while ABM platforms are adding data to their solutions. In the meantime, marketing automation platforms are 'adding traditional ABM capabilities, further blurring the line between platform types'.

Customer success management (CSM)

Nick Mehta and Allison Pickens in their book *The Customer Success Economy* (2020: 301)) explain that 'just as companies have invested in sales automation and enablement to drive sales productivity, and in marketing automation to increase lead generation and brand awareness, hundreds of organizations have invested in Customer Success Management solutions to maximize client lifetime value and advocacy'.

Analyst firm G2, in its spring 2022 report on customer success management (CSM) systems (2022), defines this software as being 'used by business to ensure, through interactions with the company, customers achieve the outcome that enterprises anticipate them to reach as they use the product. This software uses detailed analysis of past behaviour to create a "health score" to predict future satisfaction of a customer, allowing companies to systematically grow an established customer base, identify any red flags, and increase customer retention rates.' The authors explain that CSM often integrates with CRM systems, help desk software and social media management tools, and identify two leaders in this area, Gainsight and Totango.

To summarize, there is a convergence underway in the capabilities that CRM, marketing automation, ABM and customer success systems offer. Whichever flavour of these you have today, it's worth checking in with your vendor on their own product development plans and mapping out how your own systems can be used together to build the single view of data on your top customers that you need, before you explore buying anything new!

Mining data to build insight

We all know that data does not equal insight, but insights are stronger with data. Many companies are trying to be more data-led, creating actionable insight in real time for the teams who touch their biggest customers. One of their biggest challenges lies in the fact that no one off-the-shelf system can provide them with all of the data or the insights that they need, so inevitably a complex spaghetti of technologies complemented by manual extracts, analysis and processes is the result.

But some of our clients are building their own systems to integrate the data coming from their key systems, store it in one or more data lakes and analyze it with artificial intelligence (AI) and machine-learning capabilities that their data scientists have built to generate useful insights.

It all comes down to a combination of people, process, analytics and automation to understand and engage top customers in the way they expect to be treated. The objective is to build a deep understanding of a customers' priorities and desired business outcomes, as we discussed in Chapter 4, to carefully nurture them through the relationship lifecycle and to enable them to realize the value they're looking for so that they remain a customer over the long term, growing with you.

A good example of this is SAP. Its Crystal Ball initiative was sponsored by the office of the CEO to generate a state-of-the-art approach to gaining a single view of the customer across all its businesses. The case study in this chapter explores this global account intelligence and insights platform, based on modern digital analytics and delivering real-time insights and predictability both in terms of what customers have now and what they might want or need.

CASE STUDY
SAP: Gaining a single view of the customer through Crystal Ball

SAP is one of the world's leading producers of software for the management of business processes, developing solutions that facilitate effective data processing and information flow across organisations. Founded in 1972, it has grown from a small, five-person endeavour to a multinational enterprise headquartered in Walldorf, Germany. With more than 105,000 employees working in over 140 countries, the company collaborates with more than 22,000 partners to support over 200 million customers, who between them generate 87 per cent of total global commerce. SAP's 2018 purchase of Qualtrics and subsequent partnership underscores SAP's commitment to customer experience and exemplifies the strategy of SAP's initiative described below.

Building a Crystal Ball

What if every decision of every employee could be a data-driven decision, eliminating guessing? What if a 360° view of a customer created the conditions for shifting from a 'funnel-first' to 'customer-first' mission? And what if all business operations and processes – sales, marketing, customer success, to name a few – were supported with customer-centric insights to ultimately improve their experience with SAP? These were the first questions on the whiteboard of the cross-functional team missioned with transforming SAP to improve the customer experience, build awareness and demand and serve customers in a way no other technology company can.

For the past few years, the company has been investing in a state-of-the-art approach to gaining a single view of the customer across all its businesses. It began with the setup of a small global team to act as a strategic insights agency incubated in the CEO's office. The team was tasked in 2018 with designing, building and launching an innovative customer listening engine, Crystal Ball, which also included an insight engine to enable SAP to acquire a deep understanding of its customers and markets. The team assembled to build it included people from many different functional business areas, including developers and data scientists.

According to Paul Logue, SAP Senior Vice President, Customer, Competitive and Market Insights, and Crystal Ball mastermind, there were a number of key drivers behind this ambitious project.

- First was to make customer centricity the touchstone of the business: not just in the sense of being able to generate more leads but to optimize customer experience and the value the company could add to its customers' business outcomes.

- The second objective was to elevate the customer experience with SAP. If the company could really understand what Logue calls the 'true heartbeat needs' of the customer, it could improve how it addressed any concerns.

- Thirdly, by having a quality single view of the customer, the company could predict future customer needs and demands, not just current requirements.

- Finally, this sharp focus on customer centricity would prioritize customer experience as a key outcome, positively impacting business results, both in terms of pipeline and revenue.

Crystal Ball is now a global account intelligence and insights platform, based on modern digital analytics and delivering real-time insights and predictability both in terms of what customers have now and what they might want or need. The platform runs on SAP technologies and capabilities, including database, analytics and artificial intelligence and machine learning, and it is purpose built by SAP, for SAP.

The data used to feed this powerful learning machine come from a range of internal and external sources.

- Firmographic data are about defining who the customer is. Does SAP have accurate location data? What is known about them from that standpoint?

- Then there are the technographic data, which are about the customer's installed base of technology. What is their technology profile, what do they have from SAP and, importantly, what don't they have?

- Third-party insight covers a range of areas, such as intent/behavioural data, financial data, growth data and investor-related information, including identifying potentially high-growth emerging companies.

- Internally, SAP has a wealth of its own data such as frequency and method of customer contact, website visits, webinar attendance, etc. As Logue explains, 'All of these SAP domain insights help us understand what is actually going in the account and the customer's potential needs'.

Delivering insights across the business

Building Crystal Ball meant having an in-depth understanding of how it would and should be used, says Franklin Herbas, SAP Global Vice President, Customer, Competitive and Market Insights, and Crystal Ball Lead: 'We began by introducing to SAP the power of Intent signals for demand generation and account intelligence in general. We formed partnerships with key personas in marketing and sales for the most relevant line of businesses (ERP and HR) where we knew Intent signals could have the biggest impact. Since day one we've sought to elevate SAP's customer experience by delivering the best signal possible resembling what customers want and need.'

Nor has the momentum slowed down, according to Herbas: 'That's the way we still operate today, constantly co-innovating and working with different business stakeholders to understand how they are using the data and improve the engine.'

It is self-service, with insights delivered in a variety of ways and through different channels. Sales teams can download the mobile app 24/7, while there is also a desktop platform to go deeper into whatever insight is being explored. There is also a notifications process to alert account executives to any trending signals or critical insights.

Crystal Ball has been closely integrated into a variety of different tools, platforms and technologies at SAP as well, notes Bill Doyle, SAP Global Vice President, Customer, Competitive and Market Insights, and Crystal Ball Program Lead: 'We integrate into a marketing automation platform, into personalization capabilities and platforms and into digital audience platforms, along with sales engagement and workflow platforms. So, for any of those core technology watering holes that either marketing or sales consume, we are powering the insights into those different platforms.'

Marketing, for instance, wants to understand which companies are showing interest in different solutions, so they can take an account-based marketing approach in their programmes. Account executives use the insights for deeper account understanding, while sales specialists will be able to drill down to see where interest in different solutions might be heating up. Digital demand teams can be better equipped when targeting prospects through digital channels.

This constant input and feedback to monitor how customers behave and how satisfied they are is even more essential in a cloud-based environment, Doyle stresses: 'When you are no longer tied in to customers for a long time, you have to be much more proactive about consumption patterns. This is obviously really important for the sales side, but also the activity of our account-based marketers is starting to seep into the whole customer success area. They are increasingly focused on what they can bring of value to sales. For instance, we can monitor customers in line to renew in a year or two to see if they are researching the competition, and take action to improve their satisfaction and keep them as SAP customers.'

'When you think about the entire customer journey, our focus on the single view of the customer provides insights and data from the top of the funnel, and then via different strands it flows down through to customer engagement and ongoing relationship management', says Doyle. 'So, we are also going to have insights into customer satisfaction among the installed base. We want to cover our customer's whole buying journey with the Crystal Ball solution.'

Its use extends into the highest reaches of the company, with executive teams regularly seeking information to aid in their business unit decision making, such as around competitive intensity, market momentum and topical business themes such as sustainability. It can also be a source of valuable customer profile data for executives when they meet their counterparts at major industrial gatherings such as SAP's Sapphire event, with views and insights created to brief executives engaging with top customers.

Targeting accounts

The Crystal Ball engine listens to all the companies in the CRM system, with an extended version to listen to net new companies to SAP that many not be in the CRM system today but could be significant for future account-based growth.

As Herbas explains, 'If an account is in the CRM systems, it's because it was deemed worthy enough by sales to be there. For those outside the CRM, Crystal Ball surveys the potential universe and, using predictive analysis and artificial intelligence to find those accounts that marketing could engage. So, we prioritize and look at ideal customer profile but we also highlight those customers outside SAP CRM showing an interest for our solutions in the market.'

'What we deliver to the business is generally consistent no matter which account we're listening to', he adds. 'We are obviously going to provide more robust data for those companies in our CRM system though, and for top accounts we do more custom analysis where needed.'

Making progress

There were several challenges to overcome in integrating Crystal Ball into the business, says Logue. One was getting away from the traditional funnel and lead mentality in the business: 'So, rather than just saying let's fill the funnel with leads, we said, take a step back and understand what companies actually want first. It was an orientation away from a funnel-first to a customer-first motion.'

Getting cross-functional buy-in was critical for this shift in focus and encouraged by having passionate enthusiasts from across the business to help drive the initiative. That is still vital, with champions in place to promote its use and provide feedback to continue to improve and optimize its operation. Being part of the corporate strategy team within the CEO's office has also given the team a powerful mandate when promoting the need for a single view of the customer.

Another important factor has been putting pragmatism over perfection, says Logue: 'Our mantra is "crawl, walk, run". We pilot, we measure, we deliver value in short time periods and then we expand. So, it's an ongoing change management process. And we don't let perfect be the enemy of good.'

Simplicity has also been a guiding principle: 'How do you take daunting amounts of data and insights, distil them and then organize them into a single view of the customer that can be used by sales, by marketing, by customer success? By taking complex things and making them simple, we have really got traction in the business', he believes.

Measuring success

Progress is regularly tracked across a number of measures.

- Customer experience, customer outcomes. This includes whether the sales teams are having better, more relevant conversations. SAP also looks to account engagement metrics such as registrations, click-through rates and downloads, with results from two to three times greater by focusing on prioritized Crystal Ball accounts.

- Data insights, reach and scale. This includes how much Crystal Ball has grown over time, how many live accounts it covers, the amount of data flowing in, the number of signals on a weekly or monthly basis. SAP also tracks new data sources that have been added to Crystal Ball, and that have been identified by sales and marketing as critical to a great customer experience, as well as improved demand generation.

- Internal user engagement. This measures activities such as how much of the sales force is taking advantage of the insights and how many sellers are using the automation workflow platform.

- Return on investment (ROI) and conversion metrics. The impact of giving salespeople targeted account information equates to increasing deal sizes by 200–300 per cent, while there can also be a two-to-three times improvement in conversion rates from pipeline to revenue.

- Customer or strategic use cases. The team monitor activation rates, like usage out in the regions and across lines of business. How much are they using it and where? Requests from senior executives and how well they are fulfilled are tracked too.

Finally, there is a relentless focus on making the platform more efficient, effective and user-friendly for the teams, Doyle says. 'We think of ourselves as the digital artificial intelligence centre for the business, as well as a customer listening engine. So, we have tied that orientation to where we see the benefits for SAP. We never rest on our laurels.'

Looking ahead

There are a number of areas for development, including new and optimized datasets and insights, optimizing integration into the business and making continuous improvements to the AI and machine-learning model and its predictive capability. Its use is also being extended out to partners and the channel and could even one day become commercialized itself as a SAP solution out to market.

As Herbas notes, 'When we embarked on this journey in 2018, we had three core principles to do with innovation, scale and the team. We continue to innovate. We are scaling the platform intelligently with best in-market data and predictive models. And we're doing all of this with a cross-functional, nimble team. Ultimately, we want to make Crystal Ball SAP's single source of truth for account intelligence.'

Managing operational performance

In most large companies, you will find that multiple operations teams have evolved in silos, tasked with tracking and analyzing data to maximize the performance of the function in which they sit. But some are moving to build integrated operations teams. In his article 'What Is Revenue Operations and How Does It Create Value?' published in *Forbes* (14 July 2021), Stephen Diorio, Executive Director of the Revenue Enablement Institute, explains this move by saying that 'the customer experience has emerged as the primary basis of competition as digitally enabled customers armed with better information and access are putting a premium on speed, agility, personalized content, and channel integration. This has created pressure on organizations to establish a single cross-functional commercial process across the enterprise and coordinate across management systems and platforms to ensure a unified customer experience as the performance goal.'

Building a single operations team

Diorio goes on to confirm that 'there is a material move on the part of B2B organizations to better align sales, marketing, and customer support teams to sustain and accelerate growth', describing this shift to a unified approach as a Revenue Operations model (or RevOps for short).

Diorio was part of a team who conducted interviews with 106 CEOs, growth leaders and sales effectiveness professionals and experts in the first half of 2021, while also surveying 622 sales professionals and evaluating the top 100 technologies that are converging to support RevOps. They published their findings in their report *Revenue Operations in the 21st Century Commercial Model* (Revenue Enablement Institute, 2021), concluding that the nascent area of RevOps is a board-level issue for a simple reason: 'it directly impacts their primary fiduciary responsibility to protect and grow firm value'. Diorio notes that over 80 per cent of the executives interviewed were redefining their commercial architecture, consolidating the operations that support selling and reconfiguring the roles on their revenue teams. In May 2022, analyst firm Gartner (2022a) predicted that 75 per cent of the highest growth companies in the world will deploy a RevOps model by 2025.

Meredith Schmidt, Executive Vice President of Salesforce Revenue Cloud, defines RevOps as 'a B2B function that uses automation to help teams make decisions that grow the business. RevOps brings everyone together – from marketing, sales, service, customer success, and finance – around three shared goals: price for better conversion and margin, reduce revenue leakage, and use customer data to identify new revenue opportunities' (2021).

She makes the point that teams may see incomplete customer data when they make decisions. 'For example, sales may be trying to upsell a customer without knowing they're behind on payments.'

Majda Anwar, Vice President of Growth Marketing at the Pedowitz Group, has a different definition but a similar view of the importance of the single view of the customer: 'RevOps delivers one view of the customer. At its simplest level, RevOps is the end-to-end business process of driving predictable revenue through a collaboration of marketing, sales and customer success functions' (2022).

Our own research into this area shows that of the 57 companies who reflected on the statement 'Data on our top accounts is used to make better decisions about the account across sales, marketing and customer success', almost a third disagreed (Figure 5.2).

Among the two-thirds who agreed, we can't help wondering how many really have a shared 360° view of their customer and are using it to make decisions and improve their performance.

Majda Anwar suggests that RevOps is 'a multi-functional organization… not a collaboration. This is a team structure. It is a centre of excellence (CoE).' Her view of the importance of this distinction is backed up by data from analysts such as Forrester, who say that when RevOps is done right, is leads to 19 per cent faster revenue growth and 15 per cent higher profitability (2019). McKinsey has found similar results, stating that centralizing go-to-market and creating agile operating models have a domino effect that can achieve more than 20 per cent improvement in return on sales investment (Chappuis *et al*, 2020).

FIGURE 5.2 Better decision making with data

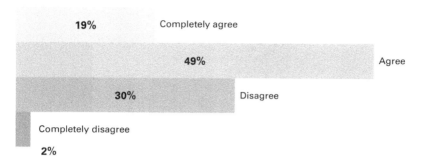

To what extent do you agree with this statement? (N=57)
Data on our top accounts are used to make better decisions about the account across sales,
marketing and customer success

19% Completely agree

49% Agree

30% Disagree

Completely disagree

2%

Anwar explains the areas of overlap that exist today between sales, marketing and customer success operations, suggesting that the removal of duplication in areas such as technology and data management, process management and reporting and analytics is a benefit of the teams being integrated into one CoE. She also identifies the distinct areas each team brings to the unified CoE in a neat Venn diagram (Figure 5.3).

Anwar states that the purpose of this integrated team is to 'drive growth through operational efficiency and keep all teams accountable to revenue', breaking down the silos between departments and 'creating one line of sight to the customer'.

Similarly, Adlard and Bausor argue for a customer operations team to become 'the nerve centre for all knowledge about the customer and help the business make the necessary plans and actions to become truly customer-led'. They believe that CRM systems may be key to this. After all, if there's one platform that can be the central nervous system for managing the performance of all teams handling your top accounts, it's your CRM system.

We've worked with several clients who bring data into their CRM platform from a range of other systems, store plans and track responses in the system and report key performance data using a series of windows into the data held in the system. But customer success management platforms may also be a contender for this role, particularly when it comes to monitoring the overall health of your relationship with your customers.

FIGURE 5.3 The functions of a revenue operations team

SOURCE Reproduced with kind permission by The Pedowitz Group

Monitoring customer 'health'

Adlard and Bausor argue for the creation of a customer health index, or CHI, drawing on Adlard's experience at fintech firm Finastra. For a cross-functional team supporting top customers, this single view of an account's 'health' at any point in time is key to managing the relationship with and outcomes for that customer, and to adapting your approach to that customer in real time to improve performance.

The great thing about a customer health index is that it draws together data from across and outside the organization to build a picture of where you stand in that account at any time. Using AI, it can be forward-looking and predictive – in the same way that Bill Doyle in the case study explained SAP's Crystal Ball being able to identify behaviour suggesting customers are

FIGURE 5.4 An illustrative customer health dashboard

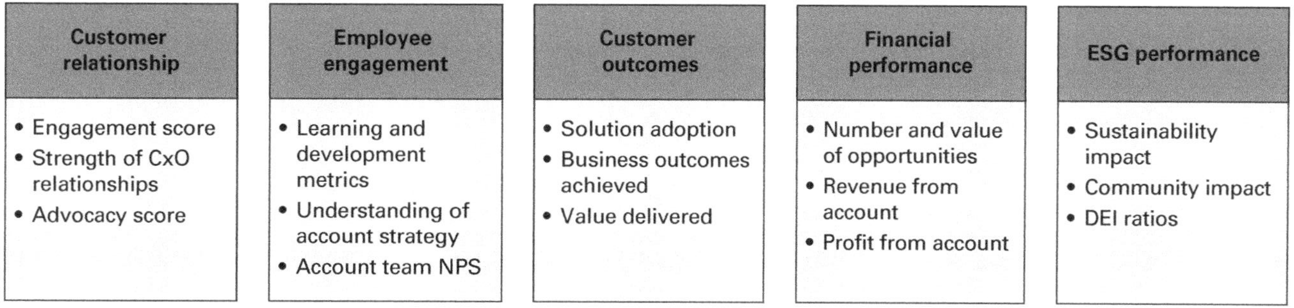

Customer relationship	Employee engagement	Customer outcomes	Financial performance	ESG performance
• Engagement score • Strength of CxO relationships • Advocacy score	• Learning and development metrics • Understanding of account strategy • Account team NPS	• Solution adoption • Business outcomes achieved • Value delivered	• Number and value of opportunities • Revenue from account • Profit from account	• Sustainability impact • Community impact • DEI ratios

considering switching their suppliers – rather than simply backward-looking in terms of satisfaction with completed projects or events. For example, you may develop scores for the level of engagement or advocacy you have with the account versus the engagement and advocacy you see your customers having with competitors, as in the SAP example.

A simple, illustrative customer health dashboard is shown in Figure 5.4.

In their book, Adlard and Bausor (2020) suggest a more complex index-based approach to customer health, with scores against factors all along the customer lifecycle, and which ultimately can be used to manage and make decisions around your complete portfolio of top accounts as well as tracking your performance in each one.

Nick Mehta and Allison Pickens recognize that customer health is one of the core functionalities companies should look for in today's customer success platforms, along with workflow, communications, analytics, surveys and applications. They agree that you need 'a capability to view a 'scorecard' of the health of a customer across many dimensions (e.g. Support health versus Adoption health versus Relationship health) and across the various entities within a customer (e.g. by product, business unit, geography, etc.)' with the ability to drill down into more detail in any area (Mehta and Pickens, 2020: 308).

Ultimately, as Kathy Macchi said in her viewpoint earlier in this chapter, the key thing is balancing what's nice to know and what information will make you act differently. The ability to respond to data on your customers in an agile way to improve your performance requires a certain style of leadership and culture, and that's what we'll explore next.

SUMMARY CHECKLIST

1 'Data is the new oil!' Building a single view of the customer is the holy grail for many B2B companies, but most face the challenge of multiple customer data sources stored in functionally siloed systems.

2 Customers expect you to recognize, understand and serve them intelligently, drawing on the data you have on them and your previous interactions with them.

3 You need to leverage firmographics, technographics, psychographics, intent and experience data on your customers, combining first-, second- and third-party data sources for a 360° view.

4 Start by leveraging your own technology infrastructure, especially your CRM, marketing automation, ABM and CSM systems.

5 Mine your data using AI and machine-learning tools to create actionable insights for the team engaging with top customers.

6 Consider combining multiple operations teams into a single team or centre of excellence that manages performance across sales, marketing and customer success or service for your top customers. RevOps and customer success management teams have made some progress towards this over recent years, but there is more integration to be done.

7 A customer health index draws together data from across and outside your company to build a picture of where you stand with each customer, providing a predictive view in some cases, and allowing you to take actions that continually strengthen your relationships.

06

Leadership, culture and change

By now, we have hopefully convinced you of the need to:

- use thoughtful, consistent selection criteria to prioritize your accounts and allocate resources appropriately;
- build and implement integrated account business plans for your top accounts;
- invest in and build towards a single view of your customers through alignment of data, technology and operations.

The benefits will be measured in sustainable, profitable growth over the long term. This chapter assumes that you will need to implement significant changes in the way you operate as a business to pursue an account-based growth strategy and explores the challenges and recommended approaches from the perspective of leadership, culture and change.

We put forward an approach for making the case for putting top customers at the heart of the company and for how new agile working practices can facilitate this change. Simon Hayward, CEO of Cirrus, an Accenture company, shares his unique perspectives on agile and connected leadership based on 30 years of research and experience of working with global leadership teams across multiple industries.

The case study in this chapter from Telstra, the Australian telco and its technology services company, Telstra Purple, describes how they have implemented agile working practices at scale.

The final section of this chapter proposes an approach to change management, drawing together proven practices from implementing account-based growth strategies across several companies, and incorporating an agile approach to governance and delivery.

The case for putting top customers at the heart of the company

A commitment to a company-wide approach for top customers to maximize the value delivered to them and drive sustainable, profitable growth has to come from the highest levels of the company. However, it can apply equally to individual business units, regions or countries. Every way a company decides to configure itself offers an opportunity to prioritize and focus. It is just the scope and scale that changes. So, if you are a business unit executive, a country manager or a sales, marketing or customer success leader, you can implement a sharpened focus with your colleagues on your top customers at any level.

Before the leadership team can articulate a vision that puts the customer at the centre of the enterprise, however, they need to understand how 80/20 applies to them based on sound analysis. It could be that this analysis is already well understood, but in our experience, as we've said, this is rare. Many leadership teams have some notion that the 80/20 rule applies to them, but most do not appreciate the fractal nature of it, nor do they have many data to support their view beyond historic revenues and sometimes revenue growth.

What we are proposing is to build a lens into those important customers that sit right at the heart of the company, one that drives a much closer connection between your company and them. As Simon Hayward points out later, typically the larger a company gets, the more likely it is that the company is disconnected from providing customer value, with executive and senior management spending the vast majority of their time on managing the business, rather than on directly delivering value to customers.

We're going to assume, for the rest of this chapter, that you think your company should be more attuned to the opportunity presented by pursuing an account-based growth strategy, and that you have taken it upon yourself to enlighten the leadership team as to what needs to be done to realize this opportunity. To do this justice, we think the best place to start is with the mathematics that underpins Pareto's analysis. And within this, we think the easiest number to get into the company vocabulary is the ratio between the size and potential of the customers right at the top tier from those in the bottom 80 per cent.

As we explained in Chapter 1, if your company follows the 80/20 rule exactly, and it is perfectly fractal, the ratio between the top 0.8 per cent (20 per cent of 20 per cent of 20 per cent of customers) will be 256 times the average size of a customer in the bottom 80 per cent. Even comparing tier one with tier two accounts, the ratio is 1:16. Your ratio may be different, but will not, in our experience, be very far from this, particularly if you are able to measure net profit rather than revenue when calculating your ratios. It is not unheard of to find that 100 per cent of your profits come from no more than 20 per cent of your customers.

Collecting these data for your own company will mean working with your CFO and finance team to determine historic and current revenues, gross margin and properly attributed direct costs – and hence net margin per customer. You might think these data are readily available, but you may well be disappointed. Even getting these as reliable revenue data is not as straightforward as you would hope, as we said in Chapter 3, because your finance systems may not recognize parent-child relationships, or your company might have grown by acquisition, with different accounting systems. Finding the net profit number at a customer level is even harder, but it is worth persevering, with some assumptions that link headcount to expense a way to get an initial handle on this. Getting the data historically is important because this gives you the ability to show churn between different tiers. Again, in many mature companies, executives are often surprised how relatively stable their top customers are. Actually, if they are stable, that's interesting and can be leveraged; if the churn is high, that's a worry and needs to be addressed.

The end result of your analysis should enable you to present data in tiers, showing the ratios across at least four if not more tiers, in a similar way to Table 6.1. The worked example uses 80/20 and is just based on revenue, not net profit, since these numbers will vary significantly between companies. We have also illustrated the churn within tiers as a percentage, but you may want to make that an actual number of accounts joining or leaving the tier.

GETTING THE MESSAGE

The 'aha' moment for many leadership teams is just how few customers (in this example, out of a total customer base of 1,000) are really that significant and just how much more significant the ones in tier one are, compared with all other tiers, but particularly tiers three and four.

The churn data will either tell you that churn within tiers is surprisingly low, which is a good thing and will get everyone's attention, or it will tell you that it is too high. Of course, there are many more pieces of analysis that can be

TABLE 6.1 The key ratios if the fractal 80/20 rule applies in your company

Company ABC Account Tiers – if 80/20 rule is fractal in your company

	Number of Accounts	% of total number of accounts	% of revenue in current year (CY)	Average revenue per account ($m)	Ratio from top tier	Churn % from CY-1	Churn % from CY-2	Churn % from CY-3
Tier 1	8	0.8%	51%	$64	1	5%	7%	9%
Tier 2	32	3.2%	13%	$4	16	12%	12%	10%
Tier 3	160	16.0%	16%	$1	64	20%	20%	15%
Tier 4	800	80.0%	20%	$0.25	256	20%	25%	25%

Total number of customers > agreed minimum size (appropriate for your company)   1,000
Total revenue from this set of customers in $m   1,000

conducted regarding churn, such as, if an account left one tier, where did it end up? Typically, in our experience, accounts move between adjacent tiers, unless you lose a major customer completely.

One of the authors, in looking to improve the business performance of a country operation, discovered that the fortunes of that particular operation (a services business with annual revenues of c. $150 million) were largely dependent on just nine customers, with only three prospects sufficiently large to make much of an impact. This was an 'aha' moment for that management team and led to a rapid change in the priorities of the team, particularly executive sponsorship, and a tighter allocation of resources. In another case, this time in a turnaround situation (a technology solutions provider and reseller), it was possible to take more than 30 per cent out of the cost base, without undue risk to revenue growth, by a careful analysis of the key accounts where sales and marketing resources should be deployed, together with a change to an indirect model for the vast majority of the company's customer base.

Many leadership teams do not realize, until the data show them, that they could focus much more around a relatively small and manageable set of top customers, allocating their own time more productively to these customers and better-qualified and more senior resources to these vital relationships. This can be a game changer for many.

Once you have the data, presenting them in such a way that they turn on a light bulb, but do not cause a defensive, negative reaction, is key. Even worse would be a dismissive attitude, where the leadership team may understand the data, but inertia and vested interests prevent the kind of radical action that may be warranted. The best way to avoid these reactions will vary, depending on the culture of the company and the characteristics of the leadership team.

OPENING LEADERSHIP'S EYES
In our experience, one of the best techniques is to immerse the leadership team in at least some aspects of the analysis, rather than just present the answer. That way they get to work through the implications as they are understanding the data.

And from this 'light bulb' or 'aha' moment, you can articulate a vision around customer centricity, not in the vague sense that 'customers are at the heart of everything we do', but in a very real sense that company executives and the resources allocated to leading and populating the top account teams are given the priority they deserve.

We believe that every B2B company should recognize the importance of their top customers and build this into their top-level governance, putting it on a par with other ways the business is run, in the way that Accenture has done with its Diamond Client Leadership Council, a key part of its corporate governance structure.

This invites top customers to, literally, help your company stay tightly connected with them and drives value creation right from the top, company-wide. It can become a test bed for your strategy and innovation and facilitate co-creation with your customers. The leadership challenge in this is significant, however, because it will require willpower and desire to make the changes needed to introduce a new element of governance at the top of the company's management system. It also means you have to stop doing some things to accommodate this.

Putting top customers at the heart of the organization requires a more agile way of working than many companies have today. The key drivers for introducing a more agile way of working are to 'declutter', simplify and focus more on providing customer value at speed. Agile leadership expert Simon Hayward explains in his viewpoint why introducing a more agile way of working is the perfect vehicle for moving and staying closer to the customer.

VIEWPOINT

Simon Hayward, Global Lead on Leadership and Culture, Accenture, CEO Cirrus, Honorary Professor, Alliance Manchester Business School

In your experience how well do company executives focus on their top customers?

I think the danger is often that the larger the company, the less easy it is for them to focus on customers. And the same goes for leadership throughout the organization, unless their job is involved with customer focus in some way through sales or service or marketing. There's increasing recognition that this needs to change, but it's very difficult because the larger the organization is, the more complex the machinations of internal management and the further away senior executives can be from customers.

When aligning around top accounts, what are the main cultural and functional challenges companies face?

Part of it is sheer willpower and what I call 'ruthless prioritization' around the customer, the importance of customer relationships and making the systems of the organization support a great customer experience. If you think about being agile, focusing on the customer vision and delivering customer value are particularly important.

I think the other factor here is simplification: large organizations tend to become more and more bureaucratic, control mechanisms become interlaced and mutually reinforcing and the conservativism of the organization often means that those rules aren't challenged and a disproportionate amount of time is spent on internal matters that aren't adding value to customers.

Simplification and de-bureaucratizing is fantastic but incredibly difficult to do. I talk to clients where they recognize their number one priority is to try to declutter the system so there can be more people focused on adding customer value. But it's very difficult because there are often vested interests in keeping all the initiatives and projects and control mechanisms and procedures that clutter the system.

Agility and agile practices are very much about reconstructing the organization to be more customer-centric. Agile thinking is fundamentally about focusing on customer value and iterative working towards maximizing that customer value. It means deconstructing the old command-and-control hierarchy, which is challenging to the incumbents.

When people are saying that a top priority for them is to simplify, are they always, in your experience, equating that with increased focus on customers? Or are they looking to do that for a variety of other reasons?

I think a lot of the motivation is very often cost related. It's about 'let's strip out cost and maybe add value to customers later by investing in other areas'. So there can be a tangential link to customer value-added activity. But more often than not, the justification is to increase shareholder value in the short term and it's not about being as customer oriented as we would hope.

Why do you think this is?

The reason executives are in their positions is often that they've been successful within the system. To disrupt that system, to break it down to be simpler and more customer oriented is actually counter-intuitive for them. Also, their primary accountability is to the board, and the board will be considering their relationship with shareholders. Short-term profit and earnings per share performance are still fundamentally a key driver of executive behaviour.

This is one of the trade-offs that our work in sustainable leadership is highlighting. There is a trade-off between short-term sales and profit versus the longer-term, purpose-driven activities about what is best for the planet or communities they serve and how to increase inclusion and diversity.

What do you think leaders can do to overcome the challenges they face and put the customer more at the centre of the management system?

It's difficult. The overwhelming shift in consumer behaviour and preference is towards more purposeful buying. Buyers increasingly look for organizations and supply chains that are ethical and that support climate change. Unilever was a pioneer in this respect, as they sought to become purpose led. If customers are voting in droves to stop buying your products, then taking a long-term purpose-driven stance starts being in line with short-term financial requirements.

Sometimes you do get a chief executive or a C-suite team that is willing to be bold and to seek to reinvent the organization, to pivot the organization into a new market or to a different ethos, and that's impressive. But it's really hard because some of these changes can take a very long time, and they don't always have that much time.

Another example is IBM, which in the '90s were forced into a pivot by its first-ever loss. It had to shift the whole organization to be more customer facing and service oriented. So sometimes a crisis is very helpful as a trigger to some of this change.

So markets typically drive a short-term focus on control and financials, whereas trying to shift the organization to be more customer-centric will deliver that but over a longer period of time. There is often a lag effect on competitive pressure to change as well. There might be new competitors in fintech or medtech, for example, who are being much more customer orientated and much more focused on the future. But for the large organization they are still just noise because the incumbent doesn't recognize the danger of being so detached from the customer. It's the same with digitization. How do you digitize a large international bank? Well, it's very slow progress compared with a fintech provider who says this is our normal state, this is how we think and how we have operated from day one.

Assuming that you do have the desire, the willpower and maybe the crisis that's caused a change of heart and people at the top want to move towards a more customer-centric organization, what do you think the critical success factors are for making that massive organizational change?

Apart from the obvious things we've already discussed, another aspect is an appreciation of the ecosystem that the organization could use to bring greater value to customers. I think digital start-ups tend to think like that anyway: let's partner with people and do something amazing for a customer, whereas a large incumbent will tend to think more self-sufficiently.

Accenture, for instance, actually embraces a massive ecosystem and says its success in delivering value to clients is partly because it is so open to partnership to create and nurture an ecosystem, so that another organization could be a competitor today and a collaborator tomorrow. But that ecosystem requires a different mindset, which involves partnering, fairness, equity and a focus on adding extra value to the customer.

In a similar way, look at disrupters like Uber. It created a different ecosystem with drivers in a way that said, in combination we can do more for the customer than trying to be the only provider. So, I think ecosystem thinking is helpful.

Have you found when you've been involved in introducing agile leadership and agile thinking into companies that it has created an opportunity to make them more customer-centric?

The majority of people that we either work with or observe who are embracing agile properly and effectively are doing it to accelerate customer value, working on customer journeys and value streams, so there is more focus on the customer outcome they are trying to deliver. They keep asking, how do they keep driving that forward? How do we align the end-to-end process behind mortgages in a bank, for instance, to make the mortgage product better and better and quicker and quicker? It is a different way of thinking about the organization: there is some thought given to cost reduction, but predominantly the objective is increased customer value and therefore greater competitiveness.

What are the ingredients that make that mind shift happen in the first place? Is that also down to a change of leader or something else?

Well, a change of leader can always be a catalyst. It's just like a crisis. But it doesn't have to be. Take ING, the Dutch multinational financial services company. About eight years ago it decided it had to learn from digital natives and went to Spotify and Uber and Google to say, teach us and let us learn. And then the company worked on how to adapt that into their organization.

I think that mindset of disruption and looking outside, which again is unusual in large corporates at senior levels, is really helpful and important. The willingness to break up the model, to shake up the operating model to say we're going to restructure around value streams focused on different customer experiences and restructure that journey and drive cost and time out of it requires a pretty radical shakeup.

Fundamental to it all is culture and risk aversion. Risk aversion is perhaps the number one barrier to agility, and risk aversion is endemic in a lot of large organizations and the control systems that drive them. At times, in certain industries, like pharmaceuticals or financial services, they might try to blame the regulator for having to be risk-averse, but that's often just an excuse.

The foundations of agile are psychological safety and a learning culture. Psychological safety is about people being willing to speak truth to power and challenge and be open and feel trusted and have high-quality relationships with their manager and their team. A learning culture is about experimentation and valuing mistakes as ways to learn and improve. If you begin to get that culture, then you can start to disrupt and you can start to expect people to be empowered. You can't make people be empowered, you can only create an environment, a climate where they feel safe to take the risk of being empowered. It creates the opportunity to focus more on the customer, which is where agile ways of working come in.

And so all of it flows from that culture of trust, safety, learning, experimentation, and it takes a very disruptively minded but very thoughtful CEO to be able to steer through that. If the climate in the organization or any part of the organization is based on fear, command and control and punishment if you make a mistake, agile fails.

When you are with a leadership team, what do you say to convince them to make what can seem to be an overwhelming transition?

There is so much evidence that if you're not adapting at least as fast as the environment in which you're operating, you're going to die. And death is quicker now than it was 20 years ago because the rate of change is so dramatic. So I think CEOs get that, largely. But changing large organizations is massively difficult because the inertia is immense. So it takes a huge determination, boldness and some very big actions like restructuring to shake up the organization and allow it to become more customer-centric. It demands massive shareholder and stakeholder management to get the support for that level of disruption.

The other thing to mention is the power of technology: technology can replace traditional control mechanisms – so you don't need managers controlling things. Reporting, control, approvals, process management, all of that can be automated. So by investing heavily in digitization, you free people up to spend more time on customer value, although I don't think a lot of digitization is done with that vision.

Any thoughts on where we are now in managing these sorts of changes in a post-pandemic hybrid world?

Some organizations have high levels of flexibility and understand that they need to be flexible and respect the preferences of individuals. And there are others who want to go back to the old world, which, in my view, is like going back to steam. It's flawed. But you can't tell the CEO of a major bank who wants everybody in the office that their judgement is flawed. Well, you can, but it's not terribly productive!

Research we did at Alliance Manchester Business School before, during and after the initial phase of COVID suggests that agile teams actually created a structure that maintained a high level of productivity when people went to work from home. We also know that social connectivity and the sense of belonging are really important to people's motivation at work. We have statistics that show that 80 per cent of people looking for jobs think culture is a massive determinant to where they want to go next. So, forcing people to work in the office no matter what becomes counterproductive.

What you can do is listen to the people and say, if we want the conditions where people are customer-centric, agile, responsive, dynamic, empowered, highly responsible, take the initiative, collaborate across the process to make it work quicker for the customer, then we need a culture that is fair, trusting, safe and encourages learning. It then becomes a partnership between all stakeholders, creating a culture that is good for customers, good for colleagues, and good for shareholders.

Finally, a key issue for many organizations is talent attraction and talent retention. If people are being forced to do something they don't want, they'll vote with their feet. So, I think there's going to be a big talent divide between the forcers and the flexible enablers. Leaders now need to be more sophisticated in their social skills and their ability to create a sense of belonging, even in hybrid environments.

Simon Hayward is the author of *The Agile Leader* (Kogan Page, 2018) and *Connected Leadership* (Financial Times/Prentice Hall, 2016)

Creating an agile culture

Simon Hayward talks about the need to create the environment where teams feel empowered. In his latest book, *The Agile Leader* (2018), he explains how the agile techniques that had developed in 2001 in the software industry and changed the way that software was developed and released are now being applied more broadly across different teams, but with the same benefits of speed and simplicity. As more aligned account teams are established for top accounts, there is an opportunity to implement agile approaches, with these teams being given the executive support and encouragement to focus the entire company on creating value for their customer.

If leaders embrace the idea that they need to orientate themselves more towards creating customer value through agile practices, they have to decide to create an agile culture. These are significant topics in their own right, and Hayward's research and publications highlight the six main factors to create an agile culture in this volatile, uncertain, complex and ambiguous (VUCA) world. He describes an agile culture as 'a connected culture, one where there is balance, strength, speed, coordination and endurance' (Hayward, 2018: 82).

The six factors to create an agile culture are:

1 *Leadership commitment*: people really feel they have the support of senior leaders working in agile ways.

2 *A shared sense of purpose and clarity of direction*: the mission is clear, the priorities are agreed, and this frees people to act quickly, safe in the knowledge that their actions are aligned with the organization's intended outcomes.

3 *Authentic leadership*: leaders are truly role models of the organization's values and instil trust around them.

4 *Devolved decision making*: decisions are consistently made as close to the customer as possible.

5 *Collaboration across teams, functions and specialisms*: there is clear commitment that teamwork and working cross-functionally are part of the company culture – that's just the way things get done around here.

6 *A focus on and encouragement of experimentation and constant feedback*: learning from customers and testing new prototypes are constant and shared widely and have a huge impact on differentiating the offer for customers.

The above are reproduced from Hayward (2018: 82).

The last three of these are highly relevant to adopting an account-based growth strategy and these points are built on in *The Agile Leader*, with case studies from start-ups, banking and telecoms to illustrate the benefits and the challenges of moving to this new, agile way of working.

The change to agile at scale across a company is a significant undertaking. Our case study in this chapter comes from Telstra, which explain how it has transformed and where it is going next on its journey.

CASE STUDY
Telstra: Agility at work

Background

Telstra is Australia's leading telecommunications and technology company and the most widely held ASX-listed company in Australia. With a long and proud history of supporting Australians for more than 100 years, the company has stayed true to its mission: to connect Australians with each other – and the world.

Telstra Purple, the company's technology services business, brings together enterprise technology service capabilities, alongside several newly acquired companies to focus on outcome-based, transformative tech solutions. Set up almost a decade ago, Telstra Purple pairs the firepower of Telstra's global network with the know-how and responsiveness of a local team to deliver a 'small company vibe' and a dynamic sense of agility to serve customers in the most impactful way.

Telstra Purple is very much a people business. In fact, the name itself derives from an amalgam of 'purpose' and 'people' to emphasize its people-centric philosophy. Chris Smith, CEO of Telstra Purple, is very proud of this fact: 'We really do believe that people bring purpose to technology, and we are definitely a people business. It's what our customers love about us.'

Building this sort of technology services business within a mainstream telecommunications company presents a huge opportunity as the different business models come together. Chris notes, 'We are involved in application-led transformations that lead us to having an outside view of opportunities beyond the traditional economics of selling networks and carriage.

'Because of this, we're able to measure things differently, we are capex light, we track our costs with revenue and we scale people with margin. It's a very different model to what some might associate the telecommunications business with.'

Redefining the mainstream business

A few years ago, amid changing financial and customer expectations and under the leadership of CEO Andy Penn, Telstra took a fundamentally different approach to what had been done before, embarking on a new three-year strategy he called T22.

This was based on four main pillars: transforming and reinventing the customer experience and its products and services; the establishment of a standalone infrastructure business; enhancing economic performance and, crucially, defining the people, culture and leadership capabilities it needed to succeed into the future.

Underpinning much of this transformation was the introduction of new ways of working across the whole company, with a shift to an agile-at-scale model being one of the most impactful. Agile working can be defined as bringing people, processes, connectivity and technology, time and place together to find the most appropriate and effective way of working to carry out a particular task and to overcome rigid functional silos.

This meant redesigning the entire Telstra organization, the simplification of its structure and an industry-leading cost-reduction program. Given the scale of these changes, this was implemented in phases, with the company's almost 30,000 team members now operating in the agile-at-scale model.

Today, Telstra has a more flexible and dynamic planning process, and instead of multiyear plans, with highly detailed annual iterations and somewhat limited ability to flex within the current trading year, the company has implemented a management system based on objectives and key results (OKRs). This helps to define clear long-term goals, as well as specific company-wide objectives that are stack ranked into an agreed and widely communicated priority order.

If this is the first time you have come across OKRs, a great reference source is the book *Measure What Matters* by John Doerr (2018), which includes more interesting case studies from Intel, Adobe, Google and many others. The Telstra OKRs then receive a relatively light-touch refresh every quarter. This means that every 90 days, Telstra's executives review the 35 or so company objectives and assess the progress made against the previously committed key results. This enables the company to re-allocate the resources it needs quickly to remain competitive in the market and meet changing customer needs, as well as better measure success or underperformance.

The clarity, transparency, and timeliness of this OKR model leaves nowhere to hide. Realities surface quickly and changes can be made where they need to be. Want to push harder on a major customer opportunity? Then shift more resources into it from the most appropriate resource pool anywhere in the company.

If there's an underperformance that's identified, then the decision gets made as to whether the company doubles down for the next quarter or steps back and shifts resources to an alternative opportunity. Too often, the performance of teams within large organizations can drift as executional weakness hides in the noise of busywork.

The management system that Telstra has successfully implemented makes this drift much easier to identify and address.

One management system, two different models

Although slightly set apart from its core telecommunications business, Telstra Purple participates fully in the quarterly planning process. Smith allocates people from the Purple teams into internal projects, while he himself is executive champion for one of the company's OKRs for enterprise growth.

Telstra Purple has been agile since it began, so integration has been easier. 'Our Purple people have worked with agile practices since the start because we are largely customer facing, with up to 90 per cent of employees working on customer projects and involved in project work. So that flow-to-work element has always been there', Smith says.

The clarity and consistency that come with this OKR-based management system have proven to be a boon in how both Telstra and Telstra Purple serve their customers. The flexibility and dynamic resourcing that were at the core of every specialist technology company Telstra Purple acquired over the past decade are now largely matched with the flexibility to allocate and shift resources at scale across the rest of Telstra.

This means that the client teams can move quickly to access the right capability from across Telstra's large pools of specialist skills and be confident that the customer opportunity can be met in a timely fashion.

T22 was a three-year transformation, with mid-2022 as its end point, but with Telstra's financial year starting in July, the team have already started to build on what's next and their revised OKRs for the next three-year journey, T25, which is focused on growth towards a more customer-centric enterprise.

Putting customers at the centre of the business

Telstra Purple is comprised of more than 2,000 experts, affectionately described by Chris as 'purple peeps', who play two main roles.

First, they help customers make the best use of the technology that Telstra offers, including value-added services, collaboration, security and cloud applications. Second, when requested, they create new technology solutions that customers need to better serve their own customers.

A good example is the application Telstra Purple developed for Transport Victoria, which enabled people to understand the density of crowds in trains in a bid to encourage the public back onto public transport.

With technology developing at such a fast pace, Telstra Purple is now strengthening their vertical industry expertise beyond its well-established horizontal capabilities and into areas like industrial automation, renewable energy and virtual reality. This is also helping to drive deeper relationships and more tuned business engagements with Telstra's top accounts.

The Telstra Purple structure reflects the emphasis on customer value. Purple's sellers are in close alignment with those at Telstra Enterprise, while business development professionals work with customers across the different segments, both geographically where Telstra Enterprise operates and according to vertical industries such as mining and energy, agriculture, supply chain and retail.

Service delivery managers also have an important part to play, with dedicated teams for the larger accounts. As engagements deepen with these top accounts, the orchestration of coordinated activities across sales, marketing, service delivery and partners becomes ever more critical.

Chris also makes sure that there is clear accountability for everyone. At the core of this is an integrated account plan that gets refreshed regularly. Telstra's agile-at-scale approach enables this to be updated and tightly aligned with the resource allocation decisions that are required to deliver on the changing needs of these major customers.

The senior leadership balances executive responsibilities and customer interactions where necessary. There is, for example, a dedicated executive for service and delivery whose job is to ensure that rigorous quality and cost standards are met, while overseeing major projects and runtime. Meanwhile, a senior technology executive does both the day job and is involved in key projects, such as being the executive sponsor for the Marvel Stadium project, the arena commissioned by the Australian Football League to become one of the world's most technologically connected and innovative sports and entertainment venues.

Defining the ecosystem

The Telstra Purple model is based on expanding partnerships, creating a channel dynamic that has contributed significantly to customer value. That has resulted in major partnerships with hyper-scalers such as Microsoft and AWS, while there are also several smaller technology partners, vendors and innovators geared towards servicing the customer base. Telstra Purple aspires to be 'the place tech comes to in Australia', Smith says.

He has embraced a modern approach to finding skills, establishing a dynamic resourcing model that taps into the gig economy and creating an extended workforce through an ecosystem of skilled technologists who have been pre-authenticated on the security frameworks: 'No one organization can find all the skills and capabilities and capacity we need any more. This is particularly the case in Australia, where our borders were closed for so long during the pandemic. So, we need to let go of the idea that we need to own our people and realize that people want to work for organizations with the best gigs and the right flexibility', he declares.

Cultural and leadership challenges

The business also has to keep up with a rapidly shifting market. 'The tech market moves so quickly that we need to always be pushing ourselves into the cloud, into new realms of IT, into security, into new vendors. Our customers trust us and want us to help them, so we need to have a leadership and team environment where all of us are constantly learning and remain relevant', Smith explains.

Yet another key challenge is finding enough talent and skills in such a tight, pandemic-affected job market. Telstra has programmes in place for retraining at scale and imparting the core skills every employee needs. Flexibility is being held out as another incentive, whereby all domestic roles can be location-agnostic, so people can work from anywhere. This has led to increased employee engagement.

Looking back to look forward

Looking back, is there anything Smith would have done differently in growing Telstra Purple? Perhaps create the single identity sooner, he reflects: 'We set out a deliberate strategy to build the company through acquisition, so we had a host of different brands with different identities and loosely coupled for a long time. But how did that fit within Telstra? Perhaps it took us too long to make the mental leap to say that we would leave those names behind and find a brand that described a people technology business that is also part of Telstra. Now we have a "tribe of tribes" model that offers the best of both worlds and feedback from our "Purple peeps" has been pretty good so far.'

What Smith is most proud of, he says, is how Telstra Purple has flourished and stuck to its purpose-led mission throughout the last few years: 'Our people are really proud of what they do because the projects that we deliver can be so meaningful, from building an emergency alert system for the country or a radio network to apps for critical healthcare.

'And I'm proud that throughout the pandemic we made the choice to do right by our people and our country as well. Purpose is in our name, and we stick to it.'

Bringing about the change

It is clear when you read the numerous case studies about companies that have moved to a more agile way of working, drawing on the inspiration of Simon Hayward and his colleagues, or review Telstra's journey to agile at scale that these undertakings are significant and long-term commitments. The question, as for any significant journey, is where to start.

In this final section, we introduce a pragmatic approach to implementing an account-based growth strategy, assuming you have done some analysis and your leadership team is convinced about the need to change. Ideally, the company will adopt agile working practices, as it will involve cross-functional teams working together to come up with the right solution.

There are four stages to consider:

1 diagnostic phase;
2 design phase;
3 definition phase;
4 implementation phase.

Diagnostic phase

The diagnostic phase has been discussed earlier in the chapter, in relation to analyzing the data to make the case to establish the 'aha' moment. However, we need to go much further, and we can use the account-based growth framework to bring clarity to the scope:

- It will need to cover account prioritization and resource allocation, no mean task in itself, particularly for a large, complex organization. From a resource allocation perspective, this will need to include an assessment of the quality and experience of individuals assigned to different individual accounts and tiers, as well as the quantity of resources.

- Account plans will have to be sampled and assessed, using the guidance and external perspectives in Chapter 4, to understand the effectiveness of the account-planning content, structure, execution and review processes.

- Our research has shown that the ability to create a single integrated view of the customer has not yet been achieved by many organizations, so a further assessment will need to be made as to how well your company is placed across the different domains as outlined in Chapter 5.

- The conduciveness of the company culture, its leadership and its impact on customer centricity are the subject of the earlier parts of this chapter, and will also be a factor to consider in the diagnostic phase.

- Finally, the way that account management and sales, marketing, customer success and company executives engage in the most important accounts all need to be understood and assessed. These four areas are covered in Part 3.

The scope of the diagnostic phase is potentially very broad, so it will be important to agree in advance which areas get priority. Similarly, it could be that the scope can be tightened by only examining the top tier of accounts initially, figuring out whether there is a better way to manage the relationships with your most important customers.

Design

Following the diagnostic phase, as you start to get a complete picture, you can turn your attention to designing what you would like the future to look like, using the clarity about your starting point from the diagnostics phase and the end point you would like to reach for each major element you have in scope – and ideally comparing your own company with best practices from others along a number of dimensions, as illustrated in Figure 6.1. This radar graph assumes you have been through a thorough account selection process, examining all the factors that contribute to the success of an account-based growth strategy.

The design will need to cover the same elements that were in scope in the diagnostic phase and will need very careful consideration and discussion between the appropriate stakeholders if the opportunity for growth is to be fully realized. There are numerous people, processes and systems that need to be included in this design, so access to the right internal teams and, potentially, external expertise in specific areas could well be needed.

FIGURE 6.1 Account-based growth key success factors

This radar graph shows the 21 key success factors grouped into seven areas, which together show what a best-in-class programme would need to cover.

Respondents were asked to indicate the extent to which they agreed with 21 separate statements, where:

1 = Strongly disagree
2 = Disagree
3 = Agree
4 = Strongly agree
(N=50-59)

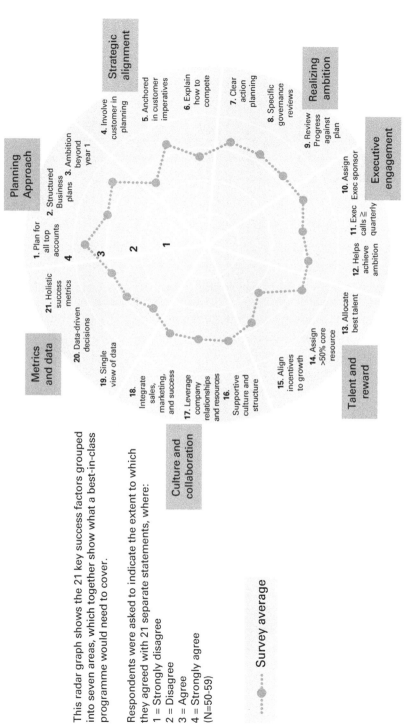

•••••••• Survey average

As the design is coming to fruition, it is important to establish an overall vision and a case for change. Often referred to by companies as their North Star, the vision needs to be simple, clear and unambiguous.

MAKE THE RIGHT CHOICES

In adopting an account-based growth strategy, the vision could be: 'Prioritize those customers where we can make the biggest impact on their success, measuring our success through customer lifetime value'.

We've thought long and hard about the statement above. The vision statement above works, we believe, because it acknowledges that choices will have to be made, allows the customer to be the determinant of whether we can play a major part in their success and focuses on the long-term creation of lifetime value.

It's an interesting conundrum for many companies. They may well come to the conclusion that they want to ruthlessly prioritize their focus and resources on some customers rather than others. But they may also not really want to declare that as a stated policy. After all, if you have a top customer list, what does this say about your service to other customers not on the list? As we will discuss further in the chapter on customer success, companies delineate between different tiers of customer and deliver service in line with the expectation that has been set, adopting different levels of cost and changing the balance of human interaction and technology.

Companies have to work out what their particular sweet spot is within the competitive landscape in which they operate. We know of some companies that deliberately avoid targeting the largest, most complex companies precisely because they know this would put them in competition with the likes of Accenture, Deloitte and IBM. And we know of companies who, once they have done the exercise in account prioritization using the directional policy matrix, come to the reluctant conclusion that while one of their most important customers may be very attractive to them, their competitive business position is very weak and they are unlikely to be able to improve it, making that customer not a strong fit for the long term. Data that lead to honest appraisal and action are all-important in this exercise.

The case for change will be very dependent on what situation your company is in as you start this journey. It could be that you are looking to accelerate growth or improve profitability or both. In turnaround situations, the case for change is often existential, so it is sometimes easier to state more precisely. We would expect that, with the right 'ruthless prioritization', to borrow the phrase from Simon Hayward, you should be able to improve growth and profitability by obsessing more about keeping and growing the largest customers you already have and minimizing the cost of serving the long tail. But in order to realize these benefits, it will require a detailed understanding of where your resources and cost base are allocated now, from the perspective of each account tier, and what it will take to refocus them more appropriately, potentially in a much more radical way than you have previously envisaged.

Pursuing an account-based growth strategy is, like any strategy, predicated on making bets, so the actual opportunity you realize will depend on your assessment of how radically you are prepared to make those bets and your assessment of the risks. The bets you are considering need to be viewed in a holistic manner, across all the teams that are responsible for growth in the broadest sense, as we said in Chapter 3.

Finally, a change of this magnitude needs the backing of the executive leadership team, with a clear sponsor with the authority to make the necessary decisions, allocate resources and actively keep key stakeholders aligned. If this is a company-wide change, it will most likely be the chief revenue officer, chief customer officer or, in some cases, the chief executive officer.

Definition

Once the vision and case for change are established, you need a structured process to define a programme that will make the link between the agreed business goals and getting the actual work done, collaboratively, across multidisciplinary teams. For this to be effective, there are some key elements that need to be included, shown below in Figure 6.2.

Programme definition can be done in a series of workshops, often held virtually in this hybrid, post-pandemic world. Given the cross-functional nature of this type of change, the selection of the programme manager and the key members of the team who are going to be charged with implementation is critical. The core programme team needs empowering and trust built across silos within a culture that is supportive, something that agile working would provide.

A programme definition report is produced at the end of the programme definition phase, which details all of the elements outlined in Figure 6.2, setting out the objectives and deliverables for each workstream in the programme. It acts as an anchor for what is being implemented. It is sometimes useful to think of the programme as a series of building blocks, as shown in the schematic in Figure 6.3.

FIGURE 6.2   An approach to programme definition

1 **Business Goals** that the programme should achieve, expressed in a SMART* format

2 **Programme objectives** it has to deliver in order to achieve these goals, together with the key metrics

3 A prioritized set of **workstreams**, with an outline of the scope of each, in terms of deliverables, timescales and ownership

4 Clarity over what is **out of scope**

5 A **resource plan** and **budget** that enables the work to be done, internally or through external suppliers

6 An approach to **programme management, programme governance** and **stakeholder engagement** to ensure the success of the program

7 The way we want to manage **risks, issues** and **dependencies**

8 An internal **communications plan**

9 **Next Steps** and **Plan Governance**

*SMART = Specific, Measurable, Attainable, Relevant and Time-bound

FIGURE 6.3   Programme definition schematic

Business Goals			
Programme Objectives and Metrics			
Workstream 1	Workstream 2	Workstream 3	Workstream 4
Budget and Resources			
Risks, Issues, and Dependencies			
Programme Management, Governance and Stakeholder Engagement			
Communications			

Implementation

Appropriate governance will have been defined in the programme definition phase, with typically a weekly core project-team meeting chaired by the programme manager and a monthly steering group chaired by the programme sponsor. If the organization is adopting agile working practices, these meetings will be augmented by the teams in each workstream employing whatever governance they need to get the work done.

In order to allow the teams who are doing the work to get on with things, we would strongly recommend an agile approach to programme implementation. This has proved very successful for us in fostering collaboration across a complex implementation of an account-based growth strategy, striking the right balance between devolved empowered teams and the need to keep everyone on the same page.

The key design elements of the approach are:

- a light-touch approach to maximize empowerment and natural collaboration;
- calls with larger audiences to focus on decisions made, outputs completed or items requiring input from others;
- a simple structure to minimize the 'timezone tax' of global working;
- eliminating 'blockers' (both anticipated and unforeseen) quickly to maintain progress towards delivery of agreed deliverable;
- maintaining a focus on the North Star vision.

In practical terms, this means:

- running the program governance as a series of team sprints, each lasting two weeks and focused on specific work packets or outcomes;
- each workstream holding a 'showcase' at the end of each sprint to present their work outputs and decisions to the full programme community and other key stakeholders;
- workstream leaders forward-planning their teams' activities to achieve deliverables by target dates, with maximum empowerment and freedom to work in the way they deem most productive.

The showcase element of this approach enables the teams from different workstreams to establish a rhythm and a momentum, and to celebrate success when a particular milestone is reached. It also creates an easy way to spot interdependencies and keeps the teams well aligned. Finally, it enables the teams to understand what each team is doing and builds trust and collaboration.

SUMMARY CHECKLIST

1 The case for adopting an account-based growth strategy needs to be built using real data from your company.

2 Once you understand the data around your account tiers, particularly the ratios between tier one and tier four, you can start to size the sustainable growth opportunity and gather support from your leadership team.

3 In parallel to understanding the data, the other major challenge facing many companies is how to get closer to their customers across the entire organization.

4 To address this, some companies are adopting a more agile way of working, bringing the customers more to the heart of the organization's management system through ruthless prioritization, decluttering and simplification in order to become more customer-centric.

5 Agile working will improve your chances of success in implementing an account-based growth strategy, putting customers at the heart of your top-level governance.

6 Moving to agile at scale requires strong leadership, a company-wide commitment and persistence in what is likely to be a multiyear journey.

7 Implementing an account-based growth strategy requires a structured change programme, and should follow a process that starts with diagnostics and design, moving on to programme definition and an implementation approach that is based on agile working practices.

PART THREE

Engaging externally for growth

Part 2 of this book looked at the internal alignment that contributes to successful account-based growth. Now we turn to those all-important external points of customer engagement: account management and sales; marketing; customer success and executive engagement. We consider each one in turn, describing how they have evolved to meet an increasingly segmented and omnichannel customer environment and where they need to improve. We take you through the process to make sure that these areas are more integrated, aligned and focused on customer outcomes.

Chapter 7 begins with an analysis of the vital role that key account management (KAM), done properly, can play in a company's fortunes. Getting it right can completely change the customer relationship and lead to long-term partnerships and trusted relationships. The other side of the coin is equally true: customers have high expectations that they will be dealt with by senior, business-trained people who have an in-depth understanding of their processes, their organization and their culture. It can be hard work to get it right. This chapter will guide you through the process and suggest further sources of help.

Chapter 8 moves on to marketing and, specifically, account-based marketing (ABM). ABM has matured over the past 20 years as a method for treating individual customers as markets in their own right with highly personalized marketing plans, particularly where complex, customized and high-consideration purchases are involved. This is a natural fit within an account-based growth strategy and its emphasis on data-based decision making and close collaboration across functions.

In Chapter 9 we turn our attention to an area that is somewhat the 'new kid on the block': customer success. This has grown out of customer service and service delivery, but goes well beyond that to ensuring that customers are deriving the best experience and outcomes from their relationship with you.

The trend first emerged from the software-as-a service market, when software companies became increasingly aware that for a subscription-based service to work, they had to invest heavily in customer success to make sure their customers were really getting value out of their investments and would stay loyal. It has now permeated many other industry sectors, driven by ever-higher customer expectations. This chapter offers practical advice for building a customer success framework that will be a key factor in a successful account-based growth model.

Finally, Chapter 10 investigates the fourth pillar of a strong account-based growth strategy: a well-organized, carefully-targeted executive engagement programme. The ability of senior executives to develop strong relationships with important customers cuts through competitive noise and can make the difference between success and failure. But it takes serious thinking about the people involved, thoughtfully designed programmes to boost engagement and thorough analysis of what works and what doesn't.

07

Account management and sales

To pursue an account-based growth strategy, there are two really important groups of customers:

- a relatively small and ideally relatively stable group of top customers (or partners) who, year after year, make up 50 per cent of revenue and, if it were measured accurately, most likely an even greater percentage of profits;
- the small set of customers in the other 97 per cent of the customer base or new prospects who could, over the next three years or so, join the top group.

This chapter starts by setting out how account management has evolved to focus on the first of these two groups into 'key account management' in many companies, and how key account management interacts with the broader sales function. Nick Wilson, an executive sales and P&L leader at six different companies spanning a 30-year career, contributes his perspective on account management and sales, particularly in relation to strategic customers.

We then include a summary of key account management in practice, drawing primarily on the research and practical advice from the Key Account Management team at Cranfield University in the UK, one of the very few business schools that has specialized in research, teaching and business partnership in this field. We will reference their excellent book, *Implementing Key Account Management: designing customer-centric processes for mutual growth* (Marcos *et al*, 2018) throughout this chapter, and draw on the lifetime experiences of Professor Malcolm McDonald, one of the world's foremost authorities on strategic marketing, market segmentation, sales and strategic/key account management, who has written extensively on the subject (2017).

We go on to examine the rise of the client partner or managing director, senior executives who represent their company's strategic interests in the largest, most complex and often global accounts. Paul Legere, from Deloitte, share his perspectives in a viewpoint on managing these long-term, critical relationships.

Finally, the chapter provides some thoughts on how to create new top customers and the important role of establishing partnerships as a route to market, particularly for younger companies trying to establish their foothold in the market.

One important point to note: as we said in Chapter 3, we're using the term 'key account manager' to mean the senior person who is given responsibility for managing a top customer relationship, which can include any of the designated job titles that companies give them, such as managing partner, global client partner, managing director, etc. This is to distinguish it from the term 'account manager', which has been used for decades and is a sales role, sometimes occupied by relatively junior sellers or within customer success.

What is key account management?

Key account management is the allocation of dedicated resources to manage, on a supplier's behalf, a specific strategic customer relationship.

Cranfield University defines key account management as 'an integrated process for the profitable management of customer relationships. The integration is a complex, multi-faceted endeavour that requires enhanced awareness of the strategic customer's intent, the gathering and transfer of specific customer knowledge, and ultimately the functional alignment to realize joint business opportunities' (Marcos *et al*, 2018: 20).

For some companies, key account management is no longer in the domain of sales, but has become a function that sits across sales, marketing, customer success and/or service delivery. Top customers, particularly the executives in these accounts, don't want a traditional sales and purely transactional relationship. They know selling is going on, but they expect suppliers to have invested sufficiently so that they know when and how to bring forward proposals that will be in their interests, based on their insights and with deep relationships developed over many years, sometimes decades.

Key account managers are not salespeople

Getting this right for top customers 'completely changes the business relationship', as one technology veteran who worked as the key account manager on a single account for over five years puts it: 'I went from running a major part of the business, with profit and loss responsibility and more than a billion dollars in revenue and with thousands of employees, to being focused on a single, significant global customer. There is an appreciation in the customer's executives that I understand what it takes to be successful in running a large business, but also, critically, that my company has invested significantly in this relationship, taking me out of a big P&L role and focusing my efforts and a large team entirely on them, the customer. They also know that I can get things done inside my own company, because of my seniority, ability to move at speed, and get the company's resources lined up to help them with their biggest challenges.'

MAKE THE RIGHT CONNECTION

This is the lesson: your most important customers want someone who understands their business intimately and brings to bear all of what your company can offer to help them deliver their business goals. They also want someone, particularly in the large global organizations that feature in this book, who can broaden and deepen the relationship by leveraging challenges and experiences in areas of common interest, such as diversity and inclusion or carbon-zero goals.

Understand your customers and their expectations

Cranfield University's McDonald has forthright views on this topic: 'Key account management requires a deep understanding of the business of major customers. This requires key account managers who are fully trained to general manager level. Instead, most companies have salespeople who are paid to sell. But unless they're paid to analyze in detail the business of their customers in order to prepare solutions that create advantage for them, they will continue to just sell, much to the annoyance of their would-be customers' (McDonald, 2022).

REINVENTING KEY ACCOUNT MANAGEMENT

According to Malcolm McDonald of Cranfield University, 'Our research at Cranfield proves clearly that important customers literally HATE being sold to. They demand senior, totally business-trained general managers who thoroughly understand finance, their processes, their organization and their culture. And our research with the European Institute of Purchasing proves beyond doubt that companies detest gangs of salespeople dressed up as key account managers descending on them to sell stuff... nothing less than a root and branch reorganization of key account management in most companies is called for' (McDonald, 2022).

In this information-rich age, it is possible to know a huge amount about your customer and the individuals that make up the decision-makers and influencers that work there. As one senior executive who is responsible for a large global industrial customer of a technology company remarked, she expects herself and, indeed, the whole account team to become 'students of the customer', meaning they become avid consumers of information, particularly in terms of the strategies, objectives and key metrics that are important to the customer.

For example, if a key objective for the customer is to reduce the carbon footprint of the company, you need to think creatively about how your solution can contribute to that, exploring ways to modify your approach to make it compatible with this key customer metric.

You should also have a good grasp of the individuals in those customers. A significant opportunity to do this exists with social media, which is dominated by applications such as LinkedIn in the B2B world. This has become so important that in some companies, senior executives, quite likely in their 50s or even 60s and now managing these top customer relationships, have had to learn new skills and habits as they are not exactly 'digital natives'.

At the individual level, this means key account managers and their teams connecting with the key customer individuals, understanding their specific business interests and personal background, and using this insight to share opinions and information that they would find interesting. There is also the potential to connect them to others in your company who have shared interests to broaden and deepen relationships.

One company we know has decided this is so important that it has established a coaching network for its executives performing the key account manager role, giving them the skills and confidence to make an impact using social media. In other cases, the account-based marketer can often take the lead on making sure that the account team have the skills, confidence and a coordinated plan to ensure they have an impactful and authentic digital presence and connections.

A well-connected digital presence can prove very powerful when new executives join or are promoted at a customer, because, through these online networks, they can rapidly be connected to the key account manager and account team, establishing new relationships very early in their tenure in a role and creating competitive advantage for the supplier.

In addition to the information that is available in the public domain, many account teams in strategic suppliers have access to a customer's internal systems, such as their intranet, providing them with even more information about the company's plans, structure and organization. This also helps cement and protect the relationship, making it harder for competitors to have anything like the same access and insights.

In short, customers now have extremely high expectations of what a strategic supplier should know about them as Ninian Wilson explained in Chapter 1. They believe that the supplier should have done their homework and be able to articulate their solution in specific terms that meet their objectives and metrics.

Capturing this information in the integrated account business plan and in systems that provide a single view of the customer is vital. It enables the key account manager and the whole account team to leverage what they know about the account, find improved ways to help the customer and act as advocates for fulfilling the customer's agenda.

Organizing around the biggest customers

Clearly, the nature of the business relationship with top customers will vary enormously, depending on the breadth of the company's portfolio, where the company is on its growth path and its maturity as an organization. But the fractal nature of the 80/20 rule seems to kick in pretty early in a company's evolution, so it is worth considering how to organize around your largest customers from the start.

As Nick Wilson of Micro Focus points out in his viewpoint, the best approach is to decide on what you can afford and design the go-to-market structure from the top tier downwards, putting in place the key account managers and giving them leadership of the sales, marketing and customer success and delivery ecosystem that gives them the maximum chances of success.

For a complex, global account, the core account team should cover multiple business units, representing different parts of the company's portfolio, as well as multiple geographies with different cultures. One big issue to resolve is that in many companies there is a likelihood that the actual reporting line for the majority of the account team is directly into a business unit, function or geography, leaving key account managers with the unenviable task of leading a group of people, the majority of whom don't have a direct reporting line into them.

Where does that leaves 'sales'?

Despite the focus on the account team, salespeople still have a vital role to play in realizing your company's ambition with top customers. If the key account manager is doing their job well, the size and scale of a proposed solution can often be larger, integrating more of what the company has to offer and bringing in innovative partners with niche but vital elements to contribute.

This crafting of the solution and bringing the whole deal together demands strong sales skills. Most large companies have adopted a single sales methodology, such as challenger sales, to create consistency in the way that sales teams pursue opportunities based on credible insights. If the customer is big enough, there could be dedicated salespeople in the account team itself, working closely with the key account manager to develop a deep understanding of the customer's priorities. Specialist salespeople will also be needed in a company with a large portfolio, because they can develop a deep understanding of how their particular set of products and services delivers value, are expert at creating strong value propositions and have a great understanding of the competitive context.

At its simplest, selling is about two things:

- access to the customer decision-makers who will, usually on a consensus basis, commit to spending money on a particular solution;
- beating the competition by putting forward the strongest value proposition.

In top customers, with a well-regarded key account manager, the first of these is made much easier because 'access' is the key account manager's job to arrange. Of course, this doesn't guarantee winning the business, but it does usually confer another great advantage for the sales teams, which is to be able to influence decision making much earlier in the buyer journey than the competition; in other words, they can shape the discussion with senior customer executives and understand what it will take for them to be success-ful months before an actual investment decision.

With much-improved access and sales teams able to engage, either alongside the key account manager or directly with customers to an orchestrated plan, the team can then really understand how a particular solution can provide competitive advantage in the context of the customer's existing landscape and all the other challenges they have. There is still no guarantee of winning, but the odds will have increased significantly against companies without this top-level customer relationship. Of course, large complex companies will have more than one relationship with key suppliers in important domains, so there will be others who have strong access too. So it is critical to make choices about 'where to play' with the customer's tacit approval.

Before we look in more detail at key account management in practice, let's understand more from Nick Wilson on some of the considerations and pitfalls in organizing a complex go-to-market team at scale and how to ensure there is an appropriate focus on the top customers.

VIEWPOINT

Nick Wilson, President of Sales, Micro Focus

Nick Wilson has held sales and P&L executive roles at IBM, Unisys, CSC, HPE and DXC, before joining Micro Focus, a $3Bn enterprise software company, where he has responsibility for sales, renewals, marketing, consulting and customer success.

How does the 80/20 role play out in your experience?

All the companies I have worked for over the years have run strategic account programmes where the 80/20 rule does by and large apply. And I have learned a few significant lessons. For instance, when you first launch strategic account programmes, you often start seeing growth over and above what you expected. But too often companies get excited about the results and start to scale up their programme by adding literally hundreds more accounts in some cases. Without fail, this over-expansion ends in unmitigated disaster. The faster you scale and dilute the programme, the greater the chance that it will fail. You need to be really disciplined on who the most important accounts are and invest in them properly, not spread your resources too thinly.

You have to keep your focus on what's important. In a mature company, the first priority may be about protecting your revenues because losing any of your large customers can be a nightmare to backfill. You may get some companies that grow, but if you analyze your revenues over a period of time, they may well be relatively stable. If you do get growth above the average, that is great. But many strategic account programmes need to have a strong focus on risk mitigation to avoid losing customers.

In younger, faster-growing companies, you are trying more likely to identify a smaller number of customers to put into a strategic account programme where you might aim for tripling or even quadrupling revenues over a relatively short time horizon, but from a lower base.

How do you determine which accounts should be in the strategic account programme?

The most successful major account programmes I have been involved with are those where 80–90 per cent of customers are existing high spenders. You have to make sure you have all the right data about what they spend and the context for making those decisions. But it's also good to place a few bets by adding in some informed intuition. Even though the data might not necessarily support it, certain accounts could become big drivers of revenue growth given the right investment.

Let's say you have 50 customers in your strategic account programme. I think you should have at least 10 per cent that have the potential to be the next big accounts, rather than them necessarily being your largest customers today. That won't be based only on historic data but also on predictive insight into these accounts, because you are trying to generate future revenues and a new relationship, based on something that hasn't been created yet with the customer, so you need to exercise judgements as to which customers are likely to be receptive, still not spreading your resources too thinly. Also, bear in mind that your big customers can fail, merge, or, in the case of governments, change the rules. So you need to be regularly gestating a stock of new strategic accounts.

There's another important point to make here about choosing the right accounts. You should take input from the sales teams, from marketing and customer success, and pull together a recommendation, usually by the head of sales or Chief Revenue Officer. However, this should be a recommendation to the company's executive committee, who have to make the final decision. If you are going to have a recognized strategic customer programme, you have to have the whole company join hands and get behind it.

So should you be making some bets over a reasonable time horizon?

It depends on your portfolio and the nature of your company. If you are talking about outsourcing contracts of anywhere between three and five years, your churn on your big accounts is going to be a lot less than in, say, software. At Micro Focus, I revisit the account list every six months but typically make any changes only every year. At a previous company, I had a three-year time scale. The danger, particularly with long-term contracts, comes when you don't keep on top of this and your revenues can take a significant hit if you lose a customer because you weren't vigilant enough.

What impact does the 80/20 rule have on strategic account programmes and account coverage models?

Compare it to promotion and relegation in sports leagues, like the Premier League in the UK. You keep an eye on both promotion and relegation prospects and adjust your bets as necessary. I have a small group called a gestation unit separate from the strategic account team looking at which companies could be the next major accounts – which team might get promoted to the top of the Premier League, to continue the analogy. The criteria for promotion and relegation have to be very clear.

You start your account coverage planning with your largest accounts and put all the resources you need into them. What do I need to protect my existing base? How many bets am I going to place within these customers? How much money do I need to spend here, within my overall cost envelope? Do I have the right level of experience and profile for managing the most important accounts? Then you work out what you can spend on the rest. Doing this properly depends on how mature and disciplined the company's planning process is as to whether they are prepared to make the big bets. It can be very easy to second-guess yourself and say, well, we can't afford to spend that. But it helps that more and more planning is based on actual data. Even just five years ago there was still a lot of gut feel and intuition, but the situation has improved significantly.

What are the most important factors in driving account-based growth from a sales leadership perspective?

You have to be very, very clear about the criteria for having a customer in the strategic account programme and regularly review it. Also, you should tell that customer that they are in it, and the criteria that have put them there, as well as what benefits they derive, such as prioritized access to key resources, improved responsiveness or early insights into product roadmaps. And you have to mean it. The biggest thing I have found with customers is they want input into where you are going with products or services and they want to see a direct result of that input. This can give you some leverage since customers want to stay in this influential group, and they also benefit from peer-to-peer conversations.

The strategic accounts have to be where the top echelon of sales jobs go. Yes, it can create something perceived of as an elite group, but you need the most experienced people on the strategic accounts. They need to be senior roles, properly supported, and portrayed as just as important as other senior roles in the company. Your incentive plans also have to reflect both short- and long-term goals.

It's slightly different for those in the gestation group, where you need a bit less account management, more emphasis on sales and different incentives and more intuition about future winners.

The strategic account programme should be global where this is appropriate for genuinely multinational customers. I have tried putting strategic accounts into regions with an 'overlay' strategic account leader acting like a programme lead. It didn't work – there were too many conflicts because of the siloed nature of the organization. So, unless you have a company that works in harmony across all geographical and business unit lines, I believe you need to keep these programmes separate, with a clear group of strategic customers who are managed separately, with empowerment and completely dedicated resources. In my experience, there are few companies where some sort of silo doesn't create conflict and where misaligned incentives get in the way of the company doing the best possible job for the customer.

How joined up are sales, marketing, executive engagement and customer success in the strategic accounts typically and what could be improved?

They're not always, but they need to be! If you don't set it up so they are, things can become very disjointed and customers will be short-changed. Large customers don't want multiple interfaces. I've known companies where the technology salespeople would be going in to the same customer actively offering an alternative solution from the services part of the business, and where there was zero contact between the two.

A lot depends on how you initially set the strategic account programme up. Ideally, you need to have tight account teams that include dedicated customer success people and specific marketing programmes based on what tiers you have put your customers in. No marketing is done to a strategic account without the authorization of the strategic account lead.

In a previous role, a large customer told me he had seen 24 salespeople in the last six months, with five of them claiming to be his account manager! I used to call it the 'ice cream van' approach: someone from the company turns up in their ice cream van in the car park, rings the bell and asks, does anyone want to buy something? It wasn't uncommon to have five of these turning up, not knowing the others were going to be there.

Following the introduction of a properly structured strategic account programme, within two years we had doubled our revenue from the customer just by getting tightly organized. It's not rocket science. The customer doesn't care about your reporting lines or structures. They just want a consistent and joined-up approach where they feel you are bringing the best of the company to bear on their challenges.

For this to work effectively, you need to have dedicated resources from all the relevant business units in the company and a well-constructed plan for the strategic accounts that everyone has bought into. You need to be regularly revisiting the investment you are making to ensure it's effective. It's also really important to make sure you communicate this broadly across the company, explaining why the programme is so vital to the company's fortunes. If that's not reinforced over time, the message can get diffused and people tend to assume you have lost focus on it.

How should companies approach growth and profitability in the remaining 80 per cent of their customers?

I am not sure there is any one answer to this. It's down to your product and services portfolio, your distribution channels, your growth ambition and your product lifecycle. It is very important to have profit in mind as well as revenue, collecting the data that enables you to track profitability at the account level. You need to be careful you are not booking revenue but losing money, with the cost of doing business outweighing the margin you're making, so constant attention to this is vital.

Finally, you need to have the insight and intelligence built into your management system to always make sure you keep a close eye on that little group of 'possibles' who could make it into the premier league and become your strategic customers of tomorrow.

Nick Wilson relates a telling anecdote of what happened in one instance when a key account manager was appointed to manage the strategic relationship and coordinate the supplier's resources across five business units: revenues doubled inside two years.

In this instance, the customer executive was willing to regard the company as a strategic supplier and saw value in a more joined-up approach. Much as we have argued elsewhere in relation to the co-creation of account plans, the deployment of a key account manager, particularly a senior one, should be based on the *customer's* wishes as well as your own company's. It is a recognition that the business relationship is worth investing in for the long haul, with business transactions the fuel that feeds the overall strategic nature of the relationship. We heard this in no uncertain terms from Ninian Wilson in Chapter 1.

But what if your top customer does not regard you as strategic to them, but you see them as strategic to you? The Strategic Account Managers Association reports that 71 per cent of B2B buyers are willing to switch suppliers whenever necessary. So the answer is to become essential to your customer. Our advice, when placing bets on where to invest, is to make an honest appraisal, based on how the customer sees you.

Key account management in practice

Key account management is multi-faceted and complex and has evolved over the past 20 years. It is hard work to get it right: many companies report they try and fail and have to regroup. But for those that stay the course, it is ultimately very worthwhile, driving sustainable, profitable long-term growth.

One of the best specialist reference books on the subject is from the University of Cranfield School of Management (Marcos *et al*, 2018), with research and practical advice on what makes successful key account management work, including numerous case studies from multiple industries. The following section is a synopsis of some of the key elements, where they have not been picked up in earlier chapters.

Key elements for successful key account management include:

- developing customer relationships;
- creating compelling customer value propositions;
- co-creating value with key customers;
- the role of the key account manager and the account team;
- measuring key account management performance;
- motivating, incentivizing and rewarding key account managers;
- key account management and procurement;
- international account management.

Developing customer relationships

Collaboration between supplier and buyers and a preference for fewer, larger, long-term, strategic relationships, rather than short-term contracts with a large number of companies, is becoming increasingly important. This continues a trend of the last several years in procurement functions to rationalize the number of suppliers their company relies upon.

From the suppliers' perspective, the benefits include reduced costs of sales over time, better insulation against competitive threats and, sometimes, higher margins. From the customer's point of view, the benefits include having access to a partner who brings broad understanding, innovation, expertise and, above all, the ability to focus this on the customer's strategic goals in a way that a supplier with a purely transactional relationship can never hope to achieve.

As the complexity of decision-making increases, with more information being available online and more people being involved in decisions, the commitment to build trust, manage conflict successfully and develop shared goals and values is vital, so trusted partners will be welcomed.

Creating compelling customer value propositions

Key account managers who build up a detailed and real appreciation of what their customer is trying to do are able to significantly influence the economic benefits of value propositions in the customer's terms. As Chapter 8 on account-based marketing outlines, creating a really strong value proposition is the vital link between the insight we have gleaned about the customer and how we translate what we have to offer into value.

> Cranfield University's authors describe the customer value proposition as 'possibly the most critical component of the strategic key account management process' (Marcos et al, 2018: 119). They stress the need to be able to articulate the customer's future state and the customer's willingness to buy into your vision of that future state, and say that this is directly linked to the trust in the relationship and track record in previous projects.

Our work with senior executives who manage large, complex customer relationships bears this out. They frequently make reference to the fact that they have to completely reframe the value proposition in the customer's language and to meet the customer's stated priorities. With the confidence that comes from a strong understanding of the customer and some imagination, this reframing can create clear differentiation from competitors who simply don't have that level of insight.

Chapter 8 offers more detail on how to create compelling value propositions. This is a very productive area for collaboration between the account-based marketers and key account managers and teams and should be a core competence.

Co-creating value with key customers

Value co-creation with top customers is elusive for many companies, but is practised widely by market leaders. It demands a high degree of trust from customer and supplier and a commitment to long-term, joint investment.

The value proposition is still an important way of framing what is being created, but the creation becomes a joint activity, rather than a supplier-initiated one. The approach to value co-creation is referred to in Chapter 10 on executive engagement and sponsorship, as it is highly probable that senior sponsorship of value co-creation will be essential.

Many companies have recognized the power of co-creating solutions with their top accounts and prospects. Capgemini, for example, has been successfully using a workshop approach it calls 'accelerated solutions environment' (ASE) for effective collaboration for almost 20 years with many FTSE 100 and *Fortune* 500 clients. It emphasizes the integration of the physical environment, work processes and technology augmentation to facilitate human creativity for large-scale change. In fact, the customer innovation officer at Capgemini has said that when the company runs an ASE with a prospect, it never loses a competitive deal.

Capgemini is not alone. Other leading companies have developed an equivalent. EY has a 'wavespace', Fujitsu has 'digital transformation centres', Accenture leverages its 360° Value framework, while Microsoft also exploits design-thinking in its 'Catalyst' approach.

They all report a significant increase in the number of sole-source deals, competitive win rates and the scale of solutions. But this is a highly resource-intensive exercise for the customer as well as the supplier, so there need to be clear criteria for when it is deployed.

The role of the key account manager

Key account managers, including those managing the biggest global customer relationships, report that they spend about 10 per cent of their time planning, 30 per cent on customer activities and fully 60 per cent of their time managing internally, trying to get their own company aligned to their customer (Marcos *et al*, 2018).

As we have already said, there are multiple aspects to this role, which is so much broader than sales. Heed the view of a senior manager from an engineering company: 'These are business managers. They are not senior salespersons. If you give the senior salesperson the title of global account manager and send them off to the customer, they can see right through them from day one. The people you need in these sorts of positions are light years away from traditional salespeople. All the competencies are the sort of skills framework we expect for rising CEOs and managing directors' (Marcos *et al*, 2018: 167).

Wipro, a global technology services company headquartered in India, has global client partners taking the lead on their most strategic accounts: 'At Wipro, we recognize the important strategic role that our Global Client Partners have in managing our most strategic clients. The competencies they need to do this are more akin to leadership and service delivery competences, but we still need them to be excellent at strategic selling and relationship building' (Marcos *et al*, 2018: 182).

Indeed, research shows that a key account manager is not wholly effective in the role until they have generally spent two years in it, as it takes them this long to really understand the customer's business environment and to build trust (Marcos *et al*, 2018).

Measuring key account management performance

With this level of investment, over a long period, a key challenge for any organization is to assess the performance of their key accounts, typically around growth, profitability, customer lifetime value and relationship strength. Cranfield's reference book also includes process-driven metrics, such as delivery, co-development and customer experience in an overall framework to measure performance (Marcos *et al*, 2018).

We believe most companies would benefit from a more joined-up approach to performance measurement, across all elements of their external engagement – not just key account management, but also account-based marketing, customer health and executive sponsorship and engagement. We made further reference to this in the customer health index in Chapter 5.

Motivating, incentivizing and rewarding key account managers

Our research has found that a significant 42 per cent of companies do not agree that they have the right incentives and rewards in place for the management of their top accounts. This could stem from the legacy of sales incentives systems, which tend to be heavily skewed towards a lower base remuneration and higher commission element for achieving short-term revenue targets, either annually or even quarterly or monthly.

The Cranfield University team have developed recommendations for how key account managers should be rewarded. It needs to start with a clear understanding of what they are expected to achieve over an appropriate timescale and working back from there to a sensible incentives and rewards package.

Companies that appoint executives to their large strategic accounts have the additional option of using long-term incentive payments as part of the compensation structure, often linked to overall company performance. This creates a better balance between the short term and long term.

Overall, it seems that this is one of the trickiest areas to get right. Sales incentives and reward systems are often inappropriate for the job of the key account manager, putting them into an invidious position when the incentives work against a course of action that is better for the customer and often, in the long run, for the supplier too.

Account management and procurement

Procurement has become much more professional. In most complex global companies, the chief procurement officer will play a strategic role in the senior leadership team and in determining whether your company becomes or remains a strategic supplier.

The procurement function in your customer will most likely use a variation of the supplier assessment framework, illustrated in Figure 7.1, to determine how they position you in the context of all their suppliers. Knowing what this looks like and how you are viewed is key to the journey to long-term security as a strategic supplier. Remember: not every supplier can be strategic, as Ninian Wilson of Vodafone pointed out in Chapter 1.

It's also vital to understand the relationship between the procurement leader and the executives and managers that make up the decision-making units for the type of solutions you provide. Getting this right is not straightforward. We often hear of examples where the strategic supplier 'tows the party line', respecting centrally made decisions and not proposing alternative solutions directly to business units, only to find that they've lost out on business because the customer's own governance was not strong enough to implement the standard, global approach they were seeking. Misunderstanding or misreading this is likely to create tension at best and loss of status or business at worst.

FIGURE 7.1 Supplier assessment framework

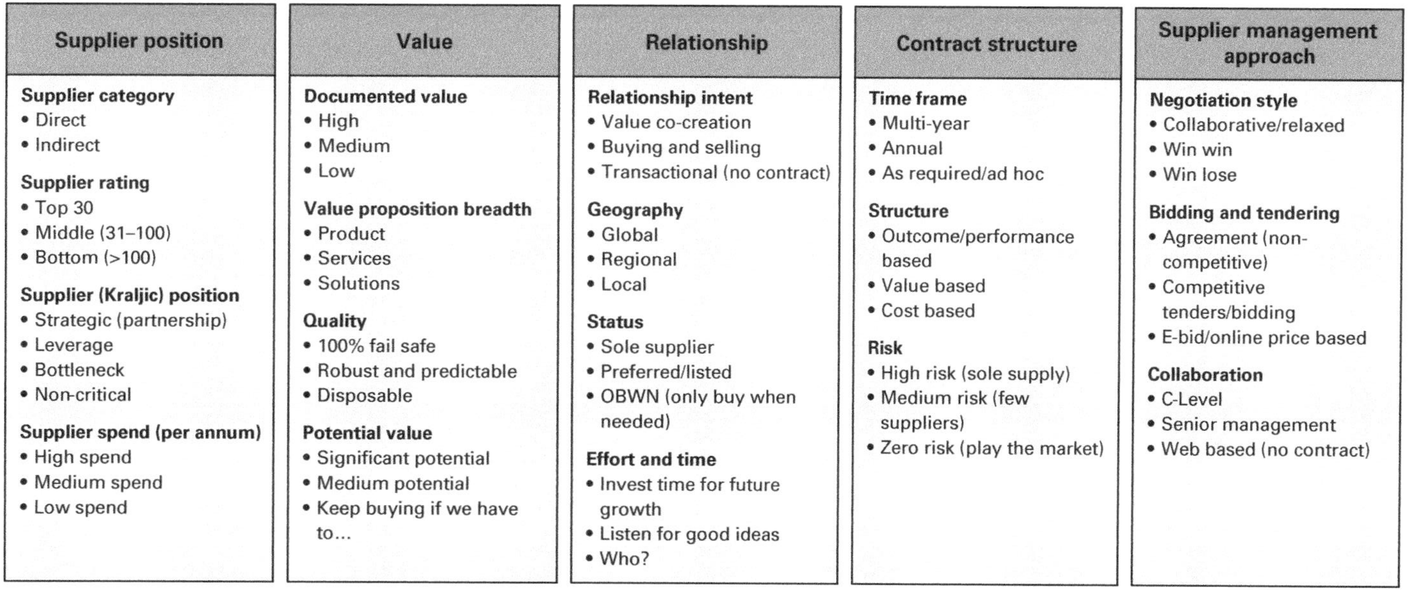

Supplier position	Value	Relationship	Contract structure	Supplier management approach
Supplier category • Direct • Indirect **Supplier rating** • Top 30 • Middle (31–100) • Bottom (>100) **Supplier (Kraljic) position** • Strategic (partnership) • Leverage • Bottleneck • Non-critical **Supplier spend (per annum)** • High spend • Medium spend • Low spend	**Documented value** • High • Medium • Low **Value proposition breadth** • Product • Services • Solutions **Quality** • 100% fail safe • Robust and predictable • Disposable **Potential value** • Significant potential • Medium potential • Keep buying if we have to….	**Relationship intent** • Value co-creation • Buying and selling • Transactional (no contract) **Geography** • Global • Regional • Local **Status** • Sole supplier • Preferred/listed • OBWN (only buy when needed) **Effort and time** • Invest time for future growth • Listen for good ideas • Who?	**Time frame** • Multi-year • Annual • As required/ad hoc **Structure** • Outcome/performance based • Value based • Cost based **Risk** • High risk (sole supply) • Medium risk (few suppliers) • Zero risk (play the market)	**Negotiation style** • Collaborative/relaxed • Win win • Win lose **Bidding and tendering** • Agreement (non-competitive) • Competitive tenders/bidding • E-bid/online price based **Collaboration** • C-Level • Senior management • Web based (no contract)

SOURCE   Reproduced with kind permission from Marcos et al (2018)

International account management

As part of understanding how a customer wishes to be 'managed' by a supplier, you need to assess whether they should be managed on an international or truly global basis. How easy that is for you as a company will depend on your own international reach and operations. The management of global accounts is not easy even for large, global companies, with management challenges across different, not necessarily well-aligned, geographic business units.

Marcos *et al* (2018: 274) have pulled out seven common pitfalls of managing strategic accounts globally or internationally.

SEVEN COMMON PITFALLS OF MANAGING STRATEGIC ACCOUNTS GLOBALLY

1 Misalignment of goals and key performance indicators (KPIs) between global and local levels.

2 Misalignment of rewards and compensation.

3 Arguments about who made the sale.

4 Global level being seen to be interfering by the local level.

5 A strategic global account may not be significant in some countries.

6 Dissatisfaction from different levels of service and price between different countries.

7 Customers themselves not adhering to global agreements or contracts.

Key account management at the account level

Many leading companies have invested significantly in senior executives to manage their most important customers. Deloitte is one such company, and Paul Legere shares his view on how managing clients has changed as markets, technology and ecosystems have changed, with many organizations making much more purposeful decisions to embrace broader societal goals.

VIEWPOINT

Paul Legere, Principal, Deloitte Consulting, Global Lead for Financial Services Industry (FSI), M&A and Restructuring Practice, US FSI Head of Strategy

How important do you think top accounts are to a company's overall profitable growth, particularly in B2B, where you've got a range of customers or clients?

In any business when you segment the customers, you have to understand the different groupings and develop your capabilities in the way that you face off with the different segments. It's all about choices, and like every business, we have to make choices about where we invest our resources. And so when you segment your business, you recognize there are some larger organizations with which you aspire to work and there are midsized and smaller organizations with which you aspire to work.

In terms of the larger organizations, they're important because you can bring to bear the kind of relationship that you want at scale, and so the investment that you're making, while it may be higher, is generally able to give greater returns. It really comes down to the fact that the big organizations with which you have relationships do have an outsized influence and outsized impact. At Deloitte, they help us evolve to be the best service provider and the best version of our firm we can be.

What does best practice look like when it comes to managing key clients? What in your view are the main ingredients for success?

Clarity of aspiration is probably top of the list. What is it that you're seeking from the relationship? What are you seeking to give to the relationship? In any productive relationship, it's a two-way street. And to me it's never been about selling to or pushing to. Instead, it's about having a clear vision for what success looks like and then working backwards from there.

Next is where do we have not only the right to play but the expectation to win in that relationship? Because in any business, with very rare exceptions, you won't be the only relationship, but it will be a potentially important relationship if the aspiration is clear and compelling enough. So you have to define the relationship parameters clearly and effectively.

Then you look beneath that and say, how can we make the platform compelling for both organizations? How does this drive the future of the organization that we're trying to work with? How can it make them a better organization in the marketplace, more able to be agile in the future, more able to transform, more organically able to adjust to a fast and rapidly changing market? And how do we each help each other so we both become more effective, more valuable and more productive?

How does it change the nature of the relationship between the two companies when you get someone senior such as yourself looking after that relationship?

Our industry, which I broadly label professional services, has changed. I think we used to do more of what I call trust-based selling. We all had our cubbyholes within which we worked and we had very specific areas of expertise and we ventured outside of those at times, but it was all about selling to clients in a trust-based way. But, as the lines between industries continue to blur and as the ability to access products and services from anywhere at a click on your screen has evolved, it has fundamentally altered the old 'handshake' sorts of deals and it demands a different level of partnering.

I think that's going to continue changing and evolving. You don't have to sit next to someone to be able to serve them. You don't have to have physical presence or the infrastructure necessarily to serve a marketplace. But you do have to, in some way, partner with the right organizations to enable all of that.

So, a senior person in that relationship can, if they're thinking the right way, bring not only the power of their organization but the power of an ecosystem of organizations together for their client. That can not only drive value that is broader and more sustainable, but can alter the factors of production and the contracts that used to be built between professional services firms and their clients.

Because of the change and the speed of change enabled by technology innovation across every dimension, it forces clients into a different kind of ecosystem play and to reconsider the boundaries of their organization: what do they do themselves, what do they do with others, what do others do for them? And so it's a challenging world because they have more options and opportunities but they also have legacy infrastructure that they have to now reconfigure, rethink and reimagine if they're really going to be effective in competing.

So why not strike a different sort of deal that not only enables the particular client organization's products and services to be sold at market, but also enables us to share in the success of that by delivering and partnering in a different sort of way? It's not about just selling to, it's about building that platform that encompasses both the professional services firm and the client organization, but also more broadly the ecosystem, and the flow of products, services and trade across all of it.

Can you say something about the importance of shared ambition and values, as well as the opportunity to take on broader challenges with these top clients?

I have long been a strong proponent of the idea that all relationships come down to shared values. I think we're attracted to individuals that not necessarily think the way we do but believe in a common set of principles that govern their lives. Institutions, companies and firms are collections of individuals, and the really effective and successful ones are those that have clarified their purpose.

Clarity around who you are, what your purpose is, both in industry as well as more broadly in community and society, is becoming intermingled. It is so difficult for me to separate shareholder value, employee value, customer value and societal value because I think increasingly they're just so intertwined.

Purpose is becoming a calling card and an attraction to the resource pool, which in my opinion is one of the most critical factors of production. The best talent has options, and they're attracted to good companies with good ethos that understand that a dollar sale or a pound sale or a euro sale is important but it's also important what that does to the environment. It's important what that does in the community. I think the winners and losers in industry are going to be more based on how well they can clearly stake their claim that they're a purpose-led organization and that they're geared up not just to make money but to make a difference.

How does that play out in your experience when you're dealing with these big client relationships?

There are companies in the marketplace that haven't yet figured out that purpose matters as much as it does. And then there are others that will surprise you, that have a tremendous grasp on the criticality of their organization-defining purpose not only for their own people but for their shareholders and their broader stakeholders. I think this comes down as much as anything to the leadership of a particular organization and their own personal value systems, and the role that they see for not only themselves and their companies but for industry in helping to shape wider society.

At the moment it's simply not a level playing field. But I think what we're going to see over time, and perhaps with increasing speed, is companies not only getting the memo, so to speak, that purpose is important (and specific elements of purpose are really important) but realizing that they're going to be held more and more accountable. It's probably going to take longer than perhaps any of us would like, but the sense that I have is that large organizations that are successful in the future are going to have to have this element of caring about a broader set of stakeholders in a meaningful way, and not just something you're ticking the box in but you're actually delivering.

How can companies help their top accounts meet this challenge?

There are entire new industries arising. Whether they're around carbon technologies or water-sharing technologies or renewables technologies, or getting plastics out of our supply chain, or educating individuals earlier on about finances. There will be entire new industries emerging that I think are going to be really exciting and very profitable.

You have to start by acknowledging it's not easy and everybody is kind of in this together. It just so happens that some are a bit more disrupter oriented, some are a bit more incumbent oriented, but in each you can have a value system that encompasses not only profit making but positive impact generation.

The challenge is always going to be to find that right mix of the fiduciary responsibility to deliver economic profit and results with the ethical responsibility of delivering goods and services that are positive for not only your shareholders and your customers but for society, the community. And that's a really tough thing to do. It's especially tough for incumbents that have far more physical infrastructure and far more history selling in an older market, where a lot of these issues weren't quite as obvious, as apparent, as visible or as urgent.

Whether you're a large incumbent with a lot of physical infrastructure or smaller, more agile and dominantly technology enabled, the question is, 'How do we produce something that's highly desired in a segment of the customer population that we're targeting that will deliver outsized profits, enable tremendous business growth and also be good for the community?' That's where these deep partnerships and wider ecosystems can help.

How does all this change what you do as the leader of a large global account day to day?

There are some constants. Hard work pays off. Honesty pays off. Transparency pays off. Accountability pays off. Measuring results pays off. Have those things in the right measure over time and you can rely on them through a whole variety of career evolution, company evolution and leadership evolution. You can't, of course, predict the unpredictable, but if you have this kind of underlying platform of values that you believe in, it doesn't matter what happens, it matters how you manage your way through it.

The most long-lasting partnerships and relationships and teams I've ever been around have been those where the common purpose that binds you isn't just doing great work, it isn't just innovating around a great concept or piece of intellectual property. It isn't just delivering a great programme or transformation. It's working with people who share a common belief around how they treat and value others, how well they work in a team. When you get that kind of culture around your organization, around the platform, and around your partnership with other organizations, you create the ability to augment your own capabilities and achieve more together. You're creating much more ability to go figure things out with more tools in the kit, more potential outcomes than you can imagine, more potential profits, and more social good.

Paul's views are consistent with those we have heard from other senior executives managing single strategic customer relationships. The signal sent to customers when someone of the seniority and experience of Paul Legere is given responsibility for a single account is highly significant and can take an already important relationship to a whole new level, to the benefit of both parties.

Targeting new top customers

We argued the case for clearer targeting of possible new prospects in Chapter 3, when discussing account prioritization, creating a tier that is for those existing smaller customers and, in some cases, prospects who could become top customers in the future. Fujitsu, in the case study in that chapter, describes 'focus' accounts, from which it expects to find new top customers, and Nick Wilson described a 'gestation unit' earlier in this chapter. Although not always explicitly stated publicly, we know of many other companies that have a similar approach: in effect, the incubation of future top customers.

This deliberate targeting is another example of placing bets, but doing so after carrying out a thorough analysis of the customers you would like to have, who fit your ideal customer profile and are chosen by using criteria that will enable a focus on a relatively small number. Then, having selected them, based on internal and external data, converting them to top customers is, in our view, another long-term play. The key ingredients for success include commitment, focused resources, a long-term, more patient approach before you can earn the right to win a transformative deal, and the imaginative use of partners where necessary.

Commitment from the senior leadership team is critical because the returns from this investment are likely to be realized over a longer time period than the current financial year. So there needs to be a tolerance of failure in individual pursuits, but with a view to success overall. It may well be necessary to dedicate a senior sales leader and ring-fence budget and resources.

Target prospecting demands a different kind of salespeople, traditionally called hunters by the sales community. Everyone involved should be made aware that these customers or prospects are to be afforded a 'special status' in terms of the attention they will be given and the quality of the resources deployed to pursue them. Investing efforts in prospects has to be a very conscious decision because all companies, however large, have finite resources and can only support a certain number of deals at one time and the number of 'A teams' to pursue them is limited.

Other important elements include an approach to account-based marketing that helps create a deeper insight and more highly personalized campaigns than would be expected for a customer of this significance. Moreover, executive engagement programmes, which are often reserved for existing top customers, need to be opened up for these carefully selected prospects, with, for example, invitations to executive roundtables and other elite events.

By way of illustration of what can often happen if this proactive targeting is not done, a senior leader in an infrastructure services company explained that an enthusiastic sales executive in their organization had put in a bid to a very large prospect in their country, but without much support from marketing or from the sales and technical team that really understood the particular solution.

Undeterred, the sales executive delivered the proposal, but it was not well received. The value proposition did not resonate and the solution was incomplete. Feedback from the customer was damning, and it changed his view completely from thinking that this was a reputable company with innovative ideas that had potential to be a significant supplier in the future. Following the inadequate proposal, his view was that, if that was the best they could do, he would not be inviting them to bid again.

Apart from the obvious issue that the sale was lost and the customer executive less than impressed, the other issue, which, unfortunately, also occurred some months later, was that this same executive then moved to another executive position, in a top customer. As by now he was disillusioned with his experience, it created a major challenge for the account team, which took several months to resolve.

QUALIFICATION AND TARGETING

Poorly qualified bidding, as well as wasting money, can be detrimental to a company's reputation and long-term growth prospects. Your goal should be to increase the amount of business you do with these prospects over three years to bring them into your top 20 per cent of customers, or even into the top three per cent.

But bear in mind that transformation on this scale, going from a small to a strategic supplier, is unlikely to happen in one giant step. With a three-year plan, your immediate objective might be to win a smaller deal in one area of the business, to earn respect and show what you can do. Some successful sales leaders have likened this to a game of chess, where everything is leading to a 'checkmate' (the big transformational deal), but where they can carefully plot their moves over months, or very often years, to earn the right to this status.

This technique has worked very well in the public sector in outsourcing, where the timeframe for contract renewal is usually known years in advance. This gives prospective bidders the opportunity to position themselves in the best possible light in the areas they think they need to prove themselves, well ahead of the time of the big, transformative deal that would catapult their relationship to one of strategic supplier.

This chess-like planning should also take account of your company's partners, who may already be working with the prospect and able to collaborate with you at a strategic level to both increase their share of wallet and help you achieve your goals. In an area where you have a very strong solution but lack access to the right decision-makers to position it correctly, partnering may well be the swiftest way to make progress, particularly for smaller companies that are earlier in their growth journey and lack brand recognition or market presence.

Creating and orchestrating this chess game, leveraging the company's capabilities and working effectively with partners to stay the course is a tough thing to get right and it will require strong leadership at the account level and senior management commitment. But the prize is worth striving for, because, if successful, you will eventually add a new top customer to your portfolio – and hopefully one you will keep for many years to come.

SUMMARY CHECKLIST

1 Customers have very high expectations of their strategic suppliers and demand a relationship that is based on a deep understanding of their business strategy and goals.

2 They don't expect the relationship to be a sales relationship, but do expect strategic suppliers to invest in a more seasoned and experienced general manager as the key account manager to manage the relationship over the long term.

3 Key account managers need to be participating fully in the digital world with their customers and partners.

4 The key account manager has to be able to coordinate and manage their own company's resources and assets effectively, so will need seniority, authority and an internal network.

5 Top customer programmes need to be carefully scoped and scaled for the long term, with investments and key resources allocated appropriately.

6 Key account management is multifaceted, complex and hard to get right, but the benefits are hugely significant for sustainable, profitable growth, bringing stability to a company's revenues and profits when done well.

7 Market leaders are investing not only in today's top customers, with executives taking the lead on these large customers, but also in future top customers, through systematic targeting and carefully crafted techniques.

08

Account-based marketing

As we noted in Chapter 1, ABM is defined as 'a structured process for developing and implementing highly customized marketing programmes to strategic accounts, partners or prospects', as fully explained by author Bev Burgess with Dave Munn in *A Practitioner's Guide to Account-Based Marketing* (Kogan Page, 2021).

But as we've already set out in this book, ABM can't operate in isolation. It has to be thought of and aligned with the way the business engages its accounts – across sales, service, customer success and the executives at the top of the company.

In this chapter, we'll look at what ABM is, why it is used, the different flavours of it that exist today, and where each potentially applies in your account-based growth strategy. Then we'll explore what's required to build and enable an ABM programme, as illustrated by the case study from ServiceNow, before looking at ABM in practice and how it is deployed to engage the customer through their buying process in collaboration with other customer-facing teams. Eric Martin, who led SAP's ABM programme in North America for many years, gives us his viewpoint on this collaboration. Finally, we delve into the specialist area of deal-based marketing, a compressed approach reserved for pursuing large opportunities with top customers or prospects.

To find out more about ABM, readers are encouraged to refer to the comprehensive *A Practitioner's Guide to ABM*, now in its second edition, which explores in detail how to set up your programme, how to execute ABM, and how to build the competencies you need to be a successful ABM-er.

What is ABM?

Accenture was one of the first companies to explore how to apply the end-to-end marketing management process to one account, treating it as a market in its own right. Dr Charles Doyle, who led marketing for the company's global high-tech practice, developed what he referred to as a 'client-centric marketing' approach back in the early 2000's. His work was driven by the belief that the company's most important accounts should have special attention, including a specific marketing plan, to build a more multifaceted relationship between Accenture and its clients over the longer term. His thinking is completely aligned with our own; a more account-based approach to marketing is needed as part of any wider account-based growth strategy.

The UK headquartered Chartered Institute for Marketing defines marketing as 'the management process responsible for identifying, anticipating and satisfying customer requirements profitably'. ABM does exactly that, one account at a time. It relies on the strategic marketing process, defined by leading marketing thinkers such as Professors Philip Kotler and Malcolm McDonald, which starts with a clear business ambition, analyzes the market (ie the account) to identify needs; segments that market to focus on the best opportunities; develops a brand position to attract the chosen segments; and designs the right marketing mix to engage them through campaigns that deliver the business ambition. As such, it is the perfect marketing strategy to support an account-based growth initiative, albeit a resource intensive approach.

The types of ABM in use today

Since the early 2000s, ABM has proved itself to deliver a consistently higher return on investment than traditional B2B marketing, with the inevitable consequence that demand for ABM surged in those companies that had adopted it. But, as most companies treat marketing as a discretionary cost that has to be carefully managed in order to maximize EBITDA, marketing leaders found themselves without the significantly increased investment in headcount or budget needed to meet this growing demand for ABM. They had three options: make a case for whatever incremental investment was available, source budgets from elsewhere in the business, such as business unit leadership or account management, or divert people and budgets from other areas of marketing. They did all three.

They also got creative, developing a lighter ABM approach to groups of accounts that shared the same goals and challenges, creating and tailoring propositions, messaging and marketing plans for these 'clusters' rather than for just one account at a time.

Those trying to expand their programmes still further were quick to grasp the usefulness of the growing number of marketing technologies and tools to scale even more widely without damaging the more individual nature of ABM. As these tools have become more sophisticated, they have offered greater scope both for scaling ABM across more accounts and for going deeper into individual accounts, in areas such as account selection and intent monitoring, stakeholder profiling and personalized digital advertising.

Today, marketing technology platforms are increasingly designed specifically to support ABM and help scale it up more cost-effectively, exploiting transformational advances such as data analytics and machine learning. In fact, in January 2022, Gartner published its first ABM Magic Quadrant report (2022b), defining ABM platforms as 'technologies that enable marketers to run ABM programs at scale, including account selection, planning, engagement and reporting'.

ABM has evolved into at least three different approaches in order to cover the tiers of priority accounts that a company wants to engage: strategic ABM, cluster ABM and programmatic ABM. It's fascinating to note that just as these three approaches have emerged in marketing over the past two decades, with various levels of resource and investment required, the same variety of approaches has emerged in customer success to invest appropriate levels of resources into different tiers of customer accounts. In customer success teams the three types are referred to as high-touch, mid-touch and tech-touch, and we explore these in Chapter 9. There is a clear correlation between the investment decisions being made across these three types of customer engagement in marketing and customer success, but we typically see an astonishing lack of alignment between these two teams. They often have two different tiering approaches for the same group of customers, hence our emphasis on collaborative account prioritization and resource allocation in Chapter 3.

STRATEGIC ABM

This first (and original) type of ABM is usually reserved for a company's most strategic accounts, providing that company's portfolio is broad enough and deal size large enough to warrant this approach.

In strategic ABM, you find one experienced marketer effectively becoming the CMO of each account as a core part of the account team, creating a bespoke marketing plan for the account. Typically, a strategic ABM-er manages between one and five accounts. Strategic ABM is the most resource intensive approach, applied to customers with a significant potential lifetime value running into tens or hundreds of millions of dollars.

CLUSTER ABM

The second type is cluster ABM. Here, one marketer works on one to five clusters of accounts, grouped for their common context and drivers, and creates a customized marketing plan for each cluster. The cluster may include both existing customers and/or prospects, but is ideally in the range of 3–15 companies, no more.

The obvious advantage of cluster ABM is that it can be scaled across more accounts, using less resource per account. It is also a more realistic type of ABM for companies whose deal size and potential customer lifetime value is in the range of hundreds of thousands or millions of dollars. Both of these reasons may be behind the current trend for companies to often start their ABM programmes with this type when at pilot stage. But inevitably, this less bespoke approach typically has correspondingly less impact than strategic ABM, albeit still a greater impact than traditional B2B marketing, thereby proving the business case in these early pilots.

PROGRAMMATIC ABM

The third type in use today is programmatic or one-to-many ABM. This is where a marketer creates personalized, usually industry aligned, persona-based campaign journeys for job roles in named accounts, and serves them up automatically in an 'always-on' approach when an account shows intent or buying signals in the market, whether through first-, second- or third party data (ie by engaging with content on the company's own website, on its partners' or suppliers' sites or on publicly available sites that sell their browsing and engagement data).

This type of ABM is typically used to target new prospects or to engage with existing customers who are in a lower tier of accounts, or indeed by companies who sell single or lower value solutions, and whose customer lifetime value may be in the range of tens to hundreds of thousands of dollars.

Allocating marketing resources across your accounts

'I know half of the money I spend on advertising is wasted; the trouble is I don't know which half.' This quote is attributed to both UK industrialist

Lord Leverhulme or US businessman and marketing pioneer, John Wanamaker. Whichever of them said it, it's an issue that has troubled many business leaders over the years, especially since many CEOs have come up the finance route and see marketing as rather a 'dark art'.

One of our own CMO clients wrestles with the same question every year at budgeting time; which marketing activities are foundational, that I have to do no matter how many customers or prospects I have; and which are more discretionary, that I could increase in good times and switch off, if I needed to, in difficult times? The joy (and difficulty) of marketing is that it is both an art and a science, making questions like these difficult to answer, and decisions about how much to invest in your marketing team and programmes hard to quantify objectively.

We would argue that the reality of the 80/20 rule, and how it plays out in your business, is an excellent starting point to answer these questions. As we said in the last chapter, there are two really important categories of account that deserve incremental investment over all others – the one to three per cent that drive half of your revenue, and the accounts who could join that group over time. Marketing has a key role to play in both of these categories.

So, to answer our CMO client's question, there are some things that you will need to do in marketing to engage all of your audiences; not just customers and prospects, but employees, partners, influencers and investors, for example. These include corporate marketing, building a clear brand positioning and narrative for your company, a digital presence that works for all audiences, plus clear and differentiated descriptions of the solutions in your portfolio and the value they deliver for various segments of buyers. But you then have a choice as to how much more you want to invest in your different tiers of customer or prospects.

What are you trying to achieve?

The first thing any CMO should do is agree with the CEO what the business is trying to achieve. Which goals need marketing support? For example, if a company is just launching or has just acquired or merged with another, there will be a significant job to do in (re)positioning the brand and telling the company's story so that its clear in the mind of all audiences.

If new customer acquisition is the main business goal, such as in the first few years of a software company's life, segment or sector-based marketing campaigns, or at best a programmatic, tech-touch approach to ABM may be the main focus for the marketing team.

Where a company selling complex, high-consideration services has set out a clear goal to build long-term customer relationships, creating loyalty and advocacy in its most important accounts, there is a clear mandate for marketing to invest in ABM to complement the business strategy. This is exactly what we've seen happen at Accenture, Fujitsu, and Infosys, among others. Their programmes are designed to defend and grow their most important accounts, driving awareness of the whole portfolio into each customer and continuing to create new value for both companies through their ongoing collaboration. This is complemented with a laser-like focus on deal-based marketing, to win the select new customers that will be part of tomorrow's top tier of accounts.

Choosing the right level of investment

As Nick Wilson said in Chapter 7, any business needs to start by deciding what it can afford to spend on accounts and organize its resources from the top down. So, just as different types of sales approaches are deployed for different tiers of customers and prospects, and customer success teams allocate different levels of investment to each tier, marketing teams may blend different types of ABM within their overall marketing strategy. The decision as to which blend is right for your business is likely to be an outcome of the collaborative account prioritization and resource allocation process described in Chapter 3.

The best way to think about this is in terms of increasing investment for each tier of account from the bottom to the top – bringing in the 80/20 rule and its fractal nature – just as the tech-touch, mid-touch and high-touch approaches to customer success do.

All audiences will see your general corporate marketing and communications messages, while the bottom 80 per cent of your accounts (Tier 5, which generate just 20 per cent of your revenue and may in fact cost you money to serve in many cases) may also receive general segment or solutions marketing campaigns. They might also receive a more tailored 'always-on' programmatic ABM approach – akin to the tech-touch offered by the customer success team, ensuring the content they receive is relevant to what they are interested in, such as for their specific industry, job role and stage in their buyer process. This does not equate to much additional investment per account.

You may also have identified new prospects that could one day be in your top tier of accounts (Tier 4). This (hopefully small and well targeted) group of prospects could be part of your programmatic or cluster ABM programmes, and of course be the subject of deal-based marketing to win your first piece of business with them.

Your top 20 per cent of accounts could also be receiving your general segment or solutions marketing campaigns, plus the more tailored 'always-on' programmatic ABM approach. However, due to the fractal nature of the 80/20 rule, there will be clusters of accounts within this top 20 per cent who generate more than their fair share of profitable revenue (Tier 3), and these could be addressed with campaigns customized for their business. Again, this may be in addition to the marketing activities all other accounts receive, or it may be instead of some of them. Either way, you are likely to be investing more per account in these clusters.

Finally, for the top 20 per cent of your top 20 per cent of accounts, you may decide that they are so important that they warrant a strategic, high-touch ABM approach (Tiers 1 and 2). As we've said, this is the most resource intensive, and yet it is the kind of bespoke approach that your most important customers deserve. It is the extraordinary focus that these accounts, which could be generating over half of your profitable revenue, need to defend them from your competitors and grow your business with them over the long term.

FIGURE 8.1 Choosing the right level of marketing investment for your accounts

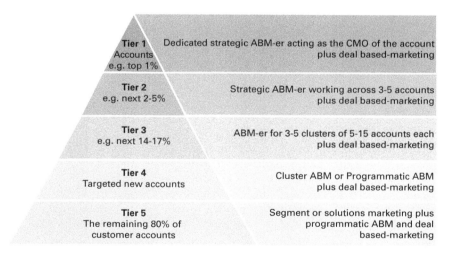

Building an ABM centre of excellence

We've watched a trend building over the past few years to create centres of excellence in specialist areas of business practice to support the community of people within a business tasked with executing that specialism. ABM is no exception. Once you have decided to invest in ABM for your most important accounts, building a centre of excellence (CoE) to enable marketers to deliver these more customized programmes can help you scale faster and more effectively.

The role of an ABM CoE spans three main areas: defining the right ABM strategy for the business, offering services that make marketers more effective and efficient in executing ABM while driving the right balance of global consistency and local flexibility, and maintaining standards through professional development and performance management (Figure 8.2).

FIGURE 8.2 The three roles of an ABM centre of excellence

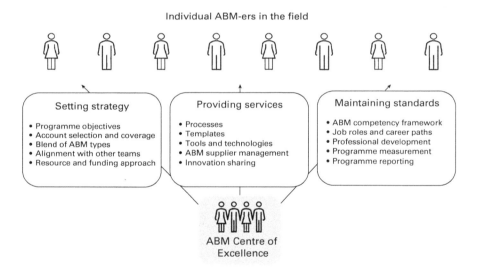

Core to the CoE's role is defining and evolving the ABM strategy for the business, including the blend of ABM types to be used across tiers of accounts, the way in which the ABM process for each type works and aligns with other customer-facing teams, and the resources required to deliver each type of ABM – both in terms of people and budgets. The CoE basically answers the question 'How do we do ABM, in all its forms, here?'

The second key role for the CoE lies in making ABM-ers across the company more efficient and effective. This involves building tools and templates that the

ABM community can leverage, sharing innovations and best practices and managing the company's ABM supplier ecosystem to deliver services that ABM-ers everywhere use on a more cost-effective basis, including technology vendors, research and insight suppliers, creative agencies and consultants.

The CoE's third role lies in maintaining the right standards of delivery, such as by recruiting and developing people with the right ABM competencies, or monitoring the business impact achieved with ABM and continually looking for improvements. The CoE defines ABM competencies and develops job roles and families within the overall marketing community, with formal onboarding and professional development in place to support career development.

Ultimately, the CoE supports a community of trained ABM-ers embedded in the business, ensuring internal alignment around objectives and key performance indicators, reporting the impact of the programme from an individual account level all the way up to a programme-wide level and maintaining a consistent approach to external engagement across the company's most important accounts and prospects.

One company that has achieved great success with an ABM programme, tightly aligned to the rest of the business and enabled by a strong CoE, is ServiceNow.

CASE STUDY
ABM as a service at ServiceNow

ServiceNow is a leading United States–based software company that offers a cloud computing platform to help companies manage digital workflows for enterprise operations. With total revenues for 2021 reaching $5.896bn, a 30 per cent increase from 2020, its customers account for almost 80 per cent of the *Fortune* 500. It employs approximately 17,000 people around the world and in 2020 was ranked number one on the *Fortune* Future 50 list of companies with the best long-term growth potential.

Engaging strategic customers

In 2018, the company hired Gemma Davies, now the senior director of Global ABM and CXO Engagement, to spearhead an ambitious ABM programme. Its objectives were to help shift ServiceNow's market perception from an IT ticketing tool to a value-based, end-to-end digital transformation platform, as well as building reputation and relevance in the C-suite.

As she recalls, 'We recognized that a small number of strategic customers were going to drive a significant amount of long-term revenue growth for the business. So, we needed a way to service and support those customers that was centered around their imperatives. At the same time, we were in the midst of transforming and developing platform capabilities that moved significantly beyond what our buyers knew of us.

'These two challenges needed a focused, fresh approach if we were going to capture that market opportunity in front of us.'

An enduring model of cross-functional collaboration was critical to success, with members of different teams from the business involved in the steering committee to establish the new ABM programme.

Becoming more customer-centric

The ABM programme has since become a driving force behind the company's 'outside-in' value-based approach, which emphasizes the core brand message that ServiceNow is a trusted advisor to the C-Suite in enterprise software, automating and orchestrating processes across core business units.

The pandemic, as well as geopolitical and social unrest, energized the company into applying its purpose and the Now Platform towards finding solutions for complex problems like emergency response management, vaccine administration and delivery and even hospital supply coordination across borders. As the company has strengthened its emphasis on customer centricity and innovation opportunities, it has won some new contracts with timely products and solutions. For example, because of the agility of the Now Platform, they were able to help NHS Scotland develop and deploy its vaccine management solution in just six weeks, and have been successful with digital solutions that enable employers to oversee the safe return of employees to the workplace.

The focus has been not just on filling up the pipeline with new business and increasing annual contract value but understanding its customers' workflow needs and making sure they realize real value, quickly, Davies explains. 'We talk about how to improve growth beyond the core by pursuing major opportunities, by changing perceptions and positioning and developing new accounts. And, significantly, asking, "How do we accelerate advocacy, adoption and time to value?"'

Evolving the global programme

While ABM has been proving its worth in terms of contributing to net new accounts and increasing average contract value, substantial progress has also been made in the more intangible but vitally important areas such as advocacy. ABM principles are seen as the basis of a go-to-market model that aligns everyone around a global solution framework geared to the customer's business requirements.

Relationship and trust across functions, and particularly with the account teams, are fundamental components to any successful ABM programme, Davies believes. This has presented new challenges during the pandemic, so, as well as being thoroughly prepared for each meeting about a strategic customer, the ABM team has worked hard to find new and creative ways to collaborate with the account teams and keep the momentum going in a virtual world.

Meanwhile, the ABM governance structure has been transformed from what had been a relatively flat structure as headcount grows and budgets increase, enabling over 100 accounts in 2022 to be treated as a 'market-of-one' and 1,000+ accounts receiving a lighter treatment through imperative-led ABM programs. ABM is no longer just a team, it is a GTM motion that the whole marketing organization is behind to help deliver and scale. There is now a more formal leadership framework to support this strategic investment, with four centres of excellence reporting to Davies.

Three of these centres are geographical, in EMEA (Europe, the Middle East, Africa), APJ (Asia, Pacific, Japan) and the Americas, with the fourth acting as the global programme office to ensure consistency as well as investing in innovative services such as video and data analytics for ABM-ers to leverage.

How to get that global/local balance right is always tricky, explains Davies, not least with defining consistent measures of success. For example, one region is focused on one-to-one ABM in top accounts and winning new logos, while another is focused on increasing C-suite advocacy to accelerate the breadth of platform adoption and value realization via a blended strategy. To drive tighter integration, the ABM directors in the regions also sit on the regional marketing management teams.

Aligning with executive engagement

Since the spring of 2020, Davies has also been given responsibility for the company's executive engagement strategy. This has entailed figuring out all the different pockets of activity across the company and working on bringing all the individual efforts into alignment to define a more holistic and impactful executive experience.

This is crucial, she notes. ABM is where you start to establish relevance in an account and build rapport and relationships. Once you do that, you can then start opening it up through executive engagement strategies, which can take you to a whole new level. But this won't happen if executives don't have a consistent experience with your company.

As Davies concludes, 'If there is one thing that the pandemic has shown us, it is that relevance is key when it comes to winning and growing our top accounts. We need to understand the business imperatives of our customers and create value-based messaging and experiences that resonate by moving to a comprehensive executive engagement strategy and focusing on the outcomes they are trying to achieve. That is how you build long-term relationships and develop loyalty and advocacy in a platform business like ServiceNow.'

ABM in practice

ServiceNow is a great example of a company collaborating across functions for the benefit of their customers. This collaboration occurs all the way through the end-to-end marketing process applied to an individual account or group of accounts. Professor Malcolm McDonald explains this strategic marketing planning process in his excellent book *Marketing Plans*, now in its eighth edition, (2016), setting out a ten-step process across four phases from goal setting, through a situation review, to strategy formulation and finally campaign planning, resource allocation, and monitoring.

Here, we set out the main phases of this marketing process as it applies to individual accounts or clusters, and the main points of collaboration with other teams engaging your top accounts.

Goal setting

We have already discussed how important it is to set out a long-term ambition for your top accounts in Chapter 4, where we introduced the integrated account business planning process. This ambition is the context in which marketing plans for individual accounts and clusters are built, ensuring alignment across the business from the very beginning.

Situation review

One of the first tasks for an ABM-er is to carry out the primary and secondary research that lies at the heart of both integrated account business planning and ABM activity.

By collaborating with the account team and leveraging the data we discussed in Chapter 5, you can build a picture of what's happening in the account. To do so, you'll need to answer some fundamental questions about the context within which the account is operating and how it is responding to its changing environment, explained in Chapter 4.

While you can leverage the systems and data you already have, and buy in additional information as needed, there's no better route to building a deep understanding of what's driving the account and the stakeholders within it than talking first to the people in your company that work with the customer, and then to the customers themselves. And yet the number of ABM-ers who use this primary market research approach to understand their accounts are few and far between.

Initial perception research will give you an understanding of how key decision makers and influencers feel about you today, and how big the gap is between what they think of you now and what you want them to think. This could be run by an independent market research company or linked to your wider brand perception or NPS surveys.

ILLUSTRATIVE DISCUSSION GUIDE FOR CUSTOMER INTERVIEWS

1. Your business objectives

- How would you describe your objectives, both currently and looking out over the next year or so?

- What are the key performance indicators you use or will use to measure your success against these objectives?

2. Challenges and obstacles

- What are the main external challenges you face in achieving your objectives?

- What are the main internal obstacles you face?

3. Priorities for XYZ services

- Looking ahead, what role will XYZ services play in helping you achieve your objectives?

- Are there any ways in which the way these services are provided will need to change to help you achieve your objectives?

4. Perceptions of current suppliers

- Thinking about the services you receive today, can you describe them and how well they are meeting your needs?

- What are your views of the suppliers who provide these services today? For example their relative strengths and weaknesses?

5. Future service needs

- Thinking about your objectives over the next year or so, are there any new XYZ services that you think will be needed to help you achieve your objectives?
- Are any of these being planned or scoped already?
- Who would you consider asking to provide these services, and why?

6. Perceptions of XYZ service companies

- Can you tell us about what value you think specific suppliers bring to you today and what makes them distinctive?

Once you have the information you need to understand the account's context, and your position within it, you can analyze it using a range of useful strategic frameworks, including:

- a PESTEL analysis – identifying the issues impacting the account across the political, economic, sociocultural, technological, environmental and legal or regulatory spheres and prioritizing them according to their likely impact on the account and thus need for a response;
- a five-forces analysis – identifying the main changes in the dynamics of power in the account's market, across buyers, suppliers, competitors, new entrants and potential substitutes, and prioritizing these as above.
- a SWOT analysis – identifying your main opportunities and threats in the account given what is happening with the customer, and your relative strengths and weaknesses compared to your competitors in the account, thereby helping you to identify the best opportunities for growth with the customer.

For a cluster or larger group of accounts, where you are unable to go into the same level of detail for individual customers or prospects, you may wish to leverage intent data from various sources and use a tool such as a heat map to identify common issues and priorities and then conduct a SWOT analysis that helps you to identify the best opportunities for your company.

Strategy formulation

This phase of the process involves collaboration with the account team to prioritize which of the issues facing the account – and the individuals dealing with them – you want to focus on as a company. Where do you have capabilities that could help, either in house or across your own ecosystem of partners and suppliers? The viewpoint from Paul Legere at Deloitte in Chapter 7 underlines how important this approach is today for your biggest customers, particularly when collaborating around some of the serious issues we all face such as climate change.

This agreed focus will drive your marketing objectives and strategy for the account or cluster: what do we want to market, and to whom? How will we position ourselves in the minds of the customer?

Developing a customized solution in response to the account's issues allows you to talk about what your organization has to offer in the context of what matters to the customer. Many companies, such as Capgemini, use design thinking or innovation workshops to work through the customer's issues, priorities, options and potential solutions, as we discussed in Chapter 7.

When applying this approach into a cluster or group of accounts, you will more likely be tailoring an existing solution to the issues the accounts have in common, working with a group of account managers and sales people. It may even be a customized solution that you initially developed for and with one of your strategic accounts.

In large, complex accounts, you may find that there are tiers of audiences you need to understand and engage with around these issues and the solutions you can offer. For example, your priority stakeholders may be one or two people within the company's leadership team, plus a few key individuals who work with or otherwise influence those stakeholders. It's important to profile and understand these key stakeholders, and your current relationship with them well. But you might also find that everyone within a specific function, or with a similar job role across the business, has some influence on the decision, and at this stage you may wish to build out buyer personas that allow you to understand this group of people without profiling them all individually.

The use of personas is valuable when running ABM for large clusters or groups of accounts, where once again it is impractical to profile every individual.

Building targeted messages for the individuals and audience segments that matter is key to positioning yourself correctly in the mind of the customer. Many successful ABM-ers start by crafting an overarching narrative for the account in collaboration with the account team; what do we want to be famous for in three years' time? Some even build a bespoke visual identity, combining elements of their own brand with that of the customer and creating a strapline that summarizes their overarching proposition to the customer.

Individual solutions propositions may sit beneath this topline message, communicating the value these solution will deliver in terms the customer will understand and care about, organized into a hierarchy or messaging house. The same hierarchy can be built for a cluster of accounts, but there is less focus on building a bespoke visual identity outside of strategic ABM.

Professor Malcolm McDonald has written extensively about how to develop strong value propositions (2019), recommending that wherever possible, your proposition should be financially quantified. This is particularly powerful when linked to a challenger sales approach or provocation to a top account or cluster, where your understanding of the customer's landscape is deep enough to model the likely business outcomes of your solution and help build the business case that gives them the confidence to buy.

Campaign planning, resource allocation and monitoring

Much of a customer's engagement with you as they research how best to solve some of the issues they face will be done before your sales people ever have a conversation with them, as explained by analyst firm, Gartner, making your marketing content and channels even more important during the early stages of the buying process. An aligned and integrated approach to the moments that matter during their buying process is critical, and many companies allocate most of their ABM budget to these pre-sales activities. But, the emphasis on customer success and successful delivery of the outcomes customers are looking for from their strategic suppliers means that ABM should not just be seen as a 'pre-sales' activity, but rather one that engages and delivers value to accounts throughout the customer lifecycle. Some companies, like Red Hat, the subject of our case study in Chapter 10, have recognized this and made the same marketing leader responsible for ABM and customer lifecycle marketing. Others have yet to do so.

The best ABM campaigns deliver the right content, through the right channels, all along the customer's journey, helping them make a decision to purchase and then get the best from that purchase for their business, such as in the example shown in Figure 8.3. Indeed, by taking an ABM approach, some companies are rethinking marketing as a provider of useful content to their most important customers; almost part of the service they offer their customers, and a key differentiator from others whose un-personalized marketing remains something to be avoided and deleted at all costs!

FIGURE 8.3 ABM in the context of the customer lifecycle

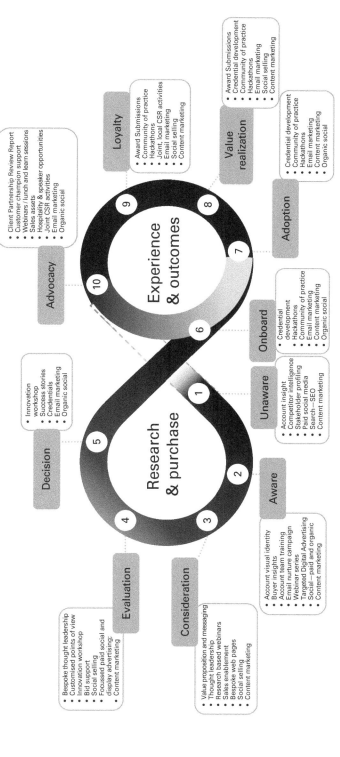

It's important to allocate marketing spend through the customer journey, monitoring how each activity lands to continually refine your approach and improve your engagement. In strategic ABM, you will likely include more high-touch activities than in cluster ABM, while programmatic ABM campaigns are likely to be mostly tech touch. These approaches are once again reflected in the way that customer success teams design their interactions with different tiers of customers, as we will explore in Chapter 9.

Along with this ongoing tracking of how the customer is engaging, you need to establish marketing metrics within the overall account dashboard or customer health index discussed in Chapter 5, to track success, measuring both qualitative and quantitative results that can also be aggregated up to an ABM programme level. Most ABM programmes include three categories of metrics linking back to the overall marketing objectives set out for the account or cluster: relationship development, reputation building, and opportunities for revenue growth.

In the relationship space, as part of the integrated account team, marketing activities can help to build contacts and start conversations with new parts of the customer's business or with more senior executives for example, deepening those relationship with valuable content and experiences along the buying journey.

Reputation is a core area for marketing to influence (brand building is one of the most significant contributions marketing makes to increase the value of any business), increasing awareness of your company and what else it could do for a customer, showcasing the value already delivered to the account to create advocates, and generally building a customer's preference for your company over any other.

Marketing's influence over revenue growth is less direct. As part of the overall team, it can identify opportunities and support them as they move through the sales cycle, sometimes accelerating that cycle and improving your win rates to reduce the cost of sale.

Pulling this end-to-end marketing process together and executing well, across multiple accounts and in close alignment with account teams, to drive long-term growth, is no mean feat! It takes a certain type of marketer and a strong ABM programme leader. One such leader is Eric Martin, who, until May 2022, led SAP's ABM team in North America and shares his views on ABM.

Eric Martin

Can you describe your approach to ABM at SAP?

In early 2015, I had the opportunity to take on the ABM program office leader role at SAP North America. My predecessor had initiated it, having seen that a third of our revenue every year came from the top strategic accounts and hypothesized that the returns would be higher if we marketed to them as individual accounts. The pilot bore this out.

Since then, ABM has evolved, with improvements made every year in the way it operates. There are now 60 accounts at a time, with five dedicated ABM marketers working on a one-to-one basis. Of course, not all of the accounts are active at any one time, since we have long sales cycles that can be very complex.

North America is the most mature region when it comes to ABM, and we are now in the process of driving more standardization globally with a new global ABM leader to promote more consistency. This is critical since many of our strategic customers are multinational. Until now, there has been a lot of coordination that goes on behind the scenes, mostly on the sales side and to a lesser extent with marketing, and we do create bespoke material for individual customers in other parts of the world. We are now building the scaffolding for a global programme, based on the learnings from North America.

How important is collaboration across functions?

It's incredibly important. SAP has a really extensive portfolio of products and services aimed at just about any line of business within a corporation. But that also makes things very complex, particularly since there are quite a few people who have relationships with strategic accounts from across SAP.

So, integration with the sales team is essential. You cannot do proper ABM without that. Otherwise, it's just marketing, not account-based marketing. We also have to know the context for a customer across the entire team. For instance, part of an account may be dormant while another part is very active, so we need that visibility in order to speak with the same voice at the same time. Collaboration works by first establishing trust and proving the value ABM can add, and then it happens organically with ABM-ers invited to discussions about the customer.

In terms of executive engagement, the account owners are the ones responsible for overseeing what's happening with the rest of the account team, gaining visibility into the deal cycle and the planning being done in other parts of the organization. They have overall responsibility for orchestrating all engagement. Where marketing helps is by understanding the business well enough to organize activities for the right individuals at the right time within the account. That might also mean stopping some marketing campaign activity from elsewhere in SAP reaching the customer if it's not related to the account plan.

Providing actionable intelligence must be an important way to add value?

Yes, and we can monitor that through a number of internal proprietary systems that can gather data and sentiment, both structured and unstructured, for accounts. That helps us identify any blind spots with the aid of the sales teams – such as which executives are SAP proponents and others who may not be – and adjust our messaging accordingly. It's definitely a two-way street of information sharing between sales and marketing.

What about other customer-facing teams, such as the delivery people?

They will often have insights too because they may know executives that our account teams don't know. What I often say to our ABM-ers is, think about this: the salespeople that you are trying to engage with as account owners are the busiest people at SAP. So don't forget the other customer-facing people who can be sources of valuable information when the account executive is just too swamped to help. Developing those relationships across the wider team focused on the customer is going to give continuity and insights.

That is a big part of the role in general and why I like to get seasoned people into these ABM roles. I tell them to use their intelligence and common sense and go where the account team needs them to, not follow a strict playbook. The more you try to reduce it to a playbook the more it resembles target marketing and the less it looks like one-to-one ABM. I feel very fortunate that we have been given the space and dedicated resources to work at this more strategic level.

Is there a place for ABM in collaborative solution development?

Currently it is the account holder and senior executives who have those conversations with customers, since it might require a strategic agreement in terms of investment. Marketing might develop communications to help sell the idea in. However, in early 2021 we hired a new chief marketing and solutions officer who is both a board member and whose title includes marketing *and* solutions. So, our approach to this is likely to look different in a year or two.

How does SAP measure customer success and feed it back into the company?

Now that over 60 per cent of SAP's revenue comes from cloud-based solutions – which was not the case 10 years ago – renewals and customer adoption and use of the products are very important and reflected in compensations plans, marketing KPIs and customer satisfaction scores that underlie all bonuses. In fact, a few years ago, because of this extended view of the customer lifecycle, we renamed the sales teams the customer success organization.

What role has ABM played in dealing with the challenges of the last few years?

ABM became much more important during the pandemic because our salespeople could no longer walk the halls of customers for months at a time leading up to an opportunity. They couldn't take them to dinner or bring them to a relevant SAP event. So, they turned to us to use our ability to communicate with customers in a personalized way, but from afar. The demand for this was such that we had to bring in others from non-ABM roles to help, giving them a playbook so they could get started more quickly. Although it was a good stopgap measure, and we responded to the needs of the business, it overstretched us and we have now moved back to our more normal number of accounts.

What the last few years have taught us is how to get real engagement. We have had to become very clever about how to nurture and condition our strategic accounts in the time leading up to a virtual event so that we do get the engagement our account teams need. It's hard work, and almost like a hidden marketing cycle we hadn't seen before. But it has shown us how to invest in ways that have incredible impact, reaching the very top of the customer's organization.

Deal-based marketing

As we said earlier in this chapter, one of the specific contexts in which an ABM approach is applied is in pursuing major opportunities, or deals. In fact, if you never identify and pursue an opportunity in your ABM accounts, you're doing something wrong! Deals may also arise as you target prospects with cluster or programmatic ABM activities.

Ideally the opportunities you identify in your strategic accounts will be co-created with your customer, and not competitive. They will be a part of the natural extension of your relationship with that account – cross- and upsell if you like. Typically, deal-based marketing will also be reserved for opportunities with your top customers, perhaps in industries where competitive tendering is required (such as the public sector), or where another supplier is the incumbent provider of a service that you wish to compete for. But it may also be used to win new accounts that you think will become your top customers of tomorrow.

In either case, if you wait to receive a request for proposal (RFP) before applying ABM to an opportunity like this, you're probably wasting your time. Particularly in large, transformational deals, someone will have already been helping to shape the customers' requirements, as expressed in the RFP, and will be in the strongest position to compete for their business. If this is not you, you might want to seriously consider 'qualifying out' of the opportunity, as we discussed in the previous chapter.

We've said before that these deals take multiple months to shape and close. Even in the case of a customer renewing a large contract, you will be able to see the opportunity coming sometimes years in advance, and so have plenty of time to prepare your approach to winning the deal, even if you aren't the incumbent. In fact, this long lead time may be the only chance you have to win the deal from an incumbent supplier, since it will give you time to build a deep understanding of the account and the key stakeholders within it, and to develop the strong, trusted relationships you'll need to win before your marketing activities are constrained by any formal procurement process.

In a deal situation, many aspects of the ABM process become heightened and more focused. Four of the key elements are around understanding the competitive landscape so that you can compete to win, really knowing the audience and what they're looking for, crafting the right win themes that draw on your differentiators and communicating throughout the bid (Figure 8.4).

FIGURE 8.4 The key aspects of deal-based marketing

Competing to win

You need to understand your competitors. Everything you say and do to engage the customer will be received in the context of what your competitors are doing. So, you need to understand their objectives, their strengths and weaknesses relative to you, their strategy to beat you and their successes so far. It's critical to find out whom they know in the account, especially at an executive level, and what those people think of them versus you. Who do they have stronger relationships with that they can call in to support them in the decision making?

You would be amazed at the number of times a sales team will be busy preparing for an opportunity without really finding out who they're competing with and what angle those competitors are likely to take. As an ABM-er, performing a thorough analysis of the competitors for the deal, even down to the profile of the individuals leading each one's approach, is one of the most useful things you can do. For example, if the opportunity you are pursuing is in a bank, you can find out:

- What messages is each competitor sending out to the banking sector in its wider marketing?

- What assets do they have, such as the number of people focused on the sector, thought leadership content, intellectual property and solutions and existing customer references (including the bank you are targeting)?

- What relationships do they have with the decision-makers or influencers for the deal? Are they already a trusted advisor to one or more executives in the account? What do they advise on?

- Who is leading the bid? Have we come up against them before? What are they talking about publicly? What experience or network will they be drawing on to win?

All of this will help you consider how your value proposition to the customer can be differentiated, drawing on your relative strengths and minimizing your weaknesses, so that it is better and more relevant than your competitors'. For example, if you find that they have more trusted advisor relationships with the customer's executive team, you may decide that the only way that you can win the bid is to work with a partner organization that also has those levels of relationships, changing the nature of the proposition you will compete with for the deal.

Really knowing your audience

Another key role for the ABM-er in a deal situation is to build real insight into the decision-makers and influencers for the opportunity. A common approach is to run an audience workshop, where the profiles of each person are shared and then added to by the account and delivery teams who know them well. Build a detailed picture of their objectives and how they will measure success, and how this opportunity plays into those measures. Use research to understand what they think of your company today and why they will or won't want to see you win this deal. Explore psychographic profiling to develop a view of how they prefer to interact with people and receive information – are they 'numbers people' or do they prefer words? Are they formal or relatively informal?

As an ABM-er, you'll be able to bring insights to the bid team working on the deal that they might not otherwise have access to, such as how are people involved in the buying process consuming content on your website, or on third-party websites? How are they engaging with you and your competitors on social media? How are they responding to outreach such as invitations to your flagship events?

All of this will help you build a communications plan with clear objectives of what you want each person or group to think, feel and do, what to say to them, and how best to engage with them.

Shaping your win themes

With this competitive context in mind, in addition to the deep understanding of the account and key stakeholders you need to engage, you'll be able to help the sales team develop your win themes against the competitors. A messaging hierarchy will be needed, where your overarching proposition for this deal is supported by win themes that differentiate you and underline why you are the best choice for the customer.

In this post-pandemic world, shaken by geopolitical turmoil like that in Ukraine, and by climate issues such as unprecedented flooding and fires in Australia, companies are increasingly looking at the fundamental values of their potential suppliers and how well those values align with their own. For example, Apple has committed to be 100 per cent carbon neutral in its supply chain and products by 2030, working with all of its suppliers to achieve this goal. Infosys is matching the environmental, social and governance (ESG) activities of its top accounts, as outlined in the case study in Chapter 2. Accenture is leading with 360° Value, looking beyond financial performance with its Diamond clients, as we saw in Chapter 1.

ABM-ers have a clear role to play here by understanding these deeply held values, and considering how best to communicate and reflect their own company's values in response. For example, in one recent opportunity, an ABM-er identified the importance of diversity, equality and inclusion (DEI) to the customer and was able to introduce their own DEI leader, recognized for their vision and accomplishments, to the executive responsible for building the customer's DEI program, demonstrating the alignment of values outside the scope of the deal on the table.

Communicating through the bid

A bid process is usually long and structured, moving through several stages including some where competitors are not meant to communicate with the account. Most are run by procurement departments, which are attempting to complete a scoring exercise of potential suppliers against an agreed set of criteria, including price. However, often there may be a favourite potential supplier who is coached to meet the criteria so that they can be awarded the project. This relies on having won the hearts and minds of the wider group of decision-makers – or perhaps the most senior of them – before the judging begins.

Throughout the bid, the ABM-er will be creating assets that communicate the value proposition and win themes across the internal account team (so that everyone is on message) and into the customer. Some of these will be sent directly to stakeholders, such as digital adverts with links to customized videos, websites or landing pages, while others will be provided to the sales or account team to take in, such as personalized invitations to events, or bid presentations.

After each communication activity, the ABM-er should review how effective it was, how well the customer engaged and what should be done differently next time. A sprint-based approach to this ongoing communication is needed, with an agile approach to learning and responding based on feedback from the customer and account team.

Finally, it is really important that, if possible, the bid is not done *to* the customer. In fact, the most successful bids for large opportunities are done *with* the customer, leveraging techniques such as innovation workshops to co-create a solution. Capgemini's 'Accelerated Solutions Environment' (ASE) is perhaps the gold standard here, having been successfully used to drive effective collaboration for almost 20 years with many FTSE 100 and *Fortune* 500 clients (Burgess, 2020: 178–180), as we saw in Chapter 7.

SUMMARY CHECKLIST

1 ABM is about treating an individual account as a market in its own right. As such, it is the perfect marketing strategy to support an account-based growth initiative.

2 Three types of ABM have evolved to cover the tiers of priority accounts that a company might want to engage – strategic ABM, cluster ABM and programmatic ABM.

3 Most companies use a blended strategy of all three types, increasing investment and personalization for each tier of account from the bottom to the top – reflecting the 80/20 rule and its fractal nature.

4 An ABM programme management office or centre of excellence can help define your ABM strategy, offer services that make ABM-ers more effective and efficient, and maintain standards through professional development and performance management.

5 ABM-ers work through the end-to-end marketing process, creating and executing plans for top accounts in alignment with account teams. Close collaboration throughout the process is key to success.

6 In a deal-based marketing context, many aspects of the ABM process become heightened and more focused, such as competitor insight, customer profiling, differentiated value propositions and messaging and campaign orchestration. An agile sprint approach works well through the bid process, as do techniques that involve supplier and customer in co-creation.

09

Customer success

'Customer success' as a term has emerged during the last decade or so primarily in the subscription, software-as-a-service industry. This business model is so dependent on reducing churn and retaining and growing revenues from existing customers that investing in customer success has become an existential necessity.

We have used the term 'customer success' throughout this book to mean going beyond just delivering what you said you would deliver in terms of the contract you have with customers to focus much more on the customer's outcomes – ie are they deriving value from their relationship with you and is it helping drive their success? It is not the same as customer service or service delivery, although clearly customer success without great service and customer experience is just not possible.

Customer success is not yet a term that has been widely adopted outside the software industry, but it is beginning to crop up elsewhere, particularly in other technology firms, as well as in the financial services, communications and media industries. This has profound implications for all customer-facing teams, particularly in account management, sales and marketing.

In this chapter, we first explore the customer success revolution, tracing its origins back to Salesforce, which really pioneered it, explaining why this has happened and spelling out some of the implications. Throughout this chapter, we've drawn on the insights and experience of Nick Mehta, CEO of Gainsight, and his colleagues who have written authoritatively on customer success (Mehta, Steinman and Murphy, 2016; Mehta and Pickens, 2020).

Picking up the constant theme in this book, which is to delineate clearly between different tiers of customers and treat them appropriately, we then look at how this has translated into 'high-touch', 'mid-touch' and 'tech-touch' in the way that companies invest in and support their customers' success.

The Salesforce case study offers us a great insight into how the company delivers different levels of customer success, particularly with its top customers.

We then broaden the discussion beyond software to look at how predominantly services companies need to focus more on customer outcomes. Graham Clark, from Cranfield University School of Management and an expert on service operations strategy and leadership, shares his perspectives.

We finish by looking at the implications for go-to-market overall, including the emergence of new organizational models and job titles.

The customer success revolution

Customer success is a business imperative for any business that depends on keeping its customers – which is every business on the planet. If you only expand by acquiring new customers, not keeping your existing ones, you will eventually run out of customers. But before that, you'll probably have run out of cash.

All businesses have companies that sit within their total addressable market (TAM) and have, over time, become customers. Their TAM might expand as they bring out new products and services, but their customers, particularly that loyal base of the 20 per cent of customers that drive 80 per cent of their revenue have to be retained and have to grow in aggregate. Otherwise, the business will almost certainly fail.

So, although the customer success revolution has become synonymous with subscription or software-as-a-service business models, the need to focus on your customers' success is equally important in pretty much every B2B business model. The underlying business trend that makes this more relevant than ever today is the transfer of power to the customer, driven by our experience as consumers and now firmly established as an unstoppable trend in B2B.

After all, as consumers, we have got used to choice and are not afraid to exercise this choice. We regularly switch between multiple providers, using the information at our fingertips to ditch some suppliers and connect with new ones in real time.

Within minutes we can go from deciding to book a holiday to choosing a destination to switching between a couple of countries depending on availability of accommodation to booking an airline to having the whole thing wrapped up – having made choices about all the essential ingredients and being impatient about which platform we use to make this all come together for us. We are willing to switch from Trip Advisor to Booking.com as we navigate our way through this, or to try an airline we've never flown with before based on recommendations from people we've never met, or to choose not to stay in an AirBnB because the photos aren't up to scratch. Until, having tried one credit card and finding we had to switch that too as we were just over our limit, we arrive triumphant with a customized holiday in a few clicks.

We've become fickle as consumers, and, as we saw in Chapter 7, 71 per cent of B2B companies say they would switch suppliers, so perhaps B2B businesses are becoming increasingly fickle too. Which is a problem if your business follows the 80/20 rule and you're dependent on retaining them.

In subscription software, however, the business model is predicated on recurring revenues, so the effects of churn on the customer base are hugely significant and potentially rapidly terminal, thus it is not surprising that this new way of 'renting' rather than 'buying' software has driven the software industry to embrace customer success. It is a phenomenon that every business can learn from, particularly as whole industries are being transformed by software companies that come to market with a subscription mindset, looking to disrupt the incumbents.

As Nick Mehta stated, when we discussed customer success with him in April 2022, 'Customer success is definitely becoming a company-wide mandate and philosophy, and not just in the subscription software business. Once the penny drops that future success depends on reducing churn and improving net retention rate (NRR), the balance shifts away from celebrating every new logo sale, important though these will continue to be, to celebrating customers who have expanded their adoption, who have gained competitive advantage as a result and who have become advocates. The emergence of the chief customer officer helps shift this balance, sending a signal to the market about what's important, giving status to customer success at least equal to sales and ensuring the internal focus on the organization is as much on customers as it is on products.'

How it all started

Back in 2005, Salesforce had 20,000 customers and a strong growth rate, but a huge problem: churn. Customers who were only renting the software were leaving at an average rate of 8 per cent per month. This was an unsustainable business dynamic, because customer acquisition is an expensive business and in subscription-based services, with no upfront licence fee, you typically do not recover the cost of this acquisition until at least two annual renewals have occurred. If it didn't address this issue, Salesforce was going to go out of business.

For its subscription-based business to flourish, it needed to acquire new customers, but, even more importantly, it needed to retain the customers it had and find ways to grow its revenues with them through upselling. And its response was a pioneering investment in customer success to make sure that customers were really getting value out of their investments and would stick around.

Building loyalty

While much has been written over the past 30 years about customer satisfaction and customer experience, it seems strange to be talking about customer success as something new. But it is the dynamics of the business model in subscription businesses that has transformed the topic from a 'nice-to-have' to an 'existential business imperative'. As we discussed in Chapter 6, often what makes a company change tack is a crisis, and as the Salesforce example has demonstrated, this was a crisis that would have engulfed the whole software industry had it not been addressed. It just happens that Salesforce got there first at scale.

The key here is loyalty. Loyalty is the antidote to churn. It's what keeps the 29 per cent who say they won't switch suppliers. And it comes in multiple forms: habitual, transactional and emotional (sometimes called attitudinal).

Consider the definition from Qualtrics (2022): 'an ongoing positive relationship between a customer and a business. It's what drives repeat purchases and prompts existing customers to choose your company over a competitor offering similar benefits. Loyalty is a result of multiple positive interactions that build up a feeling of trust over time.'

Qualtrics stresses the experience side of loyalty, but also references benefits and trust, concepts that are emphasized throughout this book. The experiences we have with a company, particularly in B2B companies where the experiences are built up over years and decades, are only part of the story, however. The other part of the loyalty equation, and, indeed, the customer success equation, is 'outcomes'. Nick Mehta defines customer success as 'customer experience + customer outcomes' (Mehta and Pickens, 2020: 126). Both are needed to drive loyalty, particularly emotional loyalty, the result of complex interactions between businesses working together and the individuals involved on both sides of the relationship figuring out how they can help each other achieve better outcomes.

In the somewhat frenetic business environment in which most companies are operating, there is another aspect of the customer success equation, which is speed. Great customer outcomes need to be delivered rapidly. The phrase that has been adopted within customer success circles, is 'time to value', ie adding a speed factor to the realization of the outcomes. You need a deliberate, thoughtful approach to be able to deliver rapid time to value, which will not only pervade product design, but also through developing methodologies that can be used with customers, bringing frameworks, templates and processes that add to the speed at which your solution can be implemented.

It may also mean that the attitude you adopt with your customers needs to be clear, pre-sale, on the joint activities that will enable rapid value realization, and that your role in the implementation is one where you go beyond simply your own implementation responsibilities, but intimately involve yourself in the customer's responsibilities, working collaboratively and, if necessary, cajoling customers to stay focused on the tasks at hand.

So, although we've borrowed the phrase 'customer success' from the subscription software industry, it works equally well in the professional services and consulting industries. How much your company can move the needle for your customers depends not only on your product and services portfolio, but also on your commitment to helping your customers achieve their desired outcomes through the innovative use of those products and services.

This trend has had another interesting result. Software companies are moving into providing services that have traditionally been provided by consulting and infrastructure services companies, thus blurring the lines between providers, and making it an imperative that they work collaboratively in an ecosystem that drives maximum value for the customer. You'll note that this idea of orchestrating ecosystems for the benefit of the customer has come up as a common theme throughout the book. If you want a perfect illustration of this, look at the partnership between Salesforce, its global systems integrators and the myriad of other software firms that have grown up to provide additional value around the Salesforce platform.

While orchestrating or participating fully in this ecosystem to achieve great outcomes for the customer is not straightforward, the ultimate prize is loyalty and customers willing to act as advocates. The alternative is to be relegated to a business where switching is common and the business is actually being sewn up elsewhere by those companies that have formed trusted long-term partnerships with their customers.

Customer success insights

Customer success drives revenue through a focus on retention and growth from the installed base. Within a relatively few years, probably five years on average, even rapidly growing software companies will have a larger percentage of their growth dependent on retaining and growing their installed base than they will obtain from new customer acquisition. And as they mature beyond that, the lines will diverge further, with net retention rate one of the critical success factors for the company.

However, a net retention rate of 100 per cent in an individual customer is only standing still, so many growth companies look for net retention rates in excess of 110 per cent, even as high as 130 or 140 per cent, particularly in their early years. In more traditional, older enterprise software companies, maintenance revenues are often as much as two-thirds of a company's revenues, but here, too, license sales are predominantly to the customer's installed base.

The other vital factor in driving an average high net retention rate is to focus on the customers who are, themselves, successful and growing, because they will drive your growth simply through their growth, particularly if you have a joint focus on their success to drive adoption and further innovation with your products and services.

Nick Mehta has written extensively on customer success and has created the 10 laws of customer success, which we have reproduced here, adding our own commentary, in italics, to put them in an account-based growth context.

THE TEN LAWS OF CUSTOMER SUCCESS

1   Customer success is a top-down, company-wide commitment. *While we are in full agreement with this statement, we would go even further. We believe that a full company-wide assessment of future growth, from an account perspective, is required in order to design the appropriate go-to-market structure, including customer success.*

2 Sell to the right customer. *We've spent the whole book arguing that you have to prioritize the accounts within your customer base and decide how to allocate resources to them. We think you need to be clinical in this assessment, because trying to hang on to customers that aren't the right fit for your business model or your capabilities is going to inhibit your ability to focus on the customers that are a perfect fit and to whom you could dedicate more effort and investment.*

3 The natural tendency for customers is towards churn. *There are all kinds of reasons that customer and supplier can 'drift apart' following a transaction, even a successful one with a solid business case: customer priorities change, key people move around, perceptions of value differ and fade. It's important to stay engaged, going above and beyond what the customer expected and find cost-effective ways to do this for smaller customers, so you can invest more people into the most important ones.*

4 Your customers expect you to make them wildly successful. *Expectations are increasing, based in part on our experience as consumers. What customers expect now is that you've invested sufficiently in understanding what success means to them and are willing to roll up your sleeves and partner with them to make them successful, in their terms. In order to do that, you need to understand how they measure success themselves, where they are now and what needs to change for them to be able to achieve their real business objectives.*

5 Relentlessly monitor and manage customer health. *Companies take a variety of approaches to understanding how their customers feel about them. It is a leading indicator and therefore gives you a chance to impact future growth. Too often companies pay lip service to what their customers are telling them and can be the afterthought on a dashboard that frequently focuses far more on lagging indicators like revenue growth, as we said in Chapter 5. But it is as important to customer success as the sales pipeline is to sales. The customer health of the top three per cent or so driving 50 per cent of the business should keep the CEO and the C-suite awake at night. It's that important.*

6 You can no longer build loyalty through personal relationships. *There are really two aspects to this of relevance to an account-based growth strategy. First, in the top customers, increasingly what matters is a trusted relationship between companies, not just individuals. The systematic investment in executives that drive these significant B2B relationships at companies like Accenture, Deloitte, IBM and Salesforce are to create the connections that enable the supplier to deliver all of its assets and capabilities and those from within its partner ecosystem, for the benefit of the customer. Second, there has to be a mixture of technology and cost-effective human interaction for 'the long tail' of customers, appropriate to the returns you expect to get from these smaller customers.*

7 Product must be priority number one. *Product or service providers that are close to their customers spend time with them and have strong feedback loops to literally create products their customers are demanding, and, in an ideal situation, can co-create with them. Customer success teams and executives, such as the chief customer officer, play a critical role in this, tipping the balance for new product or service innovation towards the wishes of the installed base, rather than the relentless pursuit of new customers.*

8 Obsessively improve time to value. *Companies are living in an environment that is changing increasingly rapidly and their ability to respond to new competitive threats and move faster than the environment they're in has put an increasing emphasis on time to value. Many of the impediments to rapid attainment of value may be the customers' responsibility, but techniques, including clear methodologies, carefully selected pilots, etc. can help to overcome this.*

9 Deeply understand the details of churn and retention. *The subscription world is, naturally, obsessed with this, but still some companies do it better than others. We are constantly surprised how few data are really analyzed about individual customers' revenue and profitability, and their use of different products and services, even for the biggest customers.*

10 Customer success teams must become metrics-driven. *Customer success, not just in the subscription software businesses, but in the broader sense we are using the term, is a huge investment for many companies. As customer success morphs from being a function or department to a company-wide philosophy, the way that we measure the 'success of customer success', in combination with investments in account management, sales and marketing, becomes an important task. These investments and metrics have to be looked at in the round, because customer success teams may be taking on responsibilities hitherto performed elsewhere, so there may be headcount and cost transfers to be made.*

Each of these ten laws has a chapter in its own right in *Customer Success* (Mehta and Pickens, 2016), and more recent perspectives on these laws and customer success more generally can be found at www.gainsight.com.

Creating customer success tiers

Companies that implement customer success have their approach to tiering, just as account management and sales have their coverage models and marketers have their account-based marketing tiers. These should be joined up as a company-wide initiative, using real data to prioritize and resource accounts appropriately (see Chapter 3).

In Nick Mehta's view, from our discussions in April 2022, 'Initially, companies have quite a simple definition of their target customers, based largely on size of opportunity, using readily available metrics like revenues or employee numbers and some rules of thumb regarding industry segment. Over time, however, as a company grows, it needs to become more sophisticated in how it defines the tiers within its addressable market, reflecting not just the relative size and attractiveness of account, but also the competitive landscape. In addition, companies start targeting smaller customers with great potential that fit their criteria of an ideal customer profile, so can "over-index" on the customer success approach, to ensure that the stage is set for significant expansion.'

This section describes an approach to tiering in customer success management, based on the experience of Nick Mehta and his Gainsight team (Mehta and Pickens, 2020). They define three tiers within the customer success model.

THREE TIERS OF CUSTOMER SUCCESS

1 High-touch – proactive, strong coordination around a client's success plan and strong collaboration with account management, sales and marketing. This is people-intensive.

2 Mid-touch – trigger driven, just-in-time, based on data, events and risk management. Less people-intensive.

3 Tech-touch – fully automated, personalized customer success based on technology.

The diagram in Figure 9.1 provides more detail.

FIGURE 9.1 Tiers within customer success unpacked

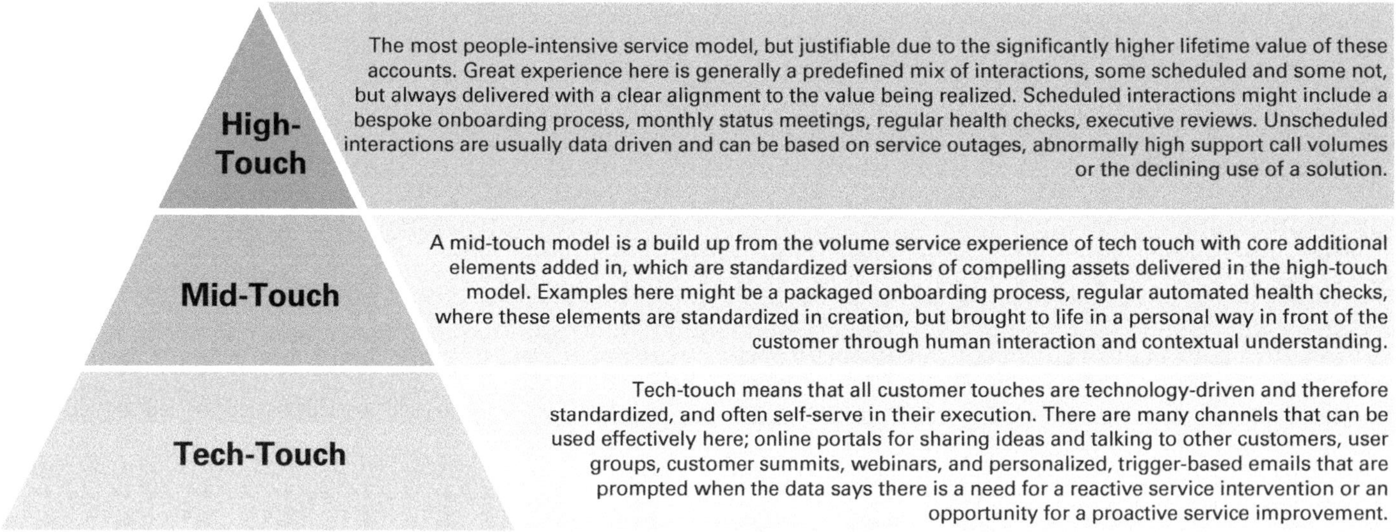

High-Touch

The most people-intensive service model, but justifiable due to the significantly higher lifetime value of these accounts. Great experience here is generally a predefined mix of interactions, some scheduled and some not, but always delivered with a clear alignment to the value being realized. Scheduled interactions might include a bespoke onboarding process, monthly status meetings, regular health checks, executive reviews. Unscheduled interactions are usually data driven and can be based on service outages, abnormally high support call volumes or the declining use of a solution.

Mid-Touch

A mid-touch model is a build up from the volume service experience of tech touch with core additional elements added in, which are standardized versions of compelling assets delivered in the high-touch model. Examples here might be a packaged onboarding process, regular automated health checks, where these elements are standardized in creation, but brought to life in a personal way in front of the customer through human interaction and contextual understanding.

Tech-Touch

Tech-touch means that all customer touches are technology-driven and therefore standardized, and often self-serve in their execution. There are many channels that can be used effectively here; online portals for sharing ideas and talking to other customers, user groups, customer summits, webinars, and personalized, trigger-based emails that are prompted when the data says there is a need for a reactive service intervention or an opportunity for a proactive service improvement.

Once a company reaches a certain level of maturity, applying the 80/20 principle to this means it is likely that no more than three per cent of customers will be provided with high-touch customer success. Perhaps the remaining customers in the top 20 per cent will be provided with mid-touch, and 80 per cent of customers with tech-touch. How this is done will vary at an individual company level, with some companies having a further tier of 'very high-touch' for the most important accounts. The analysis that goes into these decisions is important, because it gives you a model for allocating resources to each tier and, within tiers, to groups of customers.

The way you interact with each tier of customers needs coordinating with marketing in particular to create a communications strategy, cadence and calendar that is appropriate for each. Whichever tier it is, proactivity is required because customers will connect with each other whether you are involved or not, so your ability to orchestrate this and derive benefit from it is important, because customers can act as your best advocates by interacting with others.

Customer success pilots often start in the mid-touch tier, which is often the case in account-based marketing 'cluster' pilots too, so there is immediately an opportunity to synchronize better between teams. High-touch customer success managers usually manage between one and 25 customers, and mid-touch customer success managers start at 25 and can have up to a few hundred customers.

While many companies start with pilots, it is important that these are planned carefully and coordinated across different teams, because multiple pilots around different product sets will be difficult to untangle. Top customers, in particular, deserve to be treated as a customer of the whole company, not as a collection of different products or services they have acquired.

There is really strong practical advice and tips about getting started with customer success in Nick Mehta's book (Mehta and Pickens, 2020), along with examples of what can go wrong. He gave us his own perspective on positioning customer success as part of a broader go-to-market (GTM) transformation: 'Companies introducing customer success almost always invest in it as part of a broader GTM transformation. It is an acknowledgement that the installed base needs more attention and dedicated resources. In bigger companies this usually involves streamlining field sales to focus more on new logos and expansions and moves renewals to a lower cost motion. In higher-growth companies, the focus is more on net retention rate and expansion. Whichever situation you are in, you need to look at these resource investments in the round and make sure everyone is really clear what their role is.'

Some of the key points are summarized in the box below.

GETTING STARTED WITH CUSTOMER SUCCESS

- Start with a clear goal as to what you're trying to achieve, which needs to be driven from the top. A good example is Tableau, which, with its CEO, Chris Bates, built its customer success strategy from 2016 onwards around its customers' technical success, general success and ultimately around keeping its customers for life, hiring over 100 customer success managers over a two-year period. (Mehta and Pickens, 2020)

- Empower a leader for the transformation who has line of sight to the CEO and can drive a company-wide transformation, as well as coordinating the impact on other functions and teams, particularly in account management, sales and marketing. This will need a strong, hopefully agile, programme management approach, which is discussed in Chapter 6.

- Define the data and systems you will need and how you're going to source and build them, as described in Chapter 5.

- Define how you will communicate and manage stakeholders, not just internally but also how you explain the change to clients. Internally, the focus has to be on benefits overall, why the change is happening and personalized to other teams in the business. Nick Mehta's book has some useful talking points for each of these teams (Mehta and Pickens, 2020).

- Define clear and achievable success criteria, particularly leading indicators of future success in financial terms: for example, customer satisfaction, number of referenceable customers or advocates, creation of new upsell leads, etc.

Companies that embrace the concept of customer success after conducting pilots often scale this investment rapidly. Salesforce, which started all this back in 2005, now has 7,000 customer success people supporting its 150,000 customers worldwide. Recruitment of customer success managers has grown very rapidly, with LinkedIn showing there are tens of thousands of customer success manager vacancies worldwide, over 24,000 in the UK alone at the time of writing.

To get inside what the customer success teams at Salesforce actually do, we asked Aaron Tunesi, from the UK and Ireland team, to share his experience, explaining how Salesforce have structured customer success and how it works with its most important customers and partners.

CASE STUDY
Salesforce: Leading the way in delivering customer success

Salesforce is the global leader in customer relationship management (CRM) software. Companies of every size and industry use Salesforce to grow their business by building customer relationships across sales, service, marketing and commerce.

Customer success pioneers

From its very beginnings, the concept of customer success has been an integral part of the Salesforce DNA. The company was incorporated in 1999, led by Marc Benioff, who had previously spent 13 years at Oracle. He was well aware of the challenges of selling on-premises, licensed software, including the high cost to deploy and the low level of customer engagement.

Having been impressed with the emergence of the Amazon business model and its constant online engagement, he pioneered a new business model based on three pillars:

- selling software as-a-service in the cloud;
- using a monthly subscription model;
- building in philanthropy from the outset.

And those three pillars, plus three founding values – trust, customer success and innovation – were the foundation of the company's success, according to Aaron Tunesi, Vice President, Professional Services, UK and Ireland at Salesforce: 'This changed the game completely. Rather than having to buy costly servers, sign long-term software license agreements from companies like SAP or Oracle, hire a legion of IT staff to install it and then pay to upgrade to new versions every few years, businesses could pay a monthly or yearly subscription fee to access the latest software instantly in their internet browser with no more effort than it takes to purchase a book on Amazon. It also meant that after gaining customers you had to earn their trust by delivering customer success every day, as they could easily cancel their subscription.'

Structuring customer success

Salesforce has been in the vanguard of the customer success movement. Its customer success operation encompasses both breadth and depth, which reflects the expanse of the Salesforce customer base, from tactical help at the smaller end through to top-line strategic consulting services for large enterprises.

The first level is called the Standard Success Plan and offers broad support typically done through online self-guided resources. One of the main offerings is

Trailhead, an online learning platform that is gamified and where customers can earn points for participation. Customers can also submit a query online, and it goes to a centralized team for resolution. This support level offers online seminars, events and enablement sessions.

Customers can pay for more extensive support. The next level up is the Premier Success Plan, with targeted guidance and expert coaching sessions. There are 'open-door' sessions, one-to-one phone and online support at any time of the day or year, plus a named customer success manager for cases raised through the customer service portal. Customers are given help with implementation and have access to developer support.

The highest level is called Signature Success Plan, which is proactive and high-touch. It offers a dedicated technical account manager with real-time monitoring and technical health reviews to make sure customers are using the software as effectively as possible and achieving a 360° view of their customers.

Tunesi describes the Signature service as 'a one-to-one partnership where you get a group of people to help you navigate Salesforce, its products and people, and get the most out of it. It's very high-touch, offering a 15-minute response time when a case is raised. In fact, before we get back to you, we will most likely already have worked out who can best help to resolve a particular situation and they have already started work on it.'

These higher levels of service have developed over time as the company increasingly caters for much bigger customers. As he explains, 'We started in the commercial space with small to medium-sized businesses because, with our model, it was straightforward for them to buy a CRM system and start using it. And as they grew, they started asking more and more from us so we have grown and now partner with the biggest enterprises out there.'

Helping customers achieve their outcomes

As Salesforce has grown and matured, it has increasingly become a digital advisor to customers, investing in their success by helping them design a vision for their future and consider the art of the possible. This strategic engagement includes bringing together a team of strategists, researchers and designers, who focus on sparking ideas and opportunities to innovate for these customers, along with others who manage the transformation agenda.

As an example, Tunesi points to the relationship Salesforce has built with a major retail organization. It asked Salesforce to look at the quality of its end-to-end customer experience and how streamlined it was across its different channels, such as in the stores, web and mobile. It also wanted to look at the effectiveness of its loyalty programme and understand how well it was able to see a single, integrated view of each customer across every interaction.

The first step was to do some primary research, engaging with customers and staff to figure out what customers were looking to achieve and the challenges they faced. That was followed by secondary research in the marketplace to see how others were making the seamless transition from online to in-store, as well as discerning some of the major retail trends. 'We then went into the details of what the company currently had and what might be done differently', Tunesi explains. 'We considered the challenge from the initial vision right through to the target operating model.' And, crucially, it had executive sponsorship at a very senior level.

This is why Salesforce is becoming much more industry focused, says Tunesi: 'We engage with the CEOs and boards of many organizations, helping them move from the vision through to the operating model. This is part of the DNA of our organization: we have to speak the customer's language, understand their business and provide the right solution. That's a whole different level of relationship and we are bending our business more and more to achieve that.'

That also means having the right people in place to deal at that level of the business, he acknowledges: 'We are trying to get our staff to think more strategically about what's going on in the industry they are engaged with, discover what the customer needs, propose a solution and drive that either as a one-off solution to a problem or to take them on a transformation journey.'

Collaborating with partners

Projects of this scale, however, are often done in collaboration with external partners, which has to be managed by carefully balancing what each side brings to the job. The big global systems integrators (GSI) understandably tend to do the lion's share of deployment. The Salesforce objective in these partnerships is both strategic and to understand at first-hand how to drive and nurture the innovative and cutting-edge aspects of its technology, getting field experience in implementation and usage and enabling the partner ecosystem to manage outcomes successfully.

As Tunesi explains, 'In reality it is about two consulting businesses working out where the line should be drawn and how they should work together'. For example, for public sector, Salesforce will usually collaborate with three or four GSIs, and the coexistence model is wholly dependent on their capability and capacity.

Even with occasional friction, there is still plenty of this top-level work for everyone, he believes. The constant constraint is finding enough educated professionals to do the work.

Encouraging adoption and advocacy

The company is carrying through its obsession with customer success to the post-implementation stage as well, monitoring current usage in detail, down to daily login numbers and time spent, helping customers optimize their use of Salesforce and accelerate their time to value. As Tunesi points out, it is in the company's interests and the customers' interests for the Salesforce platform to be used as effectively and efficiently as possible.

The challenges of growth

One of the biggest issues currently facing large companies is to get a single view of customers across many complex systems. Salesforce uses its own technology to achieve deep customer insight. The challenge it and other companies face is how to use that insight to ensure customer success is at the heart of everything they do. Salesforce uses this insight to align with its customers on desired business outcomes and to build a path to business value and customer success in this digital-first world.

'It's key that we are true to our vision of being a strategic partner for our customers', explains Tunesi, 'understanding their business, their aspirations, and their customers. Trust is our number one value and is fundamental to our financial success.'

Keeping the customer at the centre of our decision making is critical, he concludes: 'We are 23 years old and continue to grow at pace as we deliver customer success.'

Software companies are getting into consulting

The Salesforce case study illustrates an important point: software companies are getting into high-level consulting projects, alongside partners. For this, they need a clear methodology to help their customers transform, and that's a very different business model with different skills, more typically the domain of professional services firms. The lines are becoming blurred.

Customer success is broader than the software industry

As we have explained, we have adopted the 'customer success' term to mean a more broad focus on customer experience and customer outcomes, whatever business you are in. In predominantly services companies, service delivery is often linked to service-level agreements, which have evolved over time to move from fulfilling the contractual obligations to meeting higher-level objectives that enable customers to achieve their own outcomes. This causal link between what a supplier delivers and what the customer achieves has received increasing focus, with suppliers taking on more risk and customers willing to reward suppliers who deliver more value.

In consulting engagements, the end goal of an engagement is not just to create a blueprint and roadmap of what a customer should do, but to help them see the transformation through. Increasingly this means bringing together a combination of skills from strategic and visionary people who know how to bring about change on a significant scale and who can knit together solutions. They often combine products and services from across an ecosystem to deliver a bespoke solution to a real challenge the customer has, helping that customer achieve better business outcomes. This is all done at speed, integrating with a customer's legacy systems and reducing the time to value.

The challenge for many companies that aspire to this great service delivery, as Aaron Tunesi has commented, is that they do not have the leadership nor the capacity to be able to do it across the board. There are simply not enough people to be able to do this at scale, so choices need to be made as to where to focus. Whoever you are and however many resources you have, you have to focus. A smaller company faces the same challenges in terms of how many customers it can really help achieve their outcomes.

Graham Clark of Cranfield University School of Management shares his own perspectives on this, as he discusses his experience of service operations strategy.

VIEWPOINT

Graham Clark, Visiting Fellow in Service Operations Leadership, Cranfield University School of Management

In your experience, what are the biggest challenges service delivery managers face in making their customers successful?

Fundamentally, I think it is about the difference between outcome and outputs. Traditionally customer service managers have tended to be more focused on the outputs, or those things that the customer pays for. They were not focused on customer *outcomes*, which is essentially what the customer is buying, whether that is specifically spelled out or not.

And that's not surprising. The organization as a whole may pay lip service to customer success, but those doing the bulk of the work can understandably have a quite short-term perspective, because they are probably geared to targets for this month, this quarter, this year. Much of this is about culture: how as an organization do we define success? Some organizations are much better than others at this, particularly when their defined output is closer to what the customer expects as the outcome.

There is also a challenge around scope. As a customer service manager, I am probably managed on the profitability of the contract I am responsible for. This may well include service levels I have to hit, penalties for low performance, and incentives to drive out cost against a reducing price if it is a long-term contract. That doesn't incentivise me naturally to look at how I could expand my scope to help the customer succeed! This would assume that I have spare time/capacity to think beyond the short term.

For that, I probably need investment and access to different kinds of skills, but I may be too focused on what I *have* to do rather than what I *ought* to do. In a busy operational role, that's always going to be an issue, so I really need the organization around me, particularly my executive sponsor, to help me out and get me access to what I need, or put someone alongside me who can work with me as a colleague.

Do you believe that service delivery teams should flex their approach according to the importance of the customer? If so, how?

This is a difficult question and closely related to the first one. How do you know that the one you treat less well doesn't have the potential to be a valuable customer? The reality is that we have to make some judgements, but our judgements are based on our information and experience and we may not have the broader context of the company's best interests.

It's inevitable that some customers are going to offer more long-term revenues and profits than others, so I think the people at the 'sharp end' of the business need to be given the information that enables them to make the right judgements, the right priority calls.

We don't have unlimited resource. This can lead to what I call the coping zone. The coping zone is what happens to quality when we run out of resources. My favourite example is a restaurant where your customers still get fed but no longer get the attentiveness that makes them feel special and keep coming back. It's a leadership tension: you might want to make sure you deliver on what you promised but you have to be realistic about your capacity to do that. It's important to note that we may well have capability but not capacity/resources.

There is a lot of discussion when it comes to customer success about high-tech versus high-touch, where top accounts get more of a white-glove, high-touch experience, whereas others get more self-service online support. What's your take on this?

People are increasingly comfortable with technology and it does offer choice. It depends on the scale of the issue. If it is a relatively simple enquiry, why not use technology? It's easily accessible, and, as a customer, I get the perception of control. But customers need to know someone will be there to help if things go wrong. High-value customers will usually have the option of being channelled to someone dedicated to their accounts.

However, what you should recognize is that a lot of things service providers think is important, their customers take for granted. And vice versa. To me this is the element of empathy: do I as a customer feel that you, my provider, really understand that what might seem trivial to you is actually critical for my business? I think that's the bit where technology might not be smart enough. Again, it depends how tuned we are as a company to the outcomes our customers are trying to achieve.

We need to foster connection, that sense by the customers that they are being heard. And that leads to another interesting tension between compliance in the sense that the provider will do what they say they are going to do, they will follow the process, but customers won't necessarily fit into that process. It's that ability to know when the process is working and when it isn't, which, again, technology won't easily tell us.

How can delivery managers encourage a focus on continuous improvement for the customer?

The question you have to ask is: how do I as the leader get a sense of purpose through to the heart of operations? Continuous improvement is building motivation into service delivery so that, because those people understand how things work, they are in a good place to know how to improve or adapt for the next challenge.

The worst aspect of operations is that it is too often focused on the short term: I have a job to do and I am going to do it, rather than looking at why and how the job is changing. What we should be doing is to build a wider vision of the contribution of service delivery. This is why we now tend to talk about operations strategy rather than operations management.

But can you do this for all your customers?

You have to look at your customer portfolio and decide the appropriate strategy for each segment. Set the strategy for each of these segments, and only once it is explicit can you look for improvements. We can't do everything for everyone, so we make it clear how we will deal with different demands.

And you have to give the service delivery team a sense of their importance in this process. These people relatively low down in the hierarchy have to feel they are empowered to influence outcomes. The danger, otherwise, is that delivery people make judgements based on false assumptions, rather than where the priorities are.

Given the importance of recovering well when things go wrong, how should recovery be handled for top customers?

If you have strong relationships, I would argue that you want your key customer contacts to be part of finding the solution, because you could be talking about a significant part of their business. Why should you as the provider think you can create some kind of solution without bringing in your key customer to the process? You should acknowledge the potential damage to their business and ask for their expertise, so you can co-create the right answer rather than push something out to them. Customers usually have a lot of insight into what they think should be done, and part of resolving an issue successfully is how well we interact and communicate as we're resolving it.

It takes a lot of communication, conversation and coordination. You want to encourage your key customers to be good customers through rewards and encouragement. Not everyone will want that sort of relationship, of course. You have to know when to lower expectations and just try to be as professional as you can.

What are the elements of best practice in delivering long-term customer value?

We have talked a lot about establishing partnerships and relationships over the years, but what does that actually mean? Is it that our customers seem to like us and come back to us? But that is based on a lot of assumptions. Rather than making the assumption that they seem to be happy and are paying the bills, I would like to see more suppliers checking in along the way and understanding what the world looks like to their customers.

Unless there is that sharing of insights and intelligence, we will stay being very good at delivering yesterday's value as opposed to tomorrow's or the day after's. And I would like to see service delivery people play an integral part in that. But, of course, you have to employ the people with the ability to do that.

Do you think that's why we are seeing the rise of customer success teams who can think more broadly than what they are delivering today?

Definitely. There is a fine line here, though. You don't necessarily want to create another department or function, because that can become divisive and build more silos. But to make the service delivery voice be heard and part of the broader strategy has got to be good news. What you want in that role is the type of person who actually *knows* stuff rather than someone who just passes on stuff. Someone who acts as an intelligent conduit, who is flexible and can connect with all kinds of people.

How is this field evolving? Where might it go next?

To me it is all about the emphasis on connection, on how we span the boundaries between us as the supplier and the customer. We have to enable these people to be more effective, because the stronger the relationship, the better the flow of information will be. Most of the research into these boundary spanners emphasizes the need for clarity. But too often there is ambiguity. Yes, we want to provide excellent customer service, but what does that mean? Boundary spanners have to both understand the strategy and be able to influence it. They have to have the systems capacity to support that role as well.

Also, the more we can standardize, the better. The problem is that we don't always reward consistency but instead reward those getting us out of some unique situations through cleverness. We need to reward the sort of innovation that encourages a certain degree of consistency based on our different portfolio of customer segments rather than having 100 per cent of what we do having to be unique.

Graham Clark is the author of *More than Good Enough: Insights into leadership* (independently published, 2020) and *Service Operations Management*, with R. Johnston, M. Shulver and N. Slack, 5th (Pearson, 2021, 5th edn).

Organization and leadership implications

All three major customer-facing functions – account management and sales, marketing, customer success or service delivery – aspire to understand their customers more deeply, use this insight to challenge the customer's status quo and position what they have to offer to help customers achieve better outcomes. The problem is that all these functions can operate to a greater or lesser extent in some ignorance of what the others are doing.

For instance, in many companies marketing doesn't talk much about customer success or service delivery. While multiple customer success teams are busy building success plans for their most important customers, marketers are building ABM plans too; yet our research says that, generally, account plans are the domain of sales. Everyone has their own view of customer tiers and everyone has plans. Just how many plans do you need for a top customer?

The answer is that companies need to get better aligned, so they have a company-wide view of account tiers, the resources allocated to them and plans for how to help them achieve success. However, organizationally, many companies are in flux. The rise of the chief customer officer as a new C-suite entrant is an interesting development, particularly prevalent in enterprise software, but growing in popularity. Similarly, the chief revenue officer has emerged as a more common term, usually but not always owning the entire revenue line, including renewals/installed base, and sometimes but not always including marketing, and sometimes customer success.

There are three interrelated challenges here. The first issue is the scope of a single C-suite executive reporting to the CEO. Increasingly, companies are beginning to bring together sales, marketing and customer success to report into a single executive. For the largest customers, this scope is mirrored at the individual customer level, where, as we've seen elsewhere, service delivery may also report to the client lead, with marketers allocated to the account. In other firms, service delivery will be organized more around capability, not customer.

The second issue is what this role is called. Having 'customer' or 'client' in the role title seems to convey a much clearer sense of purpose towards being interested in the customers and clients themselves and what your company can do for them, rather than 'revenue'. Perhaps over time, the tailwinds are more in favour of 'chief customer officer' rather than 'chief revenue officer' – or whatever the appropriate titles are for a C-suite executive in your particular industry sector.

The third, and perhaps most important issue, is the skills and experience of the leader, and, crucially, the biases and blind spots that this leader has, based on their background. This is a very significant point: ABM has transformed B2B marketing; challenger sales have transformed sales; key account management has transformed the way large customer relationships are managed; customer success has transformed the software industry and beyond; and, as we will see in the next chapter, executive sponsorship and engagement have transformed the way executives spend their time with customers and the impact they can have on long-term customer growth.

There is a great opportunity here to pull together cross-functional teams and use the best practices and skills available from each of the communities in such a way that they learn from each other and do the right thing for the customer over the long term.

SUMMARY CHECKLIST

1 A focus on your customers' success applies across practically every industry, but has become an existential necessity in the software-as-a-service subscription world, which is permeating every industry sector.

2 Customer success can be defined as equalling customer experience plus customer outcomes. We use the term 'customer success' in the broad sense, applying well beyond the software industry, where the term was first used.

3 Customer success has become big business since Salesforce realized over 15 years ago it had to tackle churn and retention. There is now a significant customer success movement underway.

4 There are 10 laws of customer success, all of which have a relevance to pursuing an account-based growth strategy.

5 Customer success needs to be a company-wide commitment, and agreeing the makeup of the tiers that get high-touch, mid-touch and tech-touch customer success should be company-wide too.

6 Companies such as Salesforce have structured their customer success in this way. They reveal just how 'high-touch' they have become in relation to their most important customers, charting a move to a more consulting-led approach, partnering with a broader ecosystem for the benefit of their customers.

7 Outside of the software industry, service operations are going through a transformation too, with much more of a focus on outcomes over outputs. This also demonstrates the need to prioritize which customers get a service beyond contractual promises and highlights the need for high-quality resources, better communications and sharing of information.

8 The chief customer officer is becoming more prevalent and may overtake the equally topical chief revenue officer as a new C-suite entrant. They need to take a holistic, well-informed view of best practices across all the customer-facing teams and integrate this in order to focus on customers' success.

10

Executive sponsorship and engagement

Executive sponsorship and engagement are critical for your most important customers. We heard one of these customers' perspectives in Chapter 1, from Ninian Wilson at Vodafone, who explained that one of the things he expects from his strategic suppliers is that they provide an executive sponsor to meet with his own CEO twice a year and attend quarterly governance meetings, monitoring how well their own company is delivering on its promises and exploring what new innovations could be considered to create further advantage and value.

This chapter explores the critical areas of executive sponsorship, where one of your own executives is allocated to one or more of your customer accounts, and executive engagement, where you orchestrate the various touchpoints with your customer executives across your organization, be they one-on-one meetings, small group events or peer networking and communities.

We start by defining executive sponsorship and broader executive engagement, and the reasons to engage with these senior customers. We explore the concept of executive sponsorship and how it works, and then look at how you can build a deep understanding of the executives you need to engage with – and your own executives, for that matter – before looking at the types of relationship that can emerge between the two.

Finally, we look at the various ways of engaging, from individual briefings and meetings through seminars, innovation workshops and advisory boards to networking events, peer communities and alumni groups.

Some of this chapter draws on the book *Executive Engagement Strategies* by Bev Burgess (2020). Those readers interested in understanding more about any of the topics in this chapter are referred to this book for a comprehensive guide to the topic.

Executive sponsorship

As we heard from Wilson, he expects his strategic suppliers to nominate a single executive to be the sponsor for the relationship between his company and its strategic suppliers. He expects this to be the CEO of the supplier, or a direct report to the CEO. The executive sponsor takes overall responsibility for the relationship, helps the key account manager and account team get the resources and investment they need and acts as an escalation point. This does not preclude other executive relationships being formed; in fact, it will often help facilitate them, particularly between two large, complex, global companies.

We've touched on the role of the executive sponsor in earlier chapters, particularly in taking responsibility for the level of ambition for an account, and ensuring that the integrated account business plan, described in Chapter 4, is a living document and that actions are followed through. As we argued in this earlier chapter, the executive sponsor role is not passive, but rather the executive sponsor needs to be actively engaged, 'in the account team's tent'. The very nature of the type of transformational programmes that strategic suppliers take on is that they are difficult and won't always run smoothly. As we've heard from multiple sources, sometimes relationships are strengthened in adversity, if customers see their suppliers pulling out all the stops to recover a situation and get a programme back on track.

What doesn't work, and can be very damaging, is when fingers start getting pointed and suppliers blame their customers when a project comes off the rails. The executive sponsor has a vital role to play here, taking the heat, possibly having to take a short-term financial hit, and supporting the account team.

As we will see from the case study from Red Hat, putting in place executive sponsors across top accounts is a complex business and needs the sponsorship of the CEO and the enthusiastic support of the whole C-suite. Implemented effectively, alongside appointing the right key account manager, it is one of the most powerful initiatives a company can take to raise its game with its top customers, and one of the secrets in unlocking sustainable, profitable growth. Ignore it at your peril, because some of your competitors are already doing this and some of your strategic customers regard it as mandatory for a fruitful, long-term partnership that maximizes value for both parties. And, as we discussed in Chapter 6, it is one of the actions that can be taken to create a more customer-centric, agile way of working, with all of the benefits this can bring.

Broader executive engagement

This section, leading up to the case study from Red Hat, puts executive engagement in a broader context and summarizes material from *Executive Engagement Strategies* (Burgess, 2020), which contains a much fuller commentary and many additional case studies.

Executive engagement is about building relationships with senior buyers in the organizations with which you want to do business, and with other senior executives whom those buyers trust. It is a long-term business development strategy aimed at creating mutual value for everyone involved.

Simply put, it focuses on having conversations and building relationships with your most senior clients and prospects. At its heart lies a belief that sustainable business success comes from really understanding your customers and collaborating with them to deliver value for both parties.

It enables you to cut through the noise of the market to attract the attention and engage the interest of the executives you want to serve, to secure their permission to meet and talk about their priorities and challenges and to shape their understanding of your organization and the value it can offer. Ultimately, it's about building your future business with the clients you want to work with.

Executive engagement strategies define the people who will be involved on both sides: first, the external clients, prospects and influencers who will be the focus of any engagement strategy, who are typically C-suite officers or their direct reports; second, the people within your own organization who will communicate and build relationships with these executives, usually your own C-suite officers, business leaders, subject matter experts and key account managers. Occasionally, they will include people from your partner organizations, who also bring value to a programme.

Ideally sponsored by a senior executive and orchestrated by marketing teams, executive engagement programmes cover a whole range of communication and interaction types with the executives in question, from digital marketing and online content exchange through live events and peer sharing down into small group activities or individual meetings. Managing an executive's experience through these many interactions, changing things that don't work, recovering quickly when something goes wrong and making sure that everyone who needs to be is fully briefed and debriefed for every conversation is no mean feat. It's the reason that the best companies run sophisticated programmes for executives rather than relying on ad hoc activities.

Why engage executives

In our own experience over the past few years, partly as a result of the increasing sophistication of procurement teams and partly through a heightened concern for corporate governance, executives have increasingly been involved in buying decisions. In most customers where consulting or some form of business change is involved, particularly leveraging technology, a wider group of executives gets involved in the decision-making unit, beyond the traditional IT, finance and procurement domains and into the leaders of business units or other functions.

Engaging with the C-suite is thus no longer optional for many suppliers. There are an increasing number of reasons why this is so critical to growth strategies, including the shift from selling transactional products to integrated solutions, the need to open up new buying centres in a customer organization, the need to develop loyalty and advocates in a more competitive market and the fact that large purchases – particularly in the digital transformation area – are increasingly board-level decisions.

As we heard from Stephanie Winters McConnell of Accenture in Chapter 2, building long-term partnerships with your most important customers relies on trust, especially between the executives in both companies, who want to see an ongoing commitment and investment to creating mutual, sustainable value.

Here are a few other compelling reasons why a structured executive engagement programme is essential:

- Executives have the ability to accelerate sales cycles. If as a supplier you bring them into what you are trying to achieve and show them how it aligns to their overall business strategy, they can very quickly become a key influencer in the sales cycle.

- Executives can find funding to support the initiatives that matter most to their company. They might have access to sources of budget that may not be known by those lower down in the organization and can make a case for investment that supports the strategic ambition and priorities of the leadership team.

- Executives are more likely to engage in co-creation. They will often explore a shared operational model, which may include co-creation of new products, a partnership or larger ecosystem development and even shared risk or shared value models, depending on the work being done. Most executives look to be engaged at a level that will have higher impact than just the immediate engagement on the table.

Which executives you should engage with

An executive is someone who is employed at a senior level, responsible for defining the goals and strategy of the organization and for ensuring that the strategy is executed well and the goals achieved. Typically, executive engagement programmes target the board of directors, executive officers and senior leaders in an organization – all of whom fit this description.

The executive and non-executive directors in a public, private or third-sector organization are appointed to advise the company's leadership on the organization's strategy and the way it is run, representing shareholders and owners and taking action when standards of governance or financial management don't meet regulatory requirements. Non-executive directors may advise multiple organizations, and as such are often treated as a specific peer group with targeted engagement programmes. A specific non-executive role is that of the non-executive chairperson, who takes an active leadership role in chairing the board and guiding the chief executive of the organization (CEO).

The CEO is the head of the company and of its leadership team, often known as the C-suite, so called because it covers all the roles that start with 'chief'. As the highest-level corporate executive, the CEO is the public face of the company, managing relationships with all of its key stakeholders, such as the board of directors and the company's investors, as well as customers, the media, employees and partners.

Typically, the CEO and Chief Finance Officer are members of the board, and other C-suite executives will be in the executive leadership team, which varies between companies but will most likely include the Chief Operating Officer, Chief HR Officer, Chief Legal Counsel, Chief Product Officer and Chief Information Officer, sometimes Chief Marketing Officer. Over recent years, there has been a proliferation of new C-suite roles, depending on the industry, including Chief Digital Officer, together with, as we saw in Chapter 9, Chief Revenue Officer or Chief Customer Officer. This evolving picture can cause confusion (Figure 10.1). We often hear the phrase 'we're targeting the C-suite', but we don't hear often enough 'we're targeting these three C-suite roles, and here's why…'. The key is to understand which roles each of your customers has and decide which of them you want to build a relationship with over the longer term.

Just as the number of roles in the C-suite will vary depending on the type or size of the organization, so will the senior leadership team representing the next level down from the C-suite. These 'heads of' or 'senior vice president'

FIGURE 10.1 A CMO by any other name

SOURCE Reprinted with kind permission from the Marketoonist

roles are filled with a broader range of skills and held by people responsible for planning and executing programmes that bring the C-suite's strategy for the organization to life.

Some organizations include this layer of leadership in their executive engagement programmes, particularly in the largest, most complex companies, where decision making is devolved to business units, while others do not. If they are included, they are often targeted with different activities, so that peer networking is not diluted at the C-suite level.

As with the C-suite roles, the key thing here is to be clear on which roles are important for your future growth with your top customers.

What you need to know about them

Good executive engagement strategies start with a clear understanding of the executives you plan to engage. It's all too easy to focus on your own objectives and believe that these senior buyers and influencers will be as excited about what you have to say as you are. But these are busy people who are targeted by your competitors and other suppliers, who also believe they have interesting and exciting things to say.

What is needed here is a thorough understanding of who you are targeting, their own priorities, perceptions and personality and what would make them interested in spending any of their precious time with you and your company. In existing accounts, this process of building these profiles of key stakeholders will inevitably be much easier. The account teams will know some of them already, or will know someone whom they can ask.

There are three main categories of information that you'll need to collect on the executives in your top accounts: basic profile information, their buyer persona and their psychological profile. More details on what information to collect in each category, and how, is contained in *Executive Engagement Strategies* (Burgess, 2020).

The first is basic profile information. This will tell you the facts about the executive you are targeting, such as their educational background, previous jobs, qualifications, membership of associations and networks, charity and out-of-work interests and influencers they follow. You can find out how long they've been in their current role and perhaps even details about their priority programmes in that role, including measures of success.

While this is the most basic information you'll need to start understanding your customer executives, you may want to look more closely at how and why they buy the type of solutions your company offers. This second type of information is their buyer persona, and is usually gathered through interview-based research. You can find out much more about how to build and use buyer personas for your customer executives through the Buyer Persona Institute, www.buyerpersona.com.

Armed with your personas, you'll be able to make some initial assumptions about the executives you are targeting – matching them to a particular persona – and develop the right content and engagement techniques to interest them. As you get to know them better, you'll be able to move from general personas to specific information about them as individuals, refining your assumptions into specific insights about them and their buying behaviour.

The third type of information you can use to understand your executives is built through psychological profiling. With the proliferation of information we willingly put out onto social media these days, some firms have made it their business to analyze what we say and how we say it to develop an understanding of what drives us and how we like to communicate. While this type of information is expensive, it can be very useful to understand the executives in your top accounts who are making decisions that could lead to multimillion-pound, multiyear relationships for your company.

Sponsorship and sharing the load

Executives like to engage with executives. Peer-to-peer networking is all-important in a business-to-business context, as buyers look to other buyers, industry influencers and subject matter experts to explore trends, discuss common challenges, share lessons learned and get practical advice. In fact, the quickest way to kill any executive engagement strategy is to match executives with people they don't consider peers.

Your own executives and the immediate team below them will therefore play a key role in your programme. In fact, it's worth getting one of them, preferably your CEO, to sponsor the whole initiative, since it's the CEO that many of your target executives will ultimately want to meet.

However, given the demands facing the CEO, the responsibilities of leading the programme should be shared with other C-suite members or C-1 executives. One company we work with asked different members of the executive committee to be the sponsor for different activities within the programme. So, while the CEO is the overall figurehead for the executive engagement programme, chairing the customer advisory board, for example, the COO takes the lead on an annual collaborative research project and customer summit, the CIO runs innovation days and study tours and the CMO takes the lead on a customer awards initiative.

In a similar way, other members of the C-suite or C-1 level in an organization may take responsibility for key customers in different sectors, particularly if they themselves have experience in that sector. So, the Chief Human Resources Officer may look after customers in the retail sector, while the CFO hosts utility customers. Where business unit directors are vertically aligned, this is a natural and easy choice to make. In other situations, it will be a collaborative decision as to where each executive feels most comfortable.

It is critically important that when these executives do meet with their peer executives in the programme, they are well briefed. Whether it's a one-on-one meeting to discuss the relationship between the two companies and where it may go next, or a small group meeting like an advisory council, there should be a short briefing on each target executive involved.

ELEMENTS OF AN EXECUTIVE BRIEFING PACK

1 Their name, role, and company overview.

2 Their photo.

3 Their objectives, challenges and pain points.

4 The status of your relationship with them, including annual revenues, services provided, project status and current opportunities.

5 Possible talking points.

Once the meeting has taken place, each internal executive will need to be debriefed to capture any useful intelligence for the next person to meet with that customer executive. No one, least of all busy executives, wants to tell the same organization the same thing twice, even when meeting with different representatives in different situations.

Debriefing executives can be one of the biggest challenges in executive engagement. A good approach is to work with a personal or executive assistant to understand what their preferred way of sharing feedback post-meeting would be: verbally by phone or in a quick face-to-face meeting or written in an email or straight into a CRM system. Again, more details on this are contained in *Executive Engagement Strategies* (Burgess, 2020).

The role of the account team

On the one hand, the account team (key account manager and account-based marketer in particular) are the people who know the customer best, albeit perhaps not at the executive level. On the other hand, many of the activities in an executive engagement programme will be designated a 'selling-free zone'.

But all engagement activities will likely need the support of the key account managers, sales teams and ABM-er in preparing the briefing papers for their executives. They will also be keen to hear the feedback from the executives following the meetings with customer executives in their account. And, naturally, it will fall to them, alongside the customer success and delivery teams, to follow up with any operational issues uncovered during these meetings.

So, briefing and debriefing activity can be 'contracted' with the account team, making it clear to everyone involved the commitment it demands, the format it will take and the value it will deliver. One company that has set up an executive engagement programme with real clarity on the objectives and resulting expectations of executive sponsors, account directors, customer success leaders and marketers is Red Hat.

CASE STUDY
Red Hat: Orchestrating effective executive engagement

Red Hat is the world leader in providing enterprise open-source solutions, with global reach across more than 175 countries. Founded in 1993 to revolutionize operating systems with its enterprise Linux software, it now offers a broad portfolio of open hybrid cloud technologies that enable customers to develop and manage cloud-native applications, integrate new and existing applications, automate IT processes and create a modern technology infrastructure from on-premises to multiple clouds and edge locations.

In 2019, IBM acquired the company for $34 billion, in what was the largest software acquisition in history. Red Hat continues to operate independently from IBM to deliver the neutrality expected in hybrid cloud.

Starting the journey

Red Hat's formal executive engagement initiative stems from the company's account-based marketing programme, which was developed in 2016, when the marketing team identified that a high percentage of revenue contribution came from a relatively small number of customers. Realizing the need to build even closer relationships with key executives in these accounts and encouraged by senior sales staff to strengthen the company's reach into the top offices, the company set up the executive engagement programme in late 2020.

As Kristin Nordstrom Waitkus, Senior Principal Program Manager at Red Hat, explains, 'In the past, executive engagement had been more ad hoc but now we wanted to develop deeper relationships and establish Red Hat as a trusted advisor with these customers, really delivering value to them by understanding what that meant in their terms. We also wanted to create advocates for our company.'

The timing was apt: this was the middle of the pandemic, and customers needed help from trusted sources as they navigated their way through uncertainty and rapid digital transformation in their businesses.

Executive engagement is now managed from the ABM global programme office and closely aligned with global account teams and the ABM field teams, with Waitkus working in partnership with Mark Arthur, Director of Global Accounts, and an executive sponsor from sales. This has been a critical ingredient in its success, says Kari Price, Senior Director for Global Account Based Marketing at Red Hat. As she recalls, 'What really turned the dial for ABM was showing sales how marketing could provide real value. For example, early on we began to build profiles of key people in the accounts to help sales expand account penetration. That set a benchmark.'

Waitkus agrees: 'With executive engagement, we are building on the success of what we learned from establishing the ABM programme. One of the key factors when we set up our ABM programme was having sales leadership buy-in from the beginning. We applied that same principle to our executive engagement programme. That's also why we were able to launch it in a relatively short period of time. It was a proven approach'.

Making a difference

Another important element has been in the approach to the executive sponsors. The initial session to launch the programme included those Red Hat executives who would be establishing relationships with customers and the global account managers who would be working with them in order to establish the account context, the framework and the objectives. This was about underlining the importance of consistency of approach globally in terms of deepening relationships with accounts, opening new doors, identifying opportunities and being executive advocates for customers.

Says Price, 'From the start, Kristin, Mark and team carefully defined expectations and made the objectives of the executive engagement programme explicit, thereby earning the trust of our executives involved. That has been game changing. Now, if our executives feel they need any help or coaching in their engagements, they don't hesitate to ask for it.'

The executive sponsors oversee between one and three carefully vetted accounts, the majority of which are already existing accounts covered by the ABM programme. There is a stringent process for making sure the accounts are selected for the right reasons and that everyone is on the same page.

According to Arthur, 'the most important thing is to set expectations when we start with the kick-off sessions. We emphasize that this is definitely not a sales acceleration approach, but a long-term, relationship-building activity. It is multiyear, not focused on achieving sales objectives in a single quarter or even year, but creating, building and nurturing strategic relationships and influence.'

This more formal approach to executive sponsorship and engagement has already had an impact. Metrics show that engagement has increased, while more customers are becoming advocates and seeing Red Hat as a trusted advisor. For example, having an executive sponsor turned around what had been a strained relationship with a customer, and has led to a three-year contract renewal and created a company advocate. There is also better alignment across all the executive programmes.

Encouraging consistency

There are a number of ways the company captures information critical for the customer relationship and lifecycle. There is a carefully designed process for briefing and debriefing executives, which includes templates with both general overviews of the account and also particular client issues.

Once in play, executive sponsors meet regularly with the account managers to make sure they have a grip on the account context and activity, while account managers bring valuable feedback and follow-ups back to their teams for action. In addition, there is an executive briefing centre programme, which works closely with the team to bring in other senior people where necessary to deepen the conversation with customers. To support the development of new relationships even further, executive think tanks and roundtables are being used.

The ABM team provides additional support, notes Price: 'Each of the accounts will have an ABM marketer behind the scenes thinking, how can I leverage any learnings or actions within the marketing plan to facilitate the relationship? This really helps to keep the momentum going.'

Knowing the challenges involved in orchestrating the many touchpoints included in an engagement programme of this type, the following was established to improve internal alignment and effectiveness:

- stronger alignment between executive sponsorship and the strategic advisory board, where customer executive leaders and sponsors come together to share information and drive strategy;

- best-practice sessions between executive sponsors and others to discuss insights, successes and challenges;

- a playbook including resources such as best practices, templates, content and offers to support the account managers, executive sponsors and ABM team with their executive engagements;

- the industry pulse: a quarterly, high-level executive snapshot of macrotrends in each industry, built with the help of segment experts to keep Red Hat's executives briefed on the issues facing the customer executives in the top accounts they are sponsoring.

Looking ahead

Over time, the programme will be carefully scaled up and extended and could include more regionally focused engagement and sponsorship. The company is also investigating ways to capture and collate information from executives to highlight any common issues or broader insights across sector boundaries or regions that could feed into the business strategies of their most important customers, delivering the kind of value from the programme that the team envisaged at the outset and creating long-term advocates for Red Hat.

What makes a relationship work

As we all know, chemistry is an important basis to any relationship. The ability to connect or 'click' with someone means the difference between a polite conversation and a really enjoyable meeting. It's the key to getting a second meeting. This applies to business relationships as much as to personal relationships, and so is worth taking into account in an engagement programme.

These connections can come from shared experiences, or people and places in common. They flow from shared interests and values to similar perspectives on the world. They can stem from a natural curiosity about other people, and a general respect for their views and feelings.

Some people are more open to looking for these points of connection than others, and are generally more affable and socially oriented. Others find this hard: we have met several CEOs who really don't like networking situations and abhor making small talk, and we've learned that it's best not to put them in these situations if at all possible. But, in their role, it's not always avoidable. So, it's important to look beyond their roles and job titles and think about how comfortable they will be building relationships with key customer executives.

Executives may be matched with those in buyer organizations based on their similar roles, plus shared experiences, connections or interests – or even their shared personality types, if you've gone to the trouble of a Myers Briggs–type analysis. This is a great place to start and should help decide whom to bring in.

But there will be some people who should be involved even if they don't have a natural ability to build rapport. In cases like these, it's worth looking at ways to help them navigate these social situations. At a basic level, these executives should be well briefed on the person they are going to meet, even giving them suggested talking points that will resonate with the target executive. This is good practice even for more experienced and comfortable relationship builders.

There is also the option of some soft-skills training for building rapport. There are companies that run sessions for senior people, helping them to build better questioning and listening skills, exploring behavioural techniques such as making and keeping eye contact and developing an understanding of the ways that our body language, voice and personal energy can impact others. All of these things are valuable life skills that can be used to build a better relationship with people we meet in both our business and personal lives.

Ways to engage

Broadly speaking, there are three main ways to engage with your top customer executives: individually, as a peer network or community, or in a smaller group. A well-orchestrated executive engagement programme will use all three approaches, and we'll explore some examples of each here, working from the individual through to the network (Figure 10.2).

Engaging individual executives

Business buyers are people who buy from people, especially when they're spending a significant amount of money. So, it makes sense that they need to

FIGURE 10.2 Three ways to engage executives

Individually or *one-on-one* such as through relationship governance meetings, individual briefings and hospitality, social media engagement

In small groups or *one-to few* such as through seminars and webinars, innovation workshops and advisory boards

In networks or *one-to many* such as through collaborative peer research and benchmarking, large scale events and communities such as alumni

trust those people before they'll buy from them. They need some form of relationship in place. The type of relationship they want will vary, from a meeting of equals through a professional consulting relationship, coaching or mentoring to a friendship.

It takes time to build a relationship like this, which is why one of the key risk factors in any business-to-business partnership is a change of staff – on either side. Even at work, people build relationships in the kind of stages their personal relationships go through. People are people.

The most straightforward is a peer-to-peer relationship of equals, where both parties are sharing their challenges and ideas. This can deliver great value to both parties even if it remains strictly professional and within these 'rules'. This is often the style of relationship most applicable where you have two companies in a reciprocal relationship, such as a bank providing financing and even personal wealth advice for partners in a professional service firm, who in turn are providing advisory services to the bank. When the CEOs of both companies meet to discuss how their relationship and contracts are progressing, or the executive sponsor for a customer meets with executives as part of a quarterly governance programme, it is likely to be a meeting of equals, as described by Wilson in Chapter 1.

ILLUSTRATIVE AGENDA FOR EXECUTIVE GOVERNANCE REVIEWS

Each organization will have its preferred way of running these meetings, but a good guideline of the topics to cover includes the following:

- a review of the performance of the products, services and solutions against service level agreements or contract over the previous year;

- a summary of the value delivered in terms of the business outcomes agreed at the start of the contract, such as cost savings, increased productivity, faster time to market and overall return on investment;

- in the case of reciprocal relationships, such as where a telecoms operator is buying technology solutions from an IT outsourcer, who in turn uses the communications services of the operator, a review of the 'balance of trade' between the two;

- in the case where the two organizations also go to market together, selling technology and communications solutions to other businesses, for example, a review of the business performance of the joint venture or offering;

- observations on the customer organization and suggestions for immediate improvements and near-term innovations, supported by case study examples from other companies or ROI calculators;
- observations on the market in which the organization operates and its wider environment, together with thought leadership ideas on how to take advantage of the opportunities revealed and minimize the threats arising.

Ideally a natural next step from this conversation will be a more detailed innovation or design-thinking workshop to explore the ideas further and identify potential proof-of-concept projects and the like.

There are other types of relationships that reflect a deeper engagement, such as the trusted advisor. An advisory relationship is one where the supplier executive is providing a consultancy-style service to the customer executive. There are no social meetings outside organized hospitality, and yet the customer executive will contact the supplier for advice whenever they encounter a problem.

One step on from this is the coach, or mentor. This takes the relationship on from advising the firm and the individual executive on their role within it to providing much more support for the customer executive's personal development and career. This can be an enduring way to maintain relationships with executives as they move from company to company, but the balance between advising on what's right for the individual and what's right for the company can be a tricky one to maintain in this scenario.

Of course, nowadays much of the one-on-one engagement will be online, not offline in face-to-face meetings (especially with millennial executives). Social media platforms are by far the most common means of online engagement on a one-to-one basis. The first step is to identify which platforms your customer executive is using. That's where to meet them. Predominantly today, in the West at least, it will be LinkedIn, Twitter, Instagram and, to a lesser extent, Facebook.

The next step is to understand what interests them and what they post about. This will tell you where to focus your own engagement efforts. Liking these posts and comments, sharing them, writing your own posts and sharing content they have missed is a great way to start and maintain a relationship with them online.

And don't underestimate the power of influencers. Influencers can be an important part of an executive's network, and even of their decision making. The kinds of influencers that senior buyers of complex business solutions listen to include management consultants, industry analysts, sourcing advisors, trade and professional association staff and the media. As such, while analyst or media events may be a useful way to get them together for briefings on your company's strategy and offerings, the best way to engage them is as individuals.

One company that has spent time matching its own executives to those in its top accounts, with the goal of building deep, long-term and mutually beneficial relationships, is Virgin Media O2. Mark Larwood, who leads the executive engagement and ABM programmes there, provides his perspectives on how to effectively facilitate engagement that delivers value for everyone involved.

VIEWPOINT

Mark Larwood, Head of Strategic Customer Marketing, Virgin Media O2

What is your experience in running executive sponsorship and engagement programmes?

I have been involved in and around executive engagement programmes and account-based marketing (ABM) for over 12 years, focusing on that intersect between ABM, key account activity and executive programmes. When I joined what is now Virgin Media O2 at the beginning of 2019, it was with a real desire to bring all those elements closer together, because they are mutually reinforcing.

Our ABM programme now incorporates an important emphasis on executive engagement, with multiple senior people in the business building relationships with those at the same level in customer companies, plus typically a further two or three internal executives aligned to their appropriate customer counterparts in functions such as human resources or finance. And this has obviously expanded since the merger of O2 with Virgin Media in June 2021.

How important is it, in your view, to have executive sponsors for your top accounts?

It's critical because it demonstrates a level of commitment from us and also from the customer and builds what can be a truly strategic rather than transactional relationship. It opens up lines of communication that can remove roadblocks that may at times be more perceived than real.

We tend to take the same approach as with ABM and run a tiered programme, so one-to-one, one-to-few and so on. At the top tier are the customer advisory boards, which meet quarterly and are made up of senior executives. We are constantly reviewing how we take learnings from those boards back into the business and we use them to help decision making.

The next level down is the customer innovation community. We set this up because we wanted to go deeper but also wider into those customers represented on the advisory boards. It's predominantly event driven, and the aim is to reach hundreds of people across our most important customers so we can network but also give them something back in terms of value, such as having external speakers or sharing relevant research. We have had a really good uptake from customers with this.

What was the impact of the pandemic on the programme?

When March 2020 and lockdown came along, everybody was in the same place. How do we manage this? How do we enable employees to do their work while making sure they stay safe? We had done some research towards the end of 2019 into the value of digitization and flexible working and its potential boost to the UK economy. Six months later, we got to test that out for real. There was a positive feeling that the conversations we were having on the advisory board were making a big difference, because we were all trying to deal with the same challenges.

This had to be done virtually, which meant meetings were easier to organize because they didn't involve travel. The flip side of that was you miss out on the side conversations because you are all on the same two-dimensional screen. But as a business, we have been using this technology for some time, so we have learned how to manage it.

Where do you think executive sponsors have the most impact when it comes to growing value with your key accounts?

It has to be very bespoke and depends on what needs to happen with a particular account. A peer-to-peer executive relationship works because it's about showing commitment and it opens doors. The higher up you are in an organization, the more you take a strategic view across the business, so you can join the dots. Conversations can be more candid as well. However, there is a right and wrong way to use these relationships. You cannot go to your senior executive every time there is some sort of problem. This has to be carefully managed.

What's the best way to match executive sponsors to accounts?

We try to identify where we think the best links lie. For example, if we have a chief financial officer with a retail background and we want to get to know a chief technology officer in one of our top retail accounts, we might consider that the common retailing experience is better than looking for a functional match. Or someone might know someone already. It's about understanding that dynamic and fit.

What activities work best to drive executive-to-executive conversations and relationships and how do you manage them?

That depends. There has to be a programmatic element to it to make sure our executives are talking on a quarterly basis. And we work with the account teams so they are fully briefed ahead of time. But relationships also develop, so connections don't have to be as formal. Also, over time they can blossom into friendships.

We have quarterly account reviews where we get multiple stakeholders together to review where we are with an account. A senior executive would typically be involved, along with the account and service teams. Bringing that insight into one place so that everyone understands what is going on is the holy grail. We have really strong relationships now and good evidence that what we are doing works. And, of course, having senior buy-in is crucial.

What do you think are the main challenges in orchestrating successful executive sponsorship and engagement?

You have to be very clear about what you are trying to achieve, with a central guiding principle. For us it was all about reciprocity – building long-term value for our most important customers beyond the services we deliver and, of course, building value for Virgin Media O2.

As more companies seek to build trusted relationships with customer executives, how will those executives choose whom to invest their time with? What will make the difference?

Everybody is time poor. And when so many organizations are doing the same thing, you have to keep raising the bar to continue to beat the competition. To get through to senior executives, you have to be delivering value and give them the critical information and insights that help them run their business – at every touchpoint.

Engaging executives in small groups

Executives tend to prefer small group settings. This is hardly surprising. They get to dig deeper into their issues, ask more questions and participate in hands-on activities to bring them to life and map out a route to solving them. They work side by side with their peers and your experts, with everyone benefiting.

SEMINARS

In-person business seminars are not only valued by customer executives but are perhaps one of the most cost-effective, easy-to-run ways to foster engagement. Webinars are equally well used, particularly since the pandemic, but need interactivity built in if they are to be engaging for busy customer executives with short attention spans. Most people use a combination of both to reach a wider audience, depending on their experience with that audience. Whether you are running a face-to-face or an online version, content and speakers are key for your event to be successful.

INNOVATION WORKSHOPS

The second most likely small group event for executives to participate in are innovation workshops. Suppliers are increasingly developing purpose-built innovation or briefing centres, with staff recruited to ensure their smooth running and deliver memorable experiences to the executives who visit.

Most suppliers put problem solving at the heart of the content they share during a visit, with collaborative exercises run to solve the most challenging opportunities and issues facing the executives attending. Often this will leverage research completed in advance, such as benchmarking research that highlights where the client company could focus its innovation to improve operations or build future revenue streams.

The degree of interactivity in these sessions is key. This is about collaborative problem solving after all, and techniques such as design thinking are commonly used to define a context, explore alternative ideas, develop ideas and prototypes and agree action plans that strengthen the collaboration and partnership between the two companies.

ADVISORY BOARDS

Another powerful way of engaging your target executives is through advisory boards and councils. These are strictly non-selling environments where executives can share their own views on the trends, issues and opportunities facing them, while providing you with a greater understanding of the challenges plus suggestions and feedback for your own strategy.

Many B2B organizations today have an advisory board. So, how do you make yours stand out as the one your customer executive wants to spend their precious time serving on? Companies like Microsoft are raising the game, making sure their award-winning Services Executive Board is well planned and facilitated, led by the interests of the customers themselves and delivered through immersive experiences in locations that customer executives would not normally visit.

Engaging networks of executives

Peer networks are powerful. Executives trust their peers to tell them the truth about suppliers and their solutions, and to share ideas, challenges and lessons learned in a way that they simply won't do with those they don't consider to be peers

But the way that people define and access their peer networks is changing, particularly as the pandemic has rewritten the rules of engagement. Traditionally, executives have built their networks over time and through face-to-face meetings and events – in other words, by spending time together. They may have been to the same college or university, started off in the same company or belonged to the same professional or trade association. And gradually, over time, their network has continued to expand as they meet new peers through their career. For these executives, the face-to-face exchange of information remains important, although some – the digital migrants – also engage with their peers online through social networks.

The new executives in the workforce, the millennials, are digital natives who build their peer networks online as much as offline, and rely on social media to keep themselves up to date on issues and trends that may affect them. As the way that peer networks operate continues to change, there are different techniques to use to reach and engage with your target networks, either separately or in combination: collaborating through research, running engaging events, building new communities and working with alumni.

We list below some of the key ways to engage executives in larger groups of networks.

COLLABORATIVE RESEARCH

Executives want to keep up with trends, share challenges and learn from each other, which means that research, both in terms of the process and the data generated, is a powerful tool for engaging with them. In addition to providing invaluable insights into your target executives that will advise both your own strategy and solutions development, this kind of research delivers great value to the executives involved. With this kind of research, your insights are evidence based rather than simply being points of view, and this evidence can help your target executives shape their own strategy and operations. It will help you start conversations and build relationships.

LARGE-SCALE EVENTS

The large events and conferences that suppliers attend or put on for executives are now high-quality experiences, with personalized agendas and white-glove treatment for the most important clients or prospects. Some are events within events, as smaller groups of executives are streamed into boardrooms around the main event to discuss priority issues for them. The approach taken depends on the type of event and who is running it.

BUILDING NEW COMMUNITIES

The creation of a community of peers goes one step beyond the running of a single event. One of the best examples of this is the community created by the World Economic Forum (WEF), originally the European Management Forum, formed by Klaus Schwab in 1971. Known predominantly for its annual four-day event in Davos, Switzerland, where world leaders come together to discuss some of the most pressing issues facing business and society, the forum maintains its sense of a community of peers throughout the rest of the year with an online collaboration platform, research projects, a young-leaders forum and several other topic-specific and geographically focused events around the world.

Many leading companies are now adopting a similar approach to WEF in order to build a community of peers across their most important accounts. Creating a successful community usually relies on identifying what members have in common and allowing them to share perspectives on that while delivering insights and experiences that they value.

WORKING WITH ALUMNI

Professional service firms – law, accountancy, consultancy – invest a lot in training their people. In fact, their people really are their greatest assets, since they have no tangible product or capital investment to base their offers on. These firms have worked out that when someone they have trained wants to leave them and move to another firm or another industry, this is an opportunity to build future value for both parties. Mostly, leavers will go on to develop their careers in organizations that could buy the firm's services. Or they may go into companies that could work as partners with the firm. Clearly, they may also join a competitor – but they may come back!

To maintain communication with the leavers and keep the firm front of mind for potential services, most run an alumni programme similar to academic institutions. For the alumni, there is a huge benefit in keeping up to date with the latest professional or industry news, as well as keeping their network of contacts fresh. Future jobs may be offered and secured through such a network. For the firm, it's a very real source of opportunity, with direct requests for support coming from the alumni group as well as referrals to members of their own wider networks.

Deal sponsorship

There used to be a saying in the technology industry that when a large outsourcing deal was at stake, the skies would darken with IBM executives flying in to help close it. While this may be a slight exaggeration, it's certainly true that executive sponsorship on a deal can help to get it over the line, particularly where that executive has an existing relationship with the executives in a top customer account.

There are three reasons for this: they can connect in a different way to the sales team; they bring the broadest view of what your company can do to help the customer and they help to give the deal the profile and priority it deserves inside their own company.

Connecting in a different way

As we've said in this chapter already, only executives can connect to other executives as peers. They can relate to each other's challenges in running a large, complex organization. Your own executives will be able to talk about the pressures the customer executives are facing in meeting market expectations and shareholder expectations, and will understand how the solution you are offering will meet their needs at a strategic level, improving return on capital employed and increasing the overall value of their company, for example.

Bringing a broad view of your capability

In a large business with a broad portfolio of products, services and solutions, it is hard for any salesperson or account manager to stay abreast of the full capability of the organization and how it can be brought to bear for the benefit of the customer. Often it is only at the top of the company that people have this view, and so your executives can make the connections that will bring the best of your company to the customer, and be able to articulate the total value for the account.

Making the deal a priority

In an industry where bidding for an opportunity with a customer can cost more than a million pounds, the stakes are high. Qualifying in those deals you want to bid for is a critical process, and one that has the highest levels of executive visibility. Once an executive has qualified a deal in, they will want to see the best people from across the organization working on it to maximize the chances of winning. Some of these deals can take over a year to close, and so maintaining the momentum behind the bid and keeping the best team focused on winning, rather than being pulled off to work on other priorities, can be a challenge. An executive sponsor who maintains the profile and priority of the deal, fighting for the resources needed to win, can mean the difference between winning and losing.

Of course there is one more reason executive sponsors can be useful in bid situations in your top accounts – they may be excellent salespeople who can help to close the deal!

SUMMARY CHECKLIST

1 Typically, executive engagement programmes target the board of directors, executive officers and senior leaders in an organization.

2 You need a thorough understanding of who you are targeting, their own priorities, perceptions and personality, and what would make them interested in spending any of their precious time with you and your company.

3 Executives like to engage with executives. Peer-to-peer networking is all-important in a business-to-business context, as buyers look to other buyers, industry influencers and subject matter experts to explore trends, discuss common challenges, share lessons learned and get practical advice.

4   Briefing and debriefing meetings between executives should be 'contracted' with the account management and sales community, making it clear to everyone involved the commitment it demands, the format it will take and the value it will deliver.

5   Match your own executives with customer executives based on their similar roles plus shared experiences, connections or interests – or even their shared personality types.

6   Executives like to talk about a range of things, but typically these boil down to the issues and opportunities facing them and their organization – in its internal operations, immediate environment or the wider world.

7   Orchestrate the three main ways to engage with your top customer executives: individually, as a peer network or community, or in a smaller group.

8   In a deal situation, your executives can connect powerfully with the customer executives, bring a broad view of what your company can do to help their organization and help to secure the ongoing bid the priority and resources it deserves internally. They may even close the deal!

PART FOUR

Account-based Growth assessment tool

11

How does your company stack up?

We have created a way for you to assess your own company's approach to account-based growth, building on the research we have done and the viewpoints and case studies representing best practice included in this book.

We've kept this as simple as possible, while still giving you enough breadth and depth to use it as the beginnings of a diagnostic for your company. The assessment starts with your understanding of how the fractal nature of the 80/20 rule applies to your company, and works through the internal alignment foundations and the external engagement pillars of the account-based growth framework, illustrated in figure 11.1.

We hope that this tool gives you an easy way to assess the areas that need most attention across your business, something that will help you scope a change programme, using the approach we outlined in Chapter 6. If you would like to understand how your company stacks up against others, contact us at hello@inflexiongroup.com and we will give you access to an online survey, subsequently providing you with a radar graph that compares your results with others in our database.

FIGURE 11.1 A framework for account-based growth

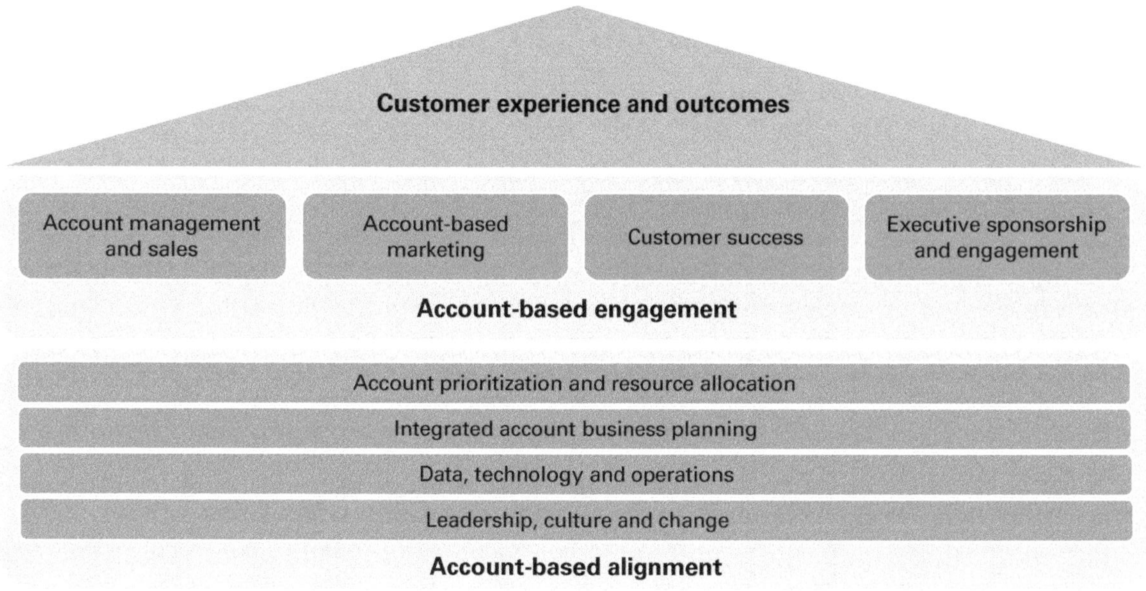

Customer experience and outcomes
Account management and sales
Account-based marketing
Customer success
Executive sponsorship and engagement
Account-based engagement
Account prioritization and resource allocation
Integrated account business planning
Data, technology and operations
Leadership, culture and change
Account-based alignment

SOURCE

Assessment tool

Assessing your own company's account-based growth strategy	Yes, strongly agree	Yes, agree	No, disagree	No, strongly disagree
A 80/20 rule in your company				
1. Do you know what percentage of customers account for 50 per cent and 80 per cent of your revenues?	☐	☐	☐	☐
2. Do you know what percentage of customers account for 50 per cent and 80 per cent of your net profits?	☐	☐	☐	☐
3. Do you analyze the revenue growth rates in your top customers?	☐	☐	☐	☐
4. Have you analyzed the churn in your top customers over the last three years?	☐	☐	☐	☐
5. Do you have a top account programme with at least two tiers, representing the different significance of these accounts?	☐	☐	☐	☐
B Account prioritization and resource allocation				
1. Do you have agreed criteria to prioritize accounts based on their market attractiveness and your competitive business position?	☐	☐	☐	☐
2. Are sales, marketing and customer success all involved in selecting your top accounts?	☐	☐	☐	☐
3. Do you have a formal process and criteria for promoting and relegating accounts between tiers?	☐	☐	☐	☐
4. Do you have an agreed way to prioritize and target future top customers?	☐	☐	☐	☐
5. Are your resources and costs allocated in proportion to the current and future profitable revenue for each tier?	☐	☐	☐	☐
C Integrated account business planning				
1. Are the account plans for your top tier of customers structured like any other business plan (eg for a market, industry or country)?	☐	☐	☐	☐

(continued)

(Continued)

Assessing your own company's account-based growth strategy	Yes, strongly agree	Yes, agree	No, disagree	No, strongly disagree
2. Are these plans anchored in a deep understanding of the customer's business issues	☐	☐	☐	☐
3. Do the plans leverage all your company's capabilities for the benefit of your customers?	☐	☐	☐	☐
4. Are you confident these plans will support your growth ambitions to take share of wallet beyond the current financial year?	☐	☐	☐	☐
5. Are plans reviewed frequently to ensure progress against actions and delivery of outcomes?	☐	☐	☐	☐
D Data, technology and operations				
1. Do your sales, marketing and customer success teams have a single view of data for your top accounts?	☐	☐	☐	☐
2. Are these data used to make better decisions about the account across sales, marketing, and customer success?	☐	☐	☐	☐
3. Is the technology stack integrated across account management, sales, marketing and customer success?	☐	☐	☐	☐
4. Is there an integrated operations team supporting the whole revenue lifecycle?	☐	☐	☐	☐
5. Have you implemented a customer health dashboard that measures key leading indicators alongside financial measures?	☐	☐	☐	☐
E Leadership, culture and change				
1. Are key account managers represented at the top of your company's governance?	☐	☐	☐	☐
2. Have you implemented agile ways of working to focus on creating customer value at speed?	☐	☐	☐	☐
3. Does your company culture and structure help with achieving sustainable, profitable growth in top accounts?	☐	☐	☐	☐

(continued)

(Continued)

Assessing your own company's account-based growth strategy	Yes, strongly agree	Yes, agree	No, disagree	No, strongly disagree
4. Is your reward, recognition and incentive system aligned with achieving sustainable, profitable growth in top accounts?	☐	☐	☐	☐
5. Do you have a change programme in place to drive a greater company-wide focus on your top customers?	☐	☐	☐	☐
F Account management and sales				
1. Have you assigned the best, experienced people to your top accounts?	☐	☐	☐	☐
2. Are your key account managers regularly bringing ideas to drive competitive advantage for your top customers?	☐	☐	☐	☐
3. Are 50 per cent of the deals with your top customers sole sourced?	☐	☐	☐	☐
4. Are you pursuing a broader, values-based approach to your top customers, incorporating environmental and societal issues?	☐	☐	☐	☐
5. Have you ring-fenced sales resources to pursue future top customers, with appropriate incentives plans?	☐	☐	☐	☐
G Account-based marketing				
1. Have you adopted an account-based marketing strategy, treating your most important customers as individual markets?	☐	☐	☐	☐
2. Do your most important customers have dedicated ABM-ers embedded in the account team?	☐	☐	☐	☐
3. Do your ABM-ers build insight into your top accounts and the individual buyers and influencers within them?	☐	☐	☐	☐
4. Do your ABM-ers deliver personalized messaging and content for top accounts through the customer's lifecycle?	☐	☐	☐	☐

(continued)

(Continued)

Assessing your own company's account-based growth strategy	Yes, strongly agree	Yes, agree	No, disagree	No, strongly disagree
5. Do you enhance the chances of winning your largest deals through deal-based marketing?	☐	☐	☐	☐
H Customer success				
1. Do you have a company-wide approach to customer success?	☐	☐	☐	☐
2. Do you delineate between high-touch, mid-touch and tech-touch tiers?	☐	☐	☐	☐
3. Are customer success managers in place for your most important customers, integrated into the overall account team?	☐	☐	☐	☐
4. Have you established the methodology and the mindset to ensure the success of your customers?	☐	☐	☐	☐
5. Are the customer success teams part of an integrated organization, led by a single chief customer or chief revenue officer?	☐	☐	☐	☐
I Executive sponsorship and engagement				
1. Have executive sponsors at CEO and C-suite level been assigned to your most important customers?	☐	☐	☐	☐
2. Does your executive sponsor call on customer executives at least quarterly?	☐	☐	☐	☐
3. Does the account team use the executive sponsor to help achieve your ambition in the account?	☐	☐	☐	☐
4. Have you identified and profiled the key executive contacts you want to engage across your top customer and prospect accounts?	☐	☐	☐	☐
5. Do you orchestrate executive engagement across individual meetings, small group events and peer networking or communities?	☐	☐	☐	☐

REFERENCES

Accenture (2021) Annual report

Accenture (2022) Accenture Investor and Analyst Conference, 7 April https:// investor.accenture.com/news-and-events/events-calendar/2022/04-07-2022 (archived at https://perma.cc/EQ69-9QUV)

Adamson, B, Dixon, M, Spenner, P and Toman, N (2015) *The Challenger Customer: Selling to the hidden influencer who can multiply your results*, Portfolio, New York

Adlard, C and Bausor, D (2020) *The Customer Catalyst: How to drive sustainable business growth in the customer economy*, Wiley, Chichester

Anwar, M (2022) [accessed 2 May 2022] How to embrace revenue operations, *The Pedowitz Group* [Blog] [Online] https://www.pedowitzgroup.com/embrace-revenue-operations/ (archived at https://perma.cc/P9K3-ZXS8)

Blissfully (2020) [accessed 2 May 2022] 2020 annual SaaS trends [Online] https:// www.blissfully.com/saas-trends/2020-annual-report/ (archived at https://perma. cc/K6XQ-78M6)

Broadcom (2021) Form 10-K, Annual report [Online] www.investors.broadcom.com

Burgess, B (2020) *Executive Engagement Strategies: How to have conversations and develop relationships that build B2B business*, Kogan Page, London

Burgess, B with Munn, D (2021) *A Practitioner's Guide to Account-Based Marketing: Accelerating growth in strategic accounts*, 2nd edn, Kogan Page, London

Chappuis, B, Cruz, G, Ellencweig, B, Valdivieso, M and Viertler, M (2020) [accessed 2 May 2022] The domino effect: How sales leaders are reinventing go-to-market in the next normal [Online] https://www.mckinsey.com/ business-functions/marketing-and-sales/our-insights/the-domino-effect-how-sales-leaders-are-reinventing-go-to-market-in-the-next-normal (archived at https://perma.cc/LKC8-8T5Z)

Chung, V, Dietz, M, Rab, I and Townsend, Z (2020) [accessed 1 May 2022] Ecosystem 2.0: Climbing to the next level [Online] https://www.mckinsey. com/business-functions/mckinsey-digital/our-insights/ecosystem-2-point-0-climbing-to-the-next-level (archived at https://perma.cc/Z7QD-Y8KX)

DeFeo, J A (2019) [accessed 1 May 2022] What is total quality management? [Online] https://www.juran.com/blog/what-is-total-quality-management/ (archived at https://perma.cc/3KG4-U663)

Dixon, M and Adamson, B (2011) *The Challenger Sale: Taking control of the customer conversation*, Portfolio, New York

Doerr, J (2018) *Measure What Matters*, Penguin Random House, New York

Forrester (2019) [accessed 5 June 2022] Introducing the Sirius7™: Seven elements to align in your revenue engine [Blog] [Online] https://www.forrester.com/blogs/how-to-align-revenue-engine/?ref_search=0_1654430156661 (archived at https://perma.cc/W8FU-GCFR)

Forrester (2022) [accessed 2 May 2022] The Forrester new wave: Account-based marketing platforms, Q1 2022 [Online] https://www.forrester.com/report/the-forrester-new-wave-tm-account-based-marketing-platforms-q1-2022/RES176331 (archived at https://perma.cc/YJ59-XGFH)

G2 (2022) Enterprise grid report for customer success

Gartner (2020) [accessed 1 May 2022] 5 ways the future of B2B buying will rewrite the rules of effective selling [Online] https://www.gartner.com/en/documents/3988440 (archived at https://perma.cc/V7SF-JHJW)

Gartner (2022a) [accessed 5 June 2022] Gartner predicts 75% of the highest growth companies in the world will deploy a RevOps model by 2025 [Press release] [Online] https://www.gartner.com/en/newsroom/press-releases/2021-05-17-gartner-predicts-75--of-the-highest-growth-companies- (archived at https://perma.cc/PBW9-L3W8)

Gartner (2022b) [accessed 1 May 2022] Magic quadrant for account-based marketing platforms (2022) [Online] https://www.gartner.com/en/documents/4009983 (archived at https://perma.cc/G3AD-GM92)

Harrison, L, Lun Plotkin, C, Reis, S and Stanley, J (2021) [accessed 1 May 2022] B2B sales: Omnichannel everywhere, every time [Online] https://www.mckinsey.com/business-functions/marketing-and-sales/our-insights/b2b-sales-omnichannel-everywhere-every-time (archived at https://perma.cc/FFA4-C6DT)

Hayward, S (2016) *Connected Leadership: How to build a more agile, customer-driven business*, Pearson, London

Hayward, S (2018) *The Agile Leader: How to create an agile business in the digital age*, Kogan Page, London

Inflexion Group (2022) Unlocking account-based growth [Online survey]

Juran, J (1951) *Quality-Control Handbook*, McGraw-Hill, New York

Koch, R (2017) *The 80/20 Principle: The secret to achieving more with less*, 3rd edn, Currency, New York

Marcos, J, Davies, M, Guesalaga, R and Holt, S (2018) *Implementing Key Account Management: Designing customer-centric processes for mutual growth*, Kogan Page, London

MacDonald, M and Oliver, G (2019) *On Value Propositions*, Kogan Page, London

McDonald, M with Rogers, B (2017) *Malcolm McDonald on Key Account Management*, Kogan Page, London

McDonald, M (2022) [accessed 2 May 2022] Why many companies get key account management hopelessly wrong [Blog] [Online] https://blog.som.cranfield.ac.uk/execdev/why-many-companies-get-key-account-management-hopelessly-wrong (archived at https://perma.cc/M76N-P4Z7)

Mehta, N and Pickens, A (2020) *The Customer Success Economy: Why every aspect of your business model needs a paradigm shift*, Wiley, Chichester

Mehta, N, Steinman, D and Murphy, L (2016) *Customer Success: How innovative companies are reducing churn and growing recurring revenue*, Wiley, Chichester

Microsoft (2022) Annual report

Palmer, M (2006) [accessed 5 June 2022] Data is the new oil [Blog] [Online] https://ana.blogs.com/maestros/2006/11/data_is_the_new.html (archived at https://perma.cc/37Z7-ETQT)

Pang, A, Markovski, M and Markovska, A (2021) [accessed 5 June 2022] Top 10 CRM software vendors, market size and market forecast 2020–2025, *Apps Run the World* [Online] https://www.appsruntheworld.com/top-10-crm-software-vendors-and-market-forecast/ (archived at https://perma.cc/9ZKA-HG97)

Qualtrics (2022) [accessed 5 June 2022] Customer loyalty definition [Online] https://www.qualtrics.com/uk/experience-management/customer/customer-loyalty/ (archived at https://perma.cc/ZB69-DAFH)

Revenue Enablement Institute (2021) *Revenue Operations in the 21st Century Commercial Model*

Schmidt, M (2021) [accessed 2 May 2022] What is revenue operations (RevOps)? A complete guide: The untold love story between CROs and CFOs [Online] https://www.salesforce.com/resources/articles/what-is-revenue-operations/ (archived at https://perma.cc/BWW5-NTT3)

Statista (2022) [accessed 6 June 2022] Worldwide desktop market share of leading search engines from January 2010 to January 2022 [Online] https://www.statista.com/statistics/216573/worldwide-market-share-of-search-engines/ (archived at https://perma.cc/Z8Q8-9ENN)

Strategic Account Managers Association (2022) https://www.strategicaccounts.org/en/ (archived at https://perma.cc/U7V4-3N8N)

Temkin, B (2020) [accessed 2 May 2022] Six types of experience data [Online] xminstitute.com/blog/six-types-experience-data (archived at https://perma.cc/39W9-6Q2J)

INDEX

Note: Page numbers in *italics* refer to figures